William Edward Hall

A treatise on the foreign powers and jurisdiction of the British Crown

William Edward Hall

A treatise on the foreign powers and jurisdiction of the British Crown

ISBN/EAN: 9783337274894

Printed in Europe, USA, Canada, Australia, Japan

Cover: Foto ©Suzi / pixelio.de

More available books at **www.hansebooks.com**

A TREATISE

ON THE

FOREIGN POWERS AND JURISDICTION

OF THE

BRITISH CROWN

BY

WILLIAM EDWARD HALL, M.A.

BARRISTER-AT-LAW

Oxford
AT THE CLARENDON PRESS
LONDON: HENRY FROWDE
OXFORD UNIVERSITY PRESS WAREHOUSE, AMEN CORNER
AND
STEVENS & SONS, LIMITED
119 & 120 CHANCERY LANE

1894

PREFACE

THE following work is an attempt to define the powers and jurisdiction which the British Crown exercises or has a right to exercise in places not within the dominions of Great Britain, whatever the source may be from which such powers and jurisdiction are derived. The subject is one in which guidance from previous writers is almost wholly wanting; it has never yet been treated as a whole; even its different parts taken separately have not received adequate attention. Little published material exists outside Acts of Parliament, Treaties, Orders in Council, some important Parliamentary Papers, and a few cases decided in the Courts. In the main the work is naturally, and indeed necessarily, based upon these. It will, however, be evident to the reader that other information has been open to me. I have had the advantage of consulting friends whose official experience and position enabled them to place at my disposal a large amount of valuable material, both in the nature of facts and of opinions. Partly for reasons of official etiquette, and partly because what I have gathered on various questions has been so fused that the elements are often indistinguishable, I have found myself in many cases unable to cite authorities. But I take this opportunity of expressing my gratitude to those who have helped me; and I will ask the reader to believe that when facts are mentioned, and when statements evidently based on facts are made, without the authority for them being given, or when views are impersonally expressed, what is said has been founded at least upon very careful inquiry. I venture to hope that little of importance will be found to be erroneous.

One well merited acknowledgement I am glad to be able to make. The work has been written in the country, and therefore under the disadvantage of remoteness from Law Reports and from foreign publications to which frequent reference was needed. The disadvantage would have been serious, had I not been able to draw upon the able assistance of my friend Mr. Beresford Atlay.

CONTENTS

PART I.

INTRODUCTORY.

CHAPTER I.

FOREIGN POWERS AND JURISDICTION IN THEIR INTERNATIONAL AND CONSTITUTIONAL ASPECTS.

SECTION		PAGE
1.	Foreign jurisdiction in its international aspect	1
2.	Rights of a state with reference to its subjects abroad	2
3.	Territorial rights of a state	2
4.	Modification of the effects of the above rights by customary practices	3
5.	The right of protection	4
6.	The various rights as factors of usage	7
7.	Foreign jurisdiction in relation to the law and constitution	8
8.	1. The prerogative	8
9.	2. Parliament	10
10.	3. Common law	12
11.	Jurisdiction in the British dominions in respect of acts done in foreign countries	12

CHAPTER II.

THE AGENTS THROUGH WHOM POWER AND JURISDICTION ARE EXERCISED.

12.	The various classes of Agents	15
13.	The Consular service	16

PART II.

POWERS AND JURISDICTION OF THE CROWN IN STATES OF EUROPEAN CIVILIZATION.

CHAPTER I.

THE PERSONS WHO ARE POSSESSED OF THE STATUS OF BRITISH SUBJECTS.

SECTION		PAGE
14.	The classes of persons who enjoy the status of British subjects	18
15.	Natural born British subjects	20
16.	Children and grandchildren born of British subjects out of the dominions of the Crown . .	21
17.	Minors obtaining a foreign nationality through the naturalization of their parents . . .	22
18.	Naturalized aliens	24
19.	Infant children of naturalized aliens . . .	26
20.	Naturalization in Colonies	28
21.	Naturalization in India	30
22.	Denization	31
23.	Conditions of loss of nationality by subjects of foreign states	34
24.	Acquisition of British nationality by marriage .	41
25.	Loss of British nationality	44
26.	Naturalization in a foreign state	45
27.	Marriage of a woman who is a British subject with an alien	49
28.	Declaration of alienage	51
29.	Recovery of British nationality	52
30.	Recovery of foreign nationality by persons naturalized in Great Britain	54

CONTENTS. xi

SECTION		PAGE
31.	Double nationality	54
32.	English law in relation to double nationality	55
33.	Foreign laws	56
34.	Questions of double nationality in their practical aspect	65
35.	Imperfect nationality	69

CHAPTER II.

GENERAL FUNCTIONS OF AGENTS OF THE BRITISH CROWN IN FOREIGN COUNTRIES.

36.	Classification of functions	72
37.	Protective functions	72
38.	Ministerial functions	75
39.	Functions of quasi-jurisdiction	77
40.	Relation of the above powers to the local law	79
41.	Limitation by territorial law of consular powers given by British law	83

CHAPTER III.

CELEBRATION OF MARRIAGE BY BRITISH AGENTS IN FOREIGN STATES.

42.	Summary of principles	85
43.	Provisions of the Marriage Act of 1892	86
44.	Restrictions upon the operation of the Act with reference to	89
45.	Persons naturalized or of double nationality	89
46.	Conditions precedent of a valid marriage	91
47.	Marriage warrants	92
48.	The official house	93
49.	Incapacity of marriage officers to use the marriage service of the Church of England	96

xii   CONTENTS.

SECTION		PAGE
50.	Order of precedence when civil and religious ceremonies are both performed	97
51.	Registration of marriages	97
52.	The relation of the Act to the laws of foreign states	101
53.	The right of a state to sanction the performance of marriages abroad in relation to the duties of comity	102
54.	Directions given by the Order in Council in restraint of the discretion of marriage officers	106
55.	Marriages *per verba de praesenti* before persons in episcopal orders	109
56.	Diplomatic, consular, and other marriages in their relation to the laws of foreign states	114
57.	Marriages on board vessels of war in foreign ports	118
58.	Marriages within the lines of a British army in foreign territory	120

PART III.

POWERS AND JURISDICTION OF THE CROWN IN EASTERN STATES, IN PROTECTORATES, AND IN BARBAROUS COUNTRIES.

CHAPTER I.

THE PERSONS WHO ARE REGARDED AS BRITISH SUBJECTS IN EASTERN STATES.

59.	The two classes of Eastern States	122
60.	General principles determining the attribution of British nationality in the East	123
61.	Effect of the Statutes and Orders in Council which are applicable	125
62.	Registration of British subjects	129
63.	Impossibility of British subjects divesting themselves of their nationality in barbarous countries	130

CHAPTER II.

POWERS AND JURISDICTION OF THE CROWN IN EASTERN STATES.

SECTION		PAGE
64.	Origin and growth of consular powers in the East	132
65.	Protective rights	134
66.	Protected persons who are not British subjects	136
67.	Double nationality	139
68.	Protection to foreign members of crews of British vessels	141
69.	Special protective privileges	143
70.	Scope and limits of British jurisdiction	146
71.	Ground of jurisdiction as between Great Britain and Eastern States and its subjects	148
72.	Criminal jurisdiction in mixed cases	152
73.	Police powers	154
74.	Civil jurisdiction in mixed cases	155
75.	Civil suits in which the plaintiff is a British subject	161
76.	Applicability of English law	162
77.	Organization and powers of the Courts	168
78.	Extent to which the divergency between the law administered in Eastern countries and in England calls for remark	172
79.	Special regulations providing for observance of treaties, &c.	173
80.	Powers of deportation	174
81.	Domicil in Oriental countries	180
82.	Bankruptcy	186
83.	Matrimonial causes	188
84.	Probate jurisdiction	190
85.	Jurisdiction of Consular Courts in respect of British officials and foreign sovereigns	191

SECTION		PAGE
86.	Marriages in Oriental countries	193
87.	*per verba de praesenti* before a person in episcopal orders	194
88.	*per verba de praesenti* in presence of witnesses .	197
89.	*Lex loci* marriages in polygamous countries .	201
90.	in monogamous Eastern countries . . .	202
91.	Registration of marriages.	202

CHAPTER III.

PROTECTORATES, SPHERES OF INFLUENCE, AND BARBAROUS COUNTRIES.

92.	Essential characteristic of a protectorate . . .	204
93.	Views formerly entertained by Great Britain as to the relation between protecting and protected states .	205
94.	Views entertained by foreign powers	207
95.	Powers actually exercised by Great Britain in her protectorates	210
96.	The true character of the relations between a protecting and a protected state or territory	218
97.	Effect of the Foreign Jurisdiction Act . . .	220
98.	The prerogative in its relation to protectorates . .	222
99.	Cyprus	225
100.	Natives of protectorates when in places under foreign jurisdiction	226
101.	Spheres of influence	228
102.	Powers which can be exercised in barbarous countries not under the protection of a civilized power . .	230
103.	Organization of British jurisdiction in barbarous territories in the Pacific	232
104.	Independent natives of barbarous places . . .	234
105.	Marriage in protectorates and barbarous countries .	235

CHAPTER IV.

JURISDICTION ON THE HIGH SEAS AND IN RESPECT OF ACTS DONE THERE.

SECTION   PAGE
106. Jurisdiction on the high seas over persons in British vessels 239
107. Fishery regulation 242
108. Revenue and quarantine jurisdiction 243
109. Classification of the foregoing instances of jurisdiction 246

APPENDICES.

                                                                                       PAGE
I. Naturalization Act, 1870 . . . 249
II. Foreign Marriage Act, 1892 . . . 263
    Foreign Marriages Order in Council, 1892 . . 276
III. Foreign Jurisdiction Act, 1890 . . 287

INDICES.

Index of Statutes 297
Index of Orders in Council 298
Index of Cases 299
Index of Treaties . . . 301
General Index 302

ERRATA

Page 12, note : *for* §§ 54 and 87, *read* §§ 55 and 87.
Page 32, line 15 : *for* in, *read* on.

FOREIGN JURISDICTION.

PART I.

CHAPTER I.

FOREIGN POWERS AND JURISDICTION IN THEIR INTERNATIONAL AND CONSTITUTIONAL ASPECTS.

§ 1. To the lawyer 'foreign jurisdiction' is an accustomed term; it is consecrated to him by a succession of Acts of Parliament; he is familiar with the working of the powers which it signifies. Even to him however the ideas which it suggests are at first sight somewhat abnormal, and to a person coming freshly upon the words they might well seem to need explanation and perhaps apology. How, it might be asked, can the exercise of jurisdiction, or, indeed, the exercise of power of whatever kind, by one state within the territory of another, be reconciled with the acknowledged principle of the equal and complete independence of all states that are not tributary or protected. Yet that the effects of the laws of a state should extend beyond its frontiers, and that it should possess certain powers within foreign territory, are almost necessary results of the modern conception of a state; and that large jurisdiction should be exercised in certain places is the almost necessary condition of peaceful intercourse

PART I.
CHAP. I.

between countries of widely differing types or grades of civilization.

Rights of a state with reference to its subjects abroad.

§ 2. At the root of state life lies the circumstance that the bond which exists between a state and its subjects is not severed when the latter issue from the national territory. The legal relations by which a person is encompassed in his country of birth and residence cannot be wholly put aside when he goes abroad for a time; many of the acts which he may do outside his native state have inevitable consequences within it. He may for many purposes be temporarily under the control of another sovereign than his own, and he may be bound to yield to a foreign government a large measure of obedience; but his own state still possesses a right to his allegiance; he is still an integral part of the national community. A state therefore can enact laws, enjoining or forbidding acts, and defining legal relations, which oblige its subjects abroad in common with those within its dominions. It can declare under what conditions it will regard as valid acts, done in foreign countries, which profess to have legal effect; it can visit others with penalties; it can estimate circumstances and facts as it chooses.

Territorial rights of a state.

§ 3. While the powers of a state over its subjects are thus absolute as between itself and them, the extent to which they actually take effect is determined by the corrective force of another fact of state life equally fundamental with the former. The authority of a state is exclusive within its own dominions; it alone prescribes what acts may, and what shall not, be done; it alone directs with what forms, and under what conditions, those which it permits shall be accomplished. While therefore any state can affix such value as it chooses to acts done by its subjects abroad, the effects of acts so done are not necessarily felt except within its own territory; if like effects follow in another country, they are produced through permission in some shape having been given by the local sovereign. He may allow foreign subjects to do certain acts in accordance with their own laws, and he may respect the incapacities which are imposed upon them; he may concede more or less of jurisdictional power to the foreign state; but whatever he does is done of pure grace. No country can insist as against another that acts performed in a manner demanded by itself shall be recognized in the country where they are accomplished, still less can it there exercise jurisdiction over the persons of its subjects without the express or implied consent of the territorial sovereign.

§ 4. The two principles that every state is absolute within its dominions, where, if it so wishes, the existence for legal purposes of every other state may be ignored, and that, for good or evil to the subject, it may appreciate as it likes whatever acts he does in foreign countries, would lend themselves ill, if the principles were crudely applied, to the necessities of international life, and would cause the infliction of great hardships on individuals. Formerly, indeed, much hardship was in fact suffered, though neither principle was ever applied with uncompromising logic; and abundant evidence will be found in the following work that the clashing laws of states of European civilization still place many persons in situations that are frequently difficult and occasionally serious. Happily, as between nations of the European type, correctives to the undue application of the principle of territorial sovereignty are supplied by permissions and consequent practices which may perhaps be taken to flow from comity. Whatever be their speculative or actual origin, the withdrawal of permissions which rest on established custom is forbidden by the usages of International Law, and those which in the following pages appear to be universal may be taken also to be obligatory.

Modification of the effects of the above rights by customary practices.

PART I.
CHAP. I.

The right of protection.

§ 5. An excessive application of the rights of territorial sovereignty is further prevented by a principle which, while itself the offspring of sovereignty, places a check on the action of its parent. The duty of protection is correlative to the rights of a sovereign over his subjects; the maintenance of the bond between a state and its subjects while they are abroad implies that the former must watch over and protect them within the due limit of the rights of other states. A government which felt inclined to push its own territorial rights too far would find itself met by the protective rights of its neighbours; and through the continuous and almost insensible pressure of this protective right much of the practice which is now usual with reference to foreigners in a state has been formed.

In its direct action.

The direct action of the right is no doubt confined within a narrow range, and inside that range it does not work as a principle of international law or ethics, or as a basis of authoritative custom. Among the group of Western states there are now only two ways in which it operates directly. It enables governments to exact reparation for oppression from which their subjects have suffered, or for injuries done to them otherwise than by process of law; and it gives the means of guarding them against the effect of unreasonable laws, of laws totally out of harmony with the nature or degree of civilization by which a foreign power affects to be characterized, and finally of an administration of the laws bad beyond a certain point. When in these directions a state grossly fails in its duties; when it is either incapable of ruling, or rules with patent injustice, the right of protection emerges in the form of diplomatic remonstrance, and in extreme cases of ulterior measures. It provides a material sanction for rights; it does not offer a theoretic foundation. It does not act within a foreign territory with the consent of the sovereign; it acts against him contentiously from without.

In another shape, however, the right of protection continually presents itself in a legal aspect; it has worked, and it continues to work, as an indirect factor of custom or convention. It is not worth while, in dealing with the present, to trace the stages of progress, and the road which has been travelled; it is enough to point out that a subtle influence of the right is constantly felt, and that its force, if the word protection be used in a wide sense as the only available term to indicate the watchfulness exercised over subjects abroad in the interest of the state no less than in that of individuals, stretches far beyond the sphere of its direct application. It is admitted to possess a reasonable moral basis, to which recognition must be given, and in this bye manner it largely determines the extent to which 'foreign jurisdiction' is permitted to exist, in other words, to which the sovereign powers of a state are waived in favour of a foreign nation, or are delegated to it.

<small>PART I. CHAP. I.

In its indirect action.</small>

In Oriental and semi-civilized countries, where the necessity of allowing the right to operate is frankly acknowledged, it gives rise to arrangements under which a state voluntarily makes a permanent surrender of some portion of its jurisdiction for the purpose of securing to the subjects of another country the means of regulating their life in conformity with their own laws and customs. A compromise, varying with the circumstances, is arrived at between the sovereign rights of the state and the jurisdictional needs of a foreign civilized power.

<small>Effects of the protective right in Oriental countries.</small>

In states of the European type the effects of the protective right may be less obviously felt, but they none the less are there. Taking the word in the large sense in which it has already been used, to the recognition of a protective right can alone be ascribed the concession to consuls of a quasi jurisdiction in mercantile disputes, or still more the exceptional position of merchant vessels within ports or territorial waters, and the jurisdiction

<small>In states of the European type.</small>

exercised by naval courts in respect of crimes, misdemeanours, and other offences, committed on board of them. These customary derogations from the fulness of local jurisdiction are not founded in indifference to the occurrence of events in a certain class; like events or incidents do not in other circumstances escape the cognizance of the local tribunals; they are founded upon a perception of the fact that maintenance of control over the men and ships of his mercantile marine is an object to a foreign sovereign of deeper importance than the assertion of jurisdiction on every occasion can be to the territorial authority. Indifference may no doubt sometimes exist, and there are customary powers which may have been tacitly granted simply because a state has no sufficient interest in taking notice of innocent acts which are unlikely in any way to affect persons or things belonging to it. Registration of births and deaths, arbitration in shipping disputes, even notarial acts, though these partake of a more public character, are matters of small concern. But when, as in the case of ships, so high a sovereign right as that of territorial jurisdiction enters into the concession made, some more active principle than indifference must supply the motive for a delegation of powers. Such a principle is found in an acknowledgement that within certain limits, varying with circumstances, it is reasonable that a state shall be allowed, in its own protective interest, to exercise powers with reference to its subjects upon the territory of another state [1].

[1] I may perhaps seem to have given too prominent a place to what I have ventured to call the 'protective' influence in the formation of modern custom, and to have attached too little importance to comity. I may be wrong, but comity appears to me to be a very unsatisfactory ground for customary practices. In analysing the sources of powers it cannot be put in the same plane with the fundamental principles of state life, such as independence, by the side of which it has to stand if the effects of the two are to be set in the balance against each other. It is itself a secondary principle, which must either flow from recognition of

§ 6. Outside the powers then which states can exercise by simply attaching a given value within their own territory to acts done in foreign countries, the nature and extent of the powers possessed by them within the dominions of other states have been mainly determined by the interacting forces of territorial sovereignty and protective rights. Each has contributed to the formation of the actual practice; in some directions one has been preponderant, in some the other may have had greater weight. It will nevertheless be readily understood that through the larger part of the following work the latter factor will hardly call for notice. It has been already observed that when the rights of protection are directly and immediately appealed to, without translation into agreement or custom having taken place, they are either used diplomatically, or in justification of precautionary or more definite ulterior measures. Exceptional action is prompted by exceptional reasons. In the case of the ordinary powers, on the other hand, which are regulated by agreement or custom, the right of protection disappears from view, whatever the part originally taken by it in their formation may have been. For practical purposes it is only essential to define the extent of the grant or concession which is made by the territorial state. In the chapters therefore which deal with the relations between

PART I.
CHAP. 1.

The various rights as factors of usage.

the facts that given conduct in certain details is morally obligatory, or from the mere egoistic feeling of reciprocal convenience between states, which must itself be caused by the more or less conscious pressure of national interests. The latter amounts to saying that one state allows another to have privileges within its territory because it has to give them in order to get like privileges from its neighbours. Of the two possible sources of practice it is assuredly that which coincides most with the usual attitude of states towards each other. It is moreover to be noticed that comity breaks down the moment that the bounds of Europe and America are overpassed. Comity implies willingness to reciprocate, and there is no reciprocity between Western and Eastern States. The Eastern State allows certain practices with the view of obtaining advantages of a totally different order from those which it grants.

PART I.
CHAP. I.

Consequent scope of the work on its international side.

Great Britain and foreign countries, whether they be of the European type or are independent Oriental states, an attempt will merely be made to define:—

(1) The powers, affecting acts intended to have effects in the British dominions, which are exercised with regard to British subjects in foreign countries irrespectively of the local laws.

(2) The derivative rights and powers enjoyed by Great Britain through custom or express agreement.

In the portion of the work which treats of the newer and more unsettled relations arising out of protectorates over more or less uncivilized territories, or connected with spheres of influence, it will be necessary to go behind the question of actual delegation, and to have recourse to ground principles for the determination of the due limits of action and of duty.

Foreign jurisdiction in its relation to the law and constitution.

§ 7. The international element in foreign jurisdiction unavoidably engages attention in the first instance; but to British subjects the legal basis of the powers exercised under their own municipal law is a matter of at least equal interest. It is time to turn to the consideration of this point.

In the British dominions there are three sources of authority whence obligations are drawn that bind a British subject, and whence rights are derived that he enjoys. The prerogative[1], Parliamentary enactments, and common law, govern him within their respective provinces. They follow him also when he enters upon foreign soil.

§ 8. So much that is connected with foreign jurisdiction

---

[1] So far as the present treatise is concerned the prerogative may be described with Dicey (Law of the Constitution, pp. 348-9) as the discretionary powers of the executive, or in other words anything that the Queen or her servants can do without the authority of an Act of Parliament. Sir W. Anson (Law and Customs of the Constitution, Pt. II. p. 3) shows that the meaning of the word prerogative is not exhausted by these powers, but its residual sense covers matter foreign to the subject in hand.

passed out of the hands of the prerogative into those of Parliament half a century ago, so much which at one time was no doubt the subject of regulation by the crown has been regulated by enactment, that the sphere within which the prerogative still works does not at once strike the eye. As however the crown represents the nation in its relations with foreign states, and is the sole channel of communication with them, its functions are still far from insignificant. All national powers and duties in foreign territory which rest upon treaty receive their international validity from its prerogative action, and are given to, or imposed upon, Great Britain independently of Parliament; by the crown moreover all protective powers are exercised, whether they are derived from treaty or rest immediately upon the sovereignty of the state. Formerly its action was wider in range, and in character much more direct and specific. In the Charter of the Levant Company the Crown made a prerogative grant of consular jurisdiction, under which general powers of fine and imprisonment were held until the dissolution of the Company in 1825; and so late as the middle of last century the Commission of the British Consul at Alicante contained a grant of judicial powers. There were other instances to the like effect. All foreign jurisdiction was in fact exercised in virtue of the mere prerogative. In 1826 the Law Officers threw doubts upon the legality of the jurisdiction which was supposed to be still vested in Consuls in the Ottoman Empire. The ultimate result of these doubts was the first of the series of Foreign Jurisdiction Acts[1]; but it does not clearly appear whether the Law Officers doubted the power of the Crown to set up Consular jurisdiction by means of the prerogative, or whether they only considered that Consular powers in Turkey were dependent upon the Charter of the Levant Company. Probably, as it was thought best to legislate,

[1] 6 & 7 Vict. cap. 94 (1843).

the former was the case; but the preamble of the Act, in saying that doubts had arisen how far the exercise of the power of the Crown was 'controlled by and dependent on the laws and customs of this realm,' suggests that another and a different reason may have contributed to bring about legislation. In any case the question of constitutional law remains undecided; and though the subsequent and continued action of Parliament has thrown the prerogative right of independently creating and regulating jurisdiction into desuetude, enough of the old prerogative may perhaps remain to cure any error of excess committed through overstepping the powers delegated by Parliament, into which an Order in Council issued under authority of an Act might possibly fall.

2. Parliament.

§ 9. In 1843 Parliament possessed itself for the first time of the domain of foreign jurisdiction, and passed the act already mentioned which, with several subsequent enactments, has formed the groundwork of the Foreign Jurisdiction Act of 1890[1]. This last Act after reciting that 'by treaty, capitulation, grant, usage, sufferance, and other lawful means, Her Majesty the Queen has jurisdiction within divers foreign countries,' enacts that 'it is and shall be lawful for Her Majesty the Queen to hold, exercise, and enjoy any jurisdiction which Her Majesty now has or may at any time hereafter have within a foreign country in the same and as ample a manner as if Her Majesty had acquired that jurisdiction by the cession or conquest of territory.' By implication this provision enables the Queen, that is to say the Queen in Council, to make such Orders as may be necessary from time to time for the purpose of giving due effect to the jurisdiction; which, be it noted, she does not hold through the Act, and which is recognized by it as having belonged anteriorly to her. To guard against a possible difficulty,

[1] 53 & 54 Vict. cap. 37.

and to secure complete freedom of action, it is declared that 'an Order in Council made in pursuance of this Act shall not be, or be deemed to have been, void on the ground of repugnancy to the law of England unless it is repugnant to the provisions' of an Act of Parliament, or of regulations made under it, which extend to British subjects in the country affected by the Order. Power is also given to apply to foreign countries certain scheduled Acts which, as passed, applied only to Great Britain or the Colonies, and to revoke or vary certain others. By this Act some pre-existing Orders in Council have been confirmed, and under its authority some fresh Orders have been issued; the two classes between them covering the whole area of Oriental States, and of protected and barbarous countries, in which British jurisdiction exists in its most developed form. With states of European civilization the Act has nothing to do; the minor powers exercised in them are otherwise provided for.

PART I.
CHAP. I.

Upon this enactment as a whole little comment need be made. It plainly recognizes in the amplest manner that the crown, independently of parliament, is in possession of jurisdictional rights abroad, which are good as between it and foreign sovereigns; but as for their enforcement against British subjects it is advisable that parliamentary sanction shall be afforded, powers of legislation are confirmed, or given by way of delegation, subject only to certain provisions contained in the Act itself, and to any special legislation that may be passed in the future.

To one detail only is it worth while to direct attention. It is specified that the jurisdiction held by the Crown shall be enjoyed 'in the same and as ample a manner as if Her Majesty had acquired that jurisdiction by the cession or conquest of territory.' It is unnecessary to say that this language does not assimilate the jurisdiction exercised in a foreign country, either in nature or degree, to that

Meaning of the provision that jurisdiction shall be as in conquered territory.

which belongs to the Crown in conquered territory. Its object is simply to provide that such jurisdiction as may have been acquired by express consent or sufferance of the foreign state shall be exercised by the Crown precisely as if it were exercised by sole virtue of the prerogative. The position of the crown relatively both to parliament and to individuals is declared to be identical with that which it holds in a country which has been conquered or ceded.

3. Common law.

§ 10. There remains the third source of capacity and obligation by which a British subject is affected when outside the dominions of the crown, viz. the common law. Upon this it is sufficient to say here that, as some Acts of Parliament do not take effect beyond England or the United Kingdom, it is possible that a person desiring to perform a given act when out of the realm may find the conditions of his act prescribed by a different rule of law to that which would govern him in the British dominions. He may find that no Act of Parliament, and no Order in Council, runs in the place where he is, and that he is consequently relegated to the sanctions of the Common Law[1].

Jurisdiction in British dominions in respect of acts done in foreign countries.

§ 11. It is an obvious consequence of the continuance of the tie between an individual and his state, notwithstanding his absence from its territory or jurisdiction, that acts done by a British subject abroad which alter his relations in the British dominions towards other individuals either in respect of person or property must, with reference to those relations, be controlled by the laws of England, or, as the case may be, of some other part of the British Empire. It is not perhaps so obvious a consequence that criminal acts, committed by him abroad, should be justiciable within the territory. They are usually left to the courts of the local sovereign, who is in general much more interested in their due punishment than is the country of the criminal. But

---

[1] See e.g. §§ 54 and 87.

there are few states which refuse to take cognizance of any criminal act done by their subjects when in foreign territory; the principle of concurrent jurisdiction is maintained; and certain crimes, ordinarily of a kind more or less affecting the state, can be punished on the return of the criminal to the jurisdiction. Though Great Britain has acted to a very limited extent upon the principle, and has not had frequent occasion to give effect to it of late years, the liability of a subject to be made answerable for crimes committed out of the jurisdiction has been affirmed by Statute for more than three centuries and a half.

Treason and misprision of treason, committed out of the realm, were rendered punishable by 35 Hen. VIII. c. 2; and by 33 Hen. VIII. c. 23, it was enacted that a commission might be issued under the Great seal for the trial of any person thought guilty of murder, in whatsoever place, within the King's dominions or without, the offence was committed; this Act was extended to accessories before the fact of murder and to manslaughter by 43 Geo. III. c. 113. By a consolidating Act of 1829 these enactments were repealed, and a provision was substituted which enabled any justice of the peace to take cognizance of the offence charged, and to proceed therein, as if it had been committed within the limits of his ordinary jurisdiction. Several cases under these Acts are reported; among them is that of Governor Wall, who was convicted under the Act of Henry VIII; and in a more recent case a native of Malta was tried and convicted under the consolidating Act of 1829[1]. Further legislation, affecting British subjects committing homicide, or being accessory thereto, on land within the dominions of foreign countries, took place in 1861[2].

---

[1] 28 State Trials, 21; R. v. Azzopardi, 2 Moody, Crown Cases, 288.
[2] 24 & 25 Vict. cap. 100. See also the Explosive Substances Act (1883), 46 & 47 Vict. cap. 3.

It has been held also from very early times that Admiralty jurisdiction extends into foreign rivers so far as the tide ebbs and flows and great ships go. In recent cases a sailor has been convicted at the Central Criminal Court of manslaughter committed on board a British vessel lying in the Garonne, and a conviction was obtained at the Central Criminal Court for receiving bonds stolen from a British ship, which at the time of the larceny was in the river Maas at Rotterdam[1]. Finally, the jurisdiction of the Admiralty is extended by enactment over offences committed in any place out of the British dominions by any master, seaman, or apprentice who at the time of, or within three months before, the offence was employed in any British ship[2].

[1] R. v. Anderson, L. R. 1 C. C. R. 161; R. v. Carr. L. R. 10 Q. B. D. 76.
[2] Merchant Shipping Act (1854), 17 & 18 Vict. cap. 104.

CHAPTER II.

The Agents through whom Power and Jurisdiction are Exercised.

§ 12. The persons through whom the rights and powers possessed by Great Britain in respect of its subjects in places under foreign sovereignty are exercised, are:—

1. Diplomatic agents.
2. Naval and military officers.
3. Consular officers.
4. In Cyprus, South Africa, and the Western Pacific an officer called a High Commissioner, and in the Oil Rivers Protectorate an Imperial Commissioner.

PART I. CHAP. 2.

The various classes of Agents.

Of the first of these classes it is enough in this place to say that, while their principal functions with reference to the subject in hand are connected with the protective rights, they have also certain ministerial powers which will be noticed in due course. The last class are chiefly concerned with protectorates, but in the Western Pacific and South Africa they, and officers dependent on them, exercise certain functions in independent barbarous territories. The Consular officers are those through whom the derivative powers generally receive effect in all independent organized states.

Subject to the qualification that a foreign state may refuse, for sufficient cause, to receive a particular diplomatic representative, the members of the first, second, and fourth of the above classes enter upon their functions

PART I.
CHAP. 2.

solely in virtue of their appointments by the British Crown. They represent its sovereignty, and consequently its independence. Consular officers stand upon a different footing. Although they possess a public official character, they are not internationally representative of their state; they are merely persons allowed by a foreign country to reside in its territory for the purpose of carrying on business on behalf of their own government, and of maintaining relations of a minor kind with local officials. They cannot act, except in the case of Pro-consuls, the limitation of whose functions places them in a class apart, until they have been duly recognized by the proper authorities of the country in which they are appointed to reside.

The Consular service.

§ 13. The Consular service consists of officers of different ranks, called respectively:—

1. Agents and Consuls General; Commissioners and Consuls General.
2. Consuls General.
3. Consuls.
4. Vice-Consuls.
5. Consular Agents.
6. Pro-Consuls.

The distinctions between the several classes are merely hierarchical, except as regards Pro-consuls; and they are of no importance otherwise than in relation to the forms of appointment, and as a consequence of these to the forms of recognition. Such consular officers as are appointed by commission from the Crown receive an 'exequatur,' usually in the form of a letter patent, from the sovereign or his equivalent in the country to which they are sent. Vice-consuls not in possession of a commission, and Consular Agents, obtain recognition in a less formal manner. Finally Pro-consuls receive no recognition from the foreign state, their functions not being considered to involve delegation of powers. Their proper office is merely notarial and was limited to performing duties of that kind under the Acts of 52 Vict. chapter 10, and 54 & 55 Vict. chapter 50, until they were enabled to celebrate marriages by the Foreign Marriage Act of 1892, if provided with marriage warrants or left in charge of consulates or vice-consulates. Their appointment as Pro-consuls confers no authority to perform any other consular duties.

Consuls being charged with duties which are necessarily local, and their powers not being locally concurrent with those of other consuls, the districts within which they are authorized to act are defined in their commissions; and their exequaturs, or in the Ottoman Empire the equivalent Berats, are by universal practice issued for the district so defined, it having always been considered that it is for the power commissioning a consul to determine within what territorial limits he should act as its representative. The right to send consuls where, and only where, the interests of a country demand their presence is in all cases of some importance; in Eastern countries, where exterritorial jurisdiction exists, freedom in this respect becomes a necessary condition of the due enjoyment of jurisdictional privileges.

PART II.

CHAPTER I.

The Persons who are possessed of the Status of British Subjects.

PART II.
CHAP. I.

Persons who enjoy the status of British subjects.

§ 14. Before considering what the powers are that can be exercised over, or in respect of, British subjects in foreign states, it is a necessary preliminary to determine to what persons the term 'British subject' applies. The matter is one, it will be seen, upon which English law is not always clear, and into which foreign laws, by giving rise to questions of double nationality, introduce considerable difficulty or at least complexity.

The persons now alive who are, or may be, possessed of the status of British subjects are:—

(1) Persons born within the British dominions, or on board British ships on the high seas or in foreign territorial waters, whether born of British or of alien parents, and whether legitimate or illegitimate, provided that, if legitimate children of alien parents, and if of the age of twenty-one years or more, they shall not have made a declaration of alienage, in accordance with the provisions of the Naturalization Act of 1870 [1].

---

[1] A few exceptions may be noted. A child born to an enemy father, at a place within the British dominions, but in military occupation of an

(2) Legitimate children and grandchildren by male descent, of British subjects, born out of the dominions of the crown [1].

(3) Persons whose father, being a British subject, or whose mother being a British subject and a widow, has become naturalized during the infancy of such persons in a country under the laws of which infant children do not become naturalized by the naturalization of their parents; and like persons, notwithstanding that they have become naturalized by the naturalization of their parents, if they have not during infancy been resident, within the meaning of Sect. 10 of the Act of 1870, in the country where the father or mother is naturalized.

(4) Persons who have become naturalized in the United Kingdom or the British Colonies in accordance with the provisions of the Act of 1870; and children of such persons who during infancy have become naturalized with their fathers or mothers in any part of the United Kingdom.

(5) Persons who have received letters of denization.

(6) Women of alien birth, married to British subjects and such women when widows, until they divest themselves of British nationality by remarriage with a subject of a foreign state, by naturalization abroad, or by resumption

---

enemy state, 'is no subject of the King though he was born within his dominions, for that he was not born under the King's ligeance or obedience.' In Calvin's case, vii. Coke, 18a. In the same position stand children of persons attainted of high treason, and of persons in the actual service of any foreign prince or state in enmity with the Crown of England or of Great Britain at the time of the birth of such children. 4 Geo. II, c. 21, s. 1 and 2.

[1] 4 Geo. II, c. 21, and 13 Geo. III, c. 21. The meaning of these Acts was decided in De Geer v. Stone (xxii. Ch. D. 243) to be that 'the grandchild born abroad, whose father was also born abroad, being respectively grandchild and child of a man who was by the common law a natural born British subject, would be himself a natural born British subject, but that his children born abroad would be aliens.'

PART II.
CHAP. I.

of their nationality of origin in the manner prescribed by the legislation of the country of their birth.

(7) Persons who, being British subjects at the date of the Act of 1870, had become naturalized in a foreign state, provided that within three years after the passing that Act, they shall have signified, in the manner prescribed by it, their wish to remain British subjects.

Natural born British subjects.

§ 15. It is to be observed of the persons enumerated in the first of the above paragraphs that they stand in a position of complete equality in their relation to the state. English law knows no distinction between different classes of natural born British subjects in respect of rights or obligations. All alike, whatever their parentage, have the same duty of allegiance, the same rights within the British dominions, and, subject only to a qualification introduced in certain cases for reasons of public policy [1], the same right to recognition and protection abroad. And as the quality of British subject is attributed to them solely in virtue of their birth on British soil or within British jurisdiction, not only is the nationality of the parents without any bearing on the nationality of the child, but the duration or the object of their sojourn, if they be foreigners, is immaterial. A child born of foreign parents even during an accidental stay of a few days is fully, and until the age of twenty-one years irretrievably, a British subject [2]. It is equally immaterial whether children are of legitimate or illegitimate origin. For the reason that they are British subjects in virtue only of the place of birth, irrespectively of any other motive for attributing

---

[1] See §§ 32 and 34.

[2] The rule appears at first sight to be a harsh one, and it would be so in fact if British national character were attended by the onerous incidents which weigh upon the subjects of most foreign countries. In the absence of conscription, and in presence of the special modifying practice, to which allusion is made above, it probably can never operate to the disadvantage of the individual, and may readily be to his advantage.

to them that status, it is unnecessary to consider whether in different circumstances the nationality of the father or mother would, or would not, determine the nationality of the child.

§ 16. In order that children, and grandchildren by male descent, of British subjects born out of the dominions of the Crown shall themselves possess British nationality, it is necessary that they be legitimate from the moment of their birth. The Act of George II[1], upon which their national character depends, declares that children thereafter born out of the ligeance of the Crown of Great Britain, 'whose fathers shall be natural born subjects of the Crown of Great Britain at the time of the birth of such children respectively,' shall be invested with British nationality. An illegitimate child has no legally ascertained father. He does not therefore satisfy the condition. If then a British subject, being domiciled in a foreign country of which the laws permit legitimation by subsequent marriage, has illegitimate children there, and afterwards legitimates them by marriage with their mother, they do not obtain the benefit of the Act, and continue to be aliens[2].

With respect to the position of persons whose legitimacy of origin primâ facie gives them the advantage of British

---

[1] 4 Geo. II, cap. 21.
[2] Shedden v. Patrick, 1 Macqueen, 535. Lord Brougham considered, apart from the legal aspect of the case, that the practical consequences of allowing legitimation to take effect might be highly inconvenient. 'It would be giving,' he said, 'to the parent of the child, the putative father of the child, the power by marrying the mother, of converting him from an alien or a foreigner into a natural born subject. If the child had done that which he had a perfect right to do at the time, namely, taken up arms against the English Crown before the marriage of his parents, it would follow from the doctrine in question that the marriage converted him from an alien enemy into a traitor to the crown of this country, thereby making him guilty of high treason, instead of being only a person taken with arms in his hands, compassing what might be on his part a perfectly innocent, and even laudable design.' The acquisition of legitimacy would of course be retroactive to the date of birth.

PART II.
CHAP. I.

nationality, a somewhat curious doubt seems to have arisen; and a disposition appears to have been shown to assume in practice that if either the father or the grandfather has lost his British nationality, the descent stops, and the children and grandchildren are aliens. It is difficult to understand the reasoning which places the persons in question under all circumstances in an identical position. They may be of full age at the date of the naturalization of their father; if so, they have an independent legal status which cannot be altered by any act of his. If they are minors at that date, they will no doubt as a general rule share the acquired national character of their father [1], for reasons to which attention will be directed later. But it is possible that the father may have become naturalized in a country by the laws of which minor children do not obtain the nationality of the state upon its acquisition by their parents. In this case, there being no law which deprives a person of British nationality otherwise than upon the assumption of another national character, the children necessarily remain British subjects.

Minors obtaining a foreign nationality through the naturalization of their parents.

§ 17. The class of persons mentioned in the latter portion of the third paragraph gives rise to more serious difficulty. The Naturalization Act of 1870 makes it a condition of the loss of British nationality by a minor child who has obtained a fresh nationality through the naturalization of his father or mother that he shall have become resident in the country to which his parent or parents have transferred their allegiance. In doing this it has left open the delicate question, in what residence consists within the meaning of the Act. Is it to be understood that any residence, anterior perhaps to the time at which a child can be first sent to school, is enough to impart an alien character, which thenceforth remains indelible except by renaturalization; or will recurrent visits, made during the

[1] But comp. § 17.

vacations of an English school, suffice for the purpose; or is it intended that residence shall be so continuous or at least habitual that the adopted country of the parents must be regarded as the definitive home of the child?

The Act itself gives little help. Nowhere is the term 'residence' defined, or so used that it can be applied with certainty in the present case. In the seventh section, where the conditions upon which aliens can be naturalized are laid down, the words 'residence' and 'reside' are no doubt employed with reference to a continued association with the United Kingdom; but even in this section they are not free from vagueness; and were their signification precise, the circumstances contemplated in the two sections are not sufficiently analogous to render it clear that the scope of the words is meant to be exactly the same in both.

Until the Courts have spoken the true intention of the Act must remain uncertain. It may, nevertheless, be worth while to suggest certain considerations by which they are not unlikely to be guided, and by which therefore the position of minor children of British parents naturalized abroad may probably be ultimately regulated.

The condition that a minor shall have become resident on foreign soil before losing his British nationality gives, and must have been intended to give, to a parent the means of settling whether his child shall or shall not retain his British national character. The loss of that character is not inevitable; it is made dependent upon a fact which is in turn dependent upon the will of the parent. Residence cannot then be looked upon as a circumstance which, though determining, is extraneous; it is an evidence of wish on the part of the parents to secure or avoid a particular nationality for their child. Such residence only in the foreign country can consequently satisfy the intention of the Act, as is enough to

PART II.
CHAP. I.

prove the wish of the parents. For this purpose a casual sojourn or an occasional visit would be inadequate. If parents bring up their child so that his association and training are calculated to fit him for life in their former country, and his visits to them are no more than are fairly explicable on the ground of natural affection, it is obvious that their desire has been to at least give him the opportunity of retaining his connexion with the country of his origin; and it would be irrational so to interpret the Act as to defeat their object. It may, for example, be reasonably expected that the Courts would be loth to refuse the status of a British subject to the possessor of a great estate, who had been educated at an English public school and an English university, and had kept up relations with his English connexions, simply because he had spent his early years in the home of a foreign stepfather, and had afterwards stayed with his mother from time to time at regular periods. It would be inconvenient, and almost absurd, that a person in this situation, on attaining his majority, should find himself a foreigner, incapable of acquiring the status of a British subject until, after the usual period of delay, he was readmitted to it by naturalization.

The principles which underlie nationality, and those which govern the attribution of domicile, are widely different from one another, and as a general rule to import anything from one of these bodies of law into the other only leads to confusion; but in this particular case they might probably with advantage be so far assimilated that, in a rough way, circumstances should be used for imputation of nationality in like manner to that in which they are used to indicate intention with regard to domicile.

Naturalized aliens.

§ 18. By the seventh section of the Naturalization Act of 1870 any alien who has resided in the United Kingdom for not less than five years, or who has been in the service of the Crown for a like period, and who intends either to reside in the United Kingdom or to serve under the Crown may, at the discretion of a Secretary of State, be granted a certificate of naturalization which carries with it all the rights and obligations of a British subject within the United Kingdom. The intention of the Act, no doubt, is to invest him with like rights and obligations when within the jurisdiction of foreign powers, subject to the important qualification that within the limits of his state of origin he is not to be deemed a British subject unless he has ceased to be a subject of that state in pursuance of the laws thereof, or in pursuance of a treaty to that effect.

The actual words of the section, however, do not go to this length. The United Kingdom, and the state of which the naturalized alien was 'previously a subject,' are the only states mentioned. His position in all other countries is left open. At the same time, as these other countries are not expressly excluded, the presumption is that he remains clothed with all the rights of a subject that he has been given in the country of his adoption. It is at least tolerably clear that the executive government may assert for him this position as between itself and foreign governments. A state, as a general rule, must take its information upon the law of a foreign country from the organ which is duly charged with the conduct of external relations; and even if there be a difficulty in the terms of the Act, it is certainly permissible for a British government, in dealing with foreign powers, to take up its ground upon the unquestionable intention. Hitherto the practice has been in accordance with this view, and naturalized persons have been invariably regarded as occupying a position identical with that of natural born subjects of the Crown in all states other than their state of origin [1].

---

[1] The instances would no doubt be extremely rare, if indeed they ever occurred, in which a person after being naturalized in a country

PART II.
CHAP. I.

Infant children of naturalized aliens.

§ 19. The position of the infant children of aliens who become British subjects is another point which is not free from difficulty. Those who become resident in the United Kingdom with their father, or with their mother if she is a widow at the time of her naturalization, are themselves naturalized British subjects, and no minimum period of residence is prescribed. A like uncertainty therefore presents itself to that which has been seen to envelop the situation of children of British subjects who have been naturalized abroad. But though the uncertainty is similar, the results in practice, and no doubt in law, are unlike. Every country proceeds on the assumption, however ill-founded the assumption may be, that in giving its nationality it confers a benefit; and a law conferring a benefit must be interpreted in a sense favourable to the person benefited. A law therefore which grants British national character must be so read as rather to include than to exclude. The period of residence which is wholly insufficient to imprint a foreign character on a child, may be amply long enough to justify him in claiming to be British, or to warrant Great Britain in taking for granted that he is a subject of her own. It is the practice to regard every child, living in the United Kingdom with the father at the date of his naturalization, as being resident; his name is inserted in the father's certificate, and no subsequent question has probably ever been raised as to his naturalization, although he may have ceased, while still an infant, to be resident with the father in the United Kingdom. The Courts not having had an opportunity of settling the

---

other than his own and other than Great Britain, became by a second change of nationality a subject of the latter state; but such cases are possible; it is therefore worth noting that the Act speaks only of 'the foreign state of which' a person 'was a subject previously to obtaining his certificate of naturalization,' so that, upon its bare terms, it would be open to the British government to protect a naturalized subject in his country of origin if he had passed through an intermediate naturalization.

question definitively, the conformity of practice to law is not of course beyond the reach of question; but there cannot be much room for doubt as to the spirit by which a decision, if one be ever made, will be inspired.

The Act is silent as to children, whether born before or after naturalization, who are not, or at least have not been, resident with the father or mother in the United Kingdom. It is to be presumed that they remain aliens. In the case of children of a father or mother residing in the United Kingdom, who have been born abroad before naturalization of the parent, this may not be unreasonable; if a father has not chosen to have his children to live with him during a sufficient part of the five years residence which necessarily precedes British naturalization, it would in the majority of instances be fair to assume that he does not wish them to follow his change of nationality. But when children are born after naturalization there are many probable circumstances in which an assumption to this effect would be manifestly unfair. If, for example, a Frenchman joins an English house of business, is naturalized in Great Britain, goes out to a British colony in charge of a branch of his house, has children there, and remains for many years, it is not to be supposed that he wishes to saddle his children with an exclusive French nationality; and an indubitable hardship is inflicted upon them, if they wish to be British subjects, when they are compelled to come to England for five years after attaining their majority before they are permitted to acquire the status of Englishmen. Cases of like kind might easily be multiplied. It would almost seem as if, by a reaction of timidity from the anterior habit of casting too wide the net of British nationality, the framers of the Act had been not disinclined in this, as in other directions, to relieve the British Crown to as large an extent as possible from the burdensome duty of protection.

PART II.
CHAP. I.

The silence of the Naturalization Act of 1870 gains in significance when the previous state of the law is remembered. The statutes of George II and of George III[1] which conferred British nationality upon children and grandchildren born abroad of British subjects, restricted the boon to the issue of natural born subjects; and the Act of 7 and 8 Victoria[2] did not enlarge the scope of the former enactments. The grant, therefore, of a certificate of naturalization, under the Act of 1844, was considered to be personal, and those children only were British who, by being born in the British dominions, were natural born subjects in any case. The Act, moreover, gave to a Secretary of State issuing a certificate of naturalization, the power of imposing restrictions by it; and after 1850 a clause was always inserted excepting 'any rights and capacities of a natural born British subject, out of and beyond the dominions of the British Crown and the limits thereof.' All children and grandchildren consequently born abroad of persons naturalized before 1870 are aliens.

Naturalization in Colonies.

§ 20. By the Act of 1870 it is provided that 'all laws, statutes, and ordinances which may be duly made by the legislature of any British possession for imparting to any person the privileges, or any of the privileges, of naturalization, to be enjoyed by such person within the limits of such possession, shall within such limits have the authority of law[3].' No language follows such as that which in the seventh section leads to the inference that a naturalized British subject must be intended to keep his British character in countries other than that of which he was a subject previously to his naturalization, and in it, also, if he has ceased to own its allegiance. A Colonial Act would seem therefore, on the terms of the Act of 1870, to be operative only within the particular colony in which it has been

[1] 4 Geo. II, cap. 21; 13 Geo. III, cap. 21.
[2] Cap. 66.   [3] Sect. 16.

enacted, and to be incapable of investing a naturalized person with the quality of a British subject in foreign states. The Naturalization Act does not however appear to have been read quite in this sense; and it has been the practice to issue passports to the holders of colonial certificates of naturalization, and to protect them in all foreign countries other than their country of origin, on the ground, it must be supposed, that when a person is treated as a subject for all purposes in any part of the British dominions, it is impossible for the state entirely to wash its hands of him and his affairs the moment that he oversteps the boundary of the empire.

PART II. CHAP. I.

Practice with regard to protecting colonially naturalized persons in foreign states.

The feeling is natural; it is even inevitable. At the same time it may well be that foreign tribunals, if called upon to weigh the effect of colonial naturalization, might refuse to regard it as possessing any international value[1]; and though, as has been already mentioned, when a question arises diplomatically, a government, as between itself and another government, must generally take its information concerning the law upon a given point from the organ of a state which is entrusted with the conduct of foreign relations, there are many contentious matters in which the Courts are first called upon to speak, and their mature judgement, save in very exceptional cases, must be supported. It is unfortunate that the Act of 1870 should have been so drawn, either from carelessness or timidity, that foreign tribunals may entertain a very legitimate doubt as to its intention.

Questions as to the view which may be taken of colonial naturalization by foreign governments.

---

[1] In a case arising in France it has already been held by the Cour de Cassation (Feb. 14, 1890) that naturalization in a British colony 'ne constitue pas une véritable naturalisation, au sens de l'Article 17, sec. 1, du Code Civil, et ne peut dès lors faire perdre à l'impétrant sa qualité de Français.' The case was one in which the appellant wished to secure advantages from the possession of a French national character; there is no reason to suppose that the decision would have been different if it had been sought to burden him with obligations.

PART II.
CHAP. I.

In any case persons naturalized in a colony would seem elsewhere to keep their nationality of birth for other purposes than that of protection; except possibly in cases when by the law of their state nationality is lost through naturalization in another country. The latter situation might result in a deprivation of all effective nationality. This however is not very likely to occur. If the country of origin took the view of colonial naturalization which is suggested above as being not improbably held, and the case were a contentious one, its agents in a third state would no doubt make a claim to consider the colonially naturalized person as a subject or citizen, which it would be hard to resist, and which, whatever the embarrassments created by itself, would at least put aside the difficulties caused by absence of national character. If on the other hand the country of origin considered the naturalized person to have lost its nationality, the third state would probably acquiesce in his being regarded as a British subject, or would attribute to him that quality in default of any other national character [1].

Naturalization in India.

§ 21. India is not mentioned in the Act of 1870, and the naturalization of foreigners, as within the Indian Empire, is provided for by a local act which differs from the former in that an applicant for naturalization is obliged only to be 'settled in the territories, or residing within the same with intent to settle,' and that it is simply stated, without mention of the position of a naturalized person in any foreign country, that he shall 'within the territories be deemed a natural born subject of Her Majesty as if he had been born within the said territories, and shall be entitled within the said territories to all rights, privileges, and

---

[1] The latter of the two solutions of the difficulty has, I believe, been arrived at on at least one occasion in Germany. The case quoted in the last note shows that the former is almost unquestionably the view which would commend itself to a French government.

capacities of a subject of Her Majesty born within the said territories [1].' What the effect of this Act might have been had it stood alone it is scarcely now worth while to consider, for there can be little doubt that the subsequent British Act of 1870 must be held to be a general statute, governing and supplementing the Indian law, so that in so far as this may not contain, or may not within its permitted range be expressly inconsistent with, the provisions of the English law in matters affecting the position of a naturalized person in foreign countries, the Indian must be read in subordination to the British Act. It is true that not merely is India unmentioned by name, but that, from the phraseology employed, its existence would not seem to have been present to the mind of the draughtsman. Had it been so, it is scarcely likely that in the definition of a 'British possession' as 'any colony, plantation, island, territory, or settlement within Her Majesty's dominions,' the only term by which the Indian Empire can be described, should have been placed in so secondary a position as that occupied by the word 'territory[2].' For all that, the intention of the British Act is too general, the scope of the term 'territory' is too wide, to permit of the Indian Act being read independently. Its effect must therefore be limited in the same manner as is the effect of Colonial laws, and the position abroad of a person naturalized under it must be the same as that of a colonially naturalized person.

§. 22. Under a very ancient practice[3], foreigners are Denization.

[1] 'An Act for the Naturalization of Aliens.' Acts of the Governor-General in Council, No. XXX of 1852.

[2] It is curious, and significant of the casual way in which Acts of Parliament have too often been drawn, that while in the Naturalization Act of 1870 a British possession is defined as 'any colony', &c., in the Foreign Jurisdiction Amendment Act of 1865, passed in order to extend certain provisions to India, the term 'British colony' is defined as including 'any of Her Majesty's possessions out of the United Kingdom.'

[3] The status is recognized by the statute of 22 Henry VIII, c. 8.

capable of acquiring a peculiar status, called that of denization, by means of letters patent issued under the Great Seal. It may be described as a sort of inferior naturalization, by which the person received into the community of British subjects enters it as 'a new man[1]', whose capacities date only from the moment of denization, and are not, as in naturalization, cast back for certain purposes to an earlier period. A denizen cannot inherit real property, and cannot transmit it to children born before his denization; but disabilities of this kind have no bearing upon his position relatively to foreign states, and in the more essential respects of equality with natural born subjects before the ordinary law from the moment of his admission, and of equality with naturalized subjects as regards political privileges, he stood until 1844 in precisely the same footing as the latter[2]. Chief Justice Cockburn does not hesitate to call denization a naturalization effected by the sovereign in virtue of the prerogative[3]. In all the circumstances, the fact that denizens have not shared in the fresh privileges which have been accorded of late years to naturalized persons does not seem to be enough to deprive them of the rights of British subjects when in foreign states other than their country of origin. This

---

[1] Bac. Abridg. Tit. Alien (B).

[2] The political equality of denizens and naturalized persons may be inferred from the language of 12 and 13 William III, cap. 2, which enacted that 'no person born out of these kingdoms (though he be naturalized or made a denizen),' the two classes, being thus coupled together, 'except such as are born of English parents, shall be capable to be of the Privy Council or a member of either House of Parliament, or to enjoy any office or place of trust either civil or military.' Denizens always enjoyed the parliamentary franchise. After 1844, when naturalized persons were relieved from their disability to hold offices and places of trust denizens, who were not touched by legislation, sank into an inferior position.

[3] 'In this country, naturalization has existed from an early period under two forms. It might be conferred (1) by the sovereign by virtue of the prerogative; (2) by Act of Parliament. The first as distinguished from the second is known under the name of denization.' Nationality, p. 28.

THE STATUS OF BRITISH SUBJECTS.

conclusion is strongly reinforced by the terms in which letters of denization are couched. While they grant to the recipient that he shall in all things exercise &c. all manner of actions &c. 'within our said United Kingdom of Great Britain and Ireland or elsewhere within our dominions.' . . . 'as any our faithful liege subjects born in our said United Kingdom may or can,' he is constituted a 'free denizen and liege subject of us our heirs and successors' without limitation of place. If this form be taken together with the fact that letters of denization can be issued to persons living out of the British dominions, it seems impossible to confine their effects within the limits of those dominions, or to deny to them an international value equal to that of a certificate of naturalization[1].

Since the acquisition of British nationality by way of naturalization has been made easy and inexpensive, applications for letters of denization have become extremely rare, and the practice of giving them has almost fallen into disuse. It would probably become obsolete, but for one circumstance which must always render it of great advantage to keep in hand the power of issuing them upon occasion. No residence in the United Kingdom is required immediately or remotely to precede denization; a person may be made a denizen without ever

---

[1] The Section of the Naturalization Act, 1870, which declares that an alien who has received a certificate of naturalization shall not be deemed to be a British subject, when within the limits of the foreign state of which he was previously a subject, unless he has ceased to be a subject of that state in pursuance of the laws thereof or in pursuance of a treaty to that effect, does not cover denizens; but an opinion of the Queen's Advocate, given in 1843, by which the British Government was always subsequently guided, is couched in such large and general terms that it would be difficult to free denizens from its application. In fact, it may be fairly said that the position of denizens, no less than that of naturalized persons, both having been born possessed of a foreign nationality only, is less favourable than that of the persons immediately contemplated by this opinion, who have a British as well as a foreign nationality by birth.

D

having set his foot upon British soil. There have been, and from time to time there no doubt will be, persons of foreign nationality, to whom it is wished to entrust functions which can only be legally exercised by British subjects. In such instances, the condition of five years' residence in the United Kingdom would generally be prohibitory. The difficulty can be avoided by the issue of letters of denization; and it is believed that on one or two occasions, letters have in fact been issued with the view of enabling persons of foreign nationality to exercise British consular jurisdiction in the East.

§ 23. It will be remembered that the seventh section of the Act of 1870 provides that a naturalized person shall not be deemed to be a British subject when within the limits of the foreign state of which he was a subject previously to obtaining his certificate of naturalization, unless he has ceased to be a subject of that state in pursuance of the laws thereof, or in pursuance of a treaty to that effect. Under the legislation of many countries their subjects or citizens lose their national character either fully or in part by being naturalized in another state or by acts which may have preceded such naturalization; but it is not always that freedom from the obligations connected with the nationality of birth accompanies the loss of its privileges. It becomes therefore necessary to determine the precise effect of the various laws dealing with the loss of national character.

By Austrian law persons who emigrate with permission wholly lose their character as Austrian subjects, and are considered to be foreigners. An Austrian therefore, emigrating with permission, becoming naturalized in Great Britain, and returning to Austria, enters the German and some other provinces of the Empire clothed with the full privileges of a British subject. If, on the other hand, he accepts a foreign national character without permission, he loses his rights of citizenship in Austria, but as it is neither said that he loses his character of Austrian subject nor that he is to be treated as a foreigner, it must be supposed that he still retains so much of his national character as will prevent him from returning to his native country in the capacity of a British subject [1].

In Hungary, nationality is lost by liberation from allegiance, which is granted, subject to conditions, varying in times of peace and war, and also by unauthorized absence from Hungarian territory for ten years without interruption, and without receipt of a new passport, certificate of domicile, or entry in the register of an Austro-Hungarian consular community [2].

By existing French law French nationality is lost by a person who becomes naturalized abroad [3], or who by operation of law acquires a foreign nationality at his own request, provided that he has attained the age of thirty or thirty-one years, and has consequently fulfilled his obligation to service in the active army. Before that age he loses his nationality only if his naturalization has been authorized by the French Government [4]. A Frenchman therefore,

[1] Report of the Royal Commissioners for inquiring into the Laws of Naturalization and Allegiance, 1869, p. 92.

[2] Law of 1879, Ap. Reports, of Her Majesty's Representatives Abroad upon the Laws of Foreign Countries, Parl. Papers, Miscell., No. 3, 1893.

[3] It has been decided more than once by the Cour de Cassation that denization in England does not deprive a person of his quality of Frenchman. Cogordan, La Nationalité, 2ᵉ éd., pp. 174 and 189. Possibly the decisions may have been given with insufficient knowledge of the obscure subject upon which they bore, and consequently of the true effect of denization.

[4] Authorization was required in all cases before 1889. Its absence however did not entail the retention of his French national character by the naturalized person; it merely subjected him to various penalties, such as loss of nobility, or degradation from the legion of honour, which do not affect his position as between Great Britain and France, and which probably are no longer inflicted, even if the law of 1887 be not in this respect retroactive. Cogordan, p. 172; and affidavit of M. Clunet in re Bourgeoise, L. R. 41 Ch. Div. 310.

On the other hand, acceptance without authorization of political,

PART II. if he be naturalized in Great Britain before accomplishing
CHAP I. his military duties, is not protected by his country of
adoption when within French territory; on the other
hand, if he be naturalized after their due fulfilment, he
returns to France as a British subject to all intents[1].

Germany. German nationality is lost,—(1) by continuous residence
abroad for a period of ten years, which can be abridged
to five years by permission of the state, provided that
a foreign nationality shall have been acquired. The required period is calculated as a rule from the date of

administrative, or judicial functions in a foreign country, before 1889, entailed complete loss of French nationality. The law was so largely construed in this respect that the pastor of a Walloon church in Holland has been held by the Courts to have ceased to be a Frenchman because his stipend was paid by the Dutch Government (Journal de Droit Int. Privé, xviii. 122); and the belief has been expressed by good authority that a doctor attached to a hospital in any way connected with the state, a person appointed municipal architect to a town or even in certain circumstances a professor in a university, or a master in a school—for example, a French master in a military academy—was cut off by his employment from his nationality of origin. Cogordan, pp. 293 and 296. Unless the law of 1889 is retroactive with regard to such persons, which hardly seems likely, there certainly have been, and there probably are, Frenchmen within the British Dominions, who have been expatriated by operation of the previous law.

[1] Before 1889 persons naturalized abroad during their minority, through the effect of the naturalization of their parents, did not lose their French nationality unless on attaining their majority they made a declaration affirming their new national character. Rev. de Droit Int. Privé, xvii. 117. It is almost certain in view of the strict and inclusive interpretation given to the law of 1889, that a declaration so made by a person naturalized as a minor since that date will be of no avail so long as French military service is not performed; and it is extremely doubtful if a person naturalized as a minor before that date, but arriving at majority subsequently, would be allowed to escape. 'Les auteurs de la loi de 1889 décidaient sinon expressément, du moins assez clairement pour qu'aucun doute sérieux ne puisse être élevé sur ce point, que la naturalisation du Français à l'étranger n'entraînerait jamais la dénationalisation de leurs enfants mineurs; ils ne se sont pas arrêtés devant cette considération que certaines législations étrangères pourraient bien conférer à la naturalisation des étrangers des effets analogues à ceux qu'ils y avaient eux-mêmes attachés.' Rev. de Droit Int. Privé, xix. 90.

departure from Federal territory, but if a person registers himself as a German subject in a Federal Consulate at any time during its continuance, it begins only when his registration is cancelled. (2) By release evidenced by a certificate from the competent authority. State officials and persons in the military or naval service are incapable of being released; as are also persons between the ages of seventeen and twenty-five years, from whom military service is due, unless they receive special permission from the district Conscription Committee. (3) By edict, as a penal measure, upon failure to respond to a summons addressed to German subjects living abroad in case of war or danger of war. Loss of German national character is in all cases absolute[1].

In Italy, citizenship is lost by formal renunciation and subsequent emigration, by naturalization in a foreign country, by employment in the service of a foreign state without previous permission of the Italian Government, or by entry into the military service of a foreign power. Persons who have thus lost their citizenship became aliens for all purposes except that they are not absolved from the obligations of military service, nor from the penalty attached to the offence of bearing arms against their native country.

Natural born Russian subjects can only be released from their national ties by the will of the Emperor. For practical purposes naturalized foreigners alone are able to escape from their allegiance. In their case, however, reversion to the former national character can be effected by the simple process of declaration, provided that they shall have first

[1] Act regulating the acquisition and loss of citizenship in the Confederation of the States, of June 1, 1870, in Reports of Her Majesty's Representatives Abroad upon the Laws of Foreign Countries. Parl. Papers, Miscell. No. 3, 1893. Except when another reference is given, the statement of foreign laws contained in the remainder of this section is derived from, or is founded on, the above reports.

PART II.
CHAP. I.

paid all debts due within the Russian dominions to the State, the provincial or other public bodies, and to private persons.

Other States.

In Belgium, Bulgaria, Denmark, Greece[1], the Netherlands, Portugal, Norway, Sweden, Servia, Brazil, Chile, Columbia[2], Peru, Roumania, Salvador, Uruguay, and no doubt the United States[3], naturalization in a foreign state carries with it loss of the national character of origin, and in all cases apparently frees the naturalized person from every obligation towards, or tie with, his native country. In several instances other circumstances produce an identical

[1] The wife and children of a person who has lost Greek nationality remain Greek.

[2] Art. 32 of the Constitution, ap. Cogordan, Annexe, S. It is, however, a condition that the naturalized person shall 'prendre domicile' in the country of which he acquires the nationality.

[3] A native born citizen of the United States, who has been naturalized in a foreign country, and has thus become a citizen thereof, is to be regarded as an alien; and in order to reacquire his original nationality, he must conform to the laws of the United States providing for the admission of aliens to citizenship. 14 Op. 295 Williams, 1873; ap. Wharton, Digest of the International Law of the United States, § 177.

A naturalized citizen of the United States may perhaps lose his acquired nationality less formally than by being again naturalized. 'Abandonment of naturalization in the United States may be inferred from a protracted stay in the country of origin after returning there, coupled with proof of *animus manendi*, and of entering into political duties in the latter country,' Mr. Frelinghuysen to Mr. Taft, Jan. 18, 1883. In the same year Mr. Frelinghuysen wrote to Mr. Fish that 'naturalization may be lost by resumption of native domicil.' (Wharton, § 176.) But it is possible that acts of abandonment of this nature may only be regarded as depriving an individual of the right to call upon the government of the United States for protection; it may reserve to itself the right to protect if it chooses. At any rate inference from facts of the above kind can never offer the certainty which is needed to satisfy the Naturalization Act of 1870. A slight shade of uncertainty indeed tinges the whole law of the United States upon the subject. The views of the Executive Government and those of the Federal Courts have not been in unison, and the Courts have refused to admit the right of expatriation (Lawrence, Commentaire sur les Éléments du Droit International de Wheaton, iii 237, and cases referred to in the note). The cases quoted appear however to be all anterior to the Bill of Protection of 1868, by which the absolute right of expatriation was affirmed.

effect; these are, in Bulgaria military service abroad, or acceptance of foreign civil employment without permission; in Greece, Brazil, and Salvador, acceptance of any public service without leave; in the Netherlands, military service without permission, civil employment in all cases, or five years' residence abroad for other than commercial purposes; in Portugal, appointment to a foreign public post, or banishment from the realm; in Chile, Peru, and Uruguay, employment in the service of a foreign state, fraudulent bankruptcy, or judicial sentences of a certain gravity; in Roumania, civil and military employment abroad, and 'submission, for however short a space of time, to the protection of a foreign power.' There seems to be some doubt as to whether emigration from Sweden causes loss of nationality, and, if so, whether there is any sufficiently definite time test of intention to abandon Swedish national character[1]. A like difficulty might perhaps be found in interpreting the Norwegian law of 1888, which provides that a Norwegian State-citizen shall lose his national character 'when he leaves the kingdom for ever'; but as he may retain his rights by making a declaration before a Norwegian consul of his intention to preserve his nationality within one year after his departure, it is probably not rash to assume that a person living out of Norway for more than a year without making the required declaration would be regarded as having no intention of returning. In Costa Rica nationality is lost by naturalization abroad, by acceptance of a post under a foreign state without consent of the national government, and by taking military service under a foreign power; a Costa Rican, however, who has been naturalized abroad can always resume his nationality by making a declaration of his intention to live in the

---

[1] Comp. p. 100 with p. 104 of Reports of Her Majesty's Representatives Abroad upon the Laws of Foreign Countries, Parl. Papers, Miscell. No. 3, 1893.

PART II.
CHAP. I.
Republic and to renounce his foreign national character; if he has been in civil employment elsewhere, he has in addition to declare that he has given it up. In Servia nationality is wholly lost by naturalization abroad, provided that the conditions prescribed by the fortieth article of the Constitution have been satisfied; these are that the obligations of service in the regular army shall have been fulfilled, as well as all duties under which the person intending to abandon Servian nationality may have lain, whether towards the State or private individuals[1].

Spain.
Spain takes up the position that loss of nationality by naturalization abroad is not accompanied with freedom from obligations to the State, unless it shall have been obtained with the knowledge and authorization of the Spanish Government. The release, in the absence of authority, being imperfect in the particular which is most essential to the permissibility of extending protection to a naturalized person in his country of origin, a naturalized subject of Great Britain, Spanish by origin, is not a British subject in Spain unless he has received permission to expatriate himself.

Switzerland.
A Swiss citizen can only lose his Swiss nationality by express renunciation, which can only be made after acquisition of a fresh national character, which is conditional upon his being domiciled abroad, and which need not be accepted by the State if objections are lodged by his commune or by other interested parties. In Luxemburg, on the other hand, naturalization in a foreign country is only recognized if the person naturalized has previously been released from his Luxemburg allegiance[2].

Luxemburg.

Argentine Confederation.
The Argentine Confederation refuses to allow any citizen to sever himself from the State; naturalization abroad subjects him to loss of political rights, but he

---

[1] M. Pavlovitch in Journal de Droit Int. Privé, xi pp. 4 and 140.
[2] Von Bar, Private International Law, trans. by Gillespie, p. 148 note.

remains burdened by every obligation. Finally, Venezuela simply ignores foreign naturalization; the Venezuelan naturalized abroad is subjected to the same duties and enjoys the same rights as citizens living upon the soil of the republic [1].

PART II.
CHAP. I.
Venezuela.

§ 24. The Naturalization Act of 1870, by a general enactment which seems to have the widest application of which the Act is capable, declares that a woman shall be deemed to be a subject of the state of which her husband is for the time being a subject, so that a foreign woman on marrying a British subject becomes herself a subject of Great Britain; and by the laws of most States a native woman, on marrying a foreigner, loses her nationality of birth, and a foreign woman on marrying a subject or citizen acquires his nationality [2].

Acquisition of British nationality by marriage.

The position, therefore, of a foreign woman married to a British subject is usually clear; there are, however, a few exceptional cases in which doubt may exist or conflict may arise.

Within the United States, for example, the position of an American woman who has married a British subject is somewhat uncertain. By the common law of the United States she retains her American nationality [3]; and the common law has never been expressly modified by legislation. It has been supposed, and it is possibly the case, that the common law has been implicitly abrogated by the Bill of Protection of 1868, which affirms

Question as to the law of the United States.

---

[1] Arts. 7 and 10 of the Venezuelan Constitution. Cogordan, Annexe L., H.H.

[2] By the laws of France, Greece, Italy, and Guatemala a widow or divorced woman who has been married to a foreigner recovers her nationality upon making a declaration of wish to do so, and taking up her residence in the country. In Russia she can reassume her Russian national character on presentation of a certificate to the effect that she is no longer a married woman. Report of Her Majesty's Representatives Abroad upon the Laws of Foreign Countries, Parl. Papers, Miscell. No. 3, 1893.

[3] Shanks v. Dupont, iii Peters 243.

the principle of the right of expatriation, and lays down amongst other things that any decision of any functionary of the Government, tending to restrain this right, is 'contrary to the fundamental principles of this government[1].' Any judgment of the Courts, therefore, in restraint of the right of expatriation, is *ipso facto* null. But a right of expatriation is a right conferred on the individual to denude himself of his nationality of birth and to adopt a foreign nationality by his own voluntary act directed to that end; it hardly seems to cover a case in which a woman on her marriage simply receives a foreign nationality by imputation of law, without being obliged to make any express renunciation of her American nationality. The acquisition of a new national character does not necessarily extinguish that which previously existed, even from the point of view of the state of which the nationality is acquired; and it might well be that an American woman in marrying a foreigner would wish to remain American as within the United States. Until the Supreme Court has decided whether the common law has in this respect been abrogated, it can hardly be prudent to assume that the American wife of a British subject is herself a British subject within the jurisdiction of her country of origin.

Exceptional provisions of French and Portuguese law. A peculiarity of French and Portuguese law leads to the necessity of also exercising caution in connexion with the wives of persons of French or Portuguese origin who have become naturalized in Great Britain. The wife of a French citizen, upon the acquisition of a new nationality by her husband, may if she chooses retain the nationality possessed by him at the date of the marriage; and the wife of a Portuguese, if herself Portuguese, keeps her nationality unless

---

[1] Fortieth Congress, Session ii, ch. 249. The United States Circuit Court in the case of Pequignot *v.* City of Detroit (16 Fed. Reporter, 212) seems to have held on this ground that a woman, naturalized in the United States by marriage with an American citizen, resumed her alienage by marriage with a subject of her native country.

she declares it to be her wish to follow that of her husband. Hence, while a Frenchman naturalized in Great Britain is a British subject within the British Empire, in third states, and in France if no impediment to his naturalization has existed under French law, his wife, who is considered by Great Britain to be a naturalized subject in virtue of her marriage, may also be claimed by France, whether she be of French or of other origin, if, having been married while her husband was French, she has elected to retain her French nationality. In the case of Portuguese, the same result follows from nearly identical circumstances. In cases where the interests of the husband and wife are in collision, it is obvious that jurisdictional questions of some difficulty might arise[1]. PART II. CHAP. I.

It seems to be uncertain whether a woman who is a native of Uruguay loses her nationality in marrying a foreigner, but the weight of opinion seems to be in favour of its retention. In Ecuador a native woman retains her nationality so long as she remains in the country; and in Venezuela and Haiti she keeps it in all circumstances[2]. Countries in which marriage with a foreigner does not involve change of nationality.

Under the Act of 1844 a curious question has arisen, to which it may not yet be superfluous to refer. It was usual, in certificates of naturalization granted under that Act, to insert a clause providing for forfeiture of the naturalization by residence abroad. Was this condition personal to the man; or did the wife, naturalized through him, become subject to it? It seems reasonable to suppose that, as the wife follows the status of the husband, she would lose her nationality by his forfeiture; but that if he died without forfeiture, the widow would retain the status freed from the condition by which she has only been bound through him, and by breach of which on her part independently of Effect of the Act of 1844 upon widows infringing a forfeiture condition in the naturalization of their husbands.

[1] Von Bar, p. 173. Report on Nationality and Nationalization, Parl. Papers, Miscell. No. 3, 1893.

[2] Report on Nationality and Naturalization, Parl. Papers, Miscell. No. 3, 1893, and Cogordan, 262 of ed. 1, and Annexe H. H.

him, it is evident that during his life she could never have lost her British national character.

Effect of nullity of marriage. It may be noted that if a marriage is null by the law which has the right of deciding upon its validity, the naturalization effected by the marriage is also null, the declaration of nullity having a retrospective effect; but until the nullity is judicially declared, the woman, if proceeded against by the putative husband, must be assumed to be invested with his nationality; if, on the other hand, the proceedings are taken by her, it may be doubtful whether she has not the alternative right, as may be more to her advantage, of going upon the supposition that she retains her nationality of origin, or of availing herself of the presumption that the marriage is real until its reality is disproved, and so of acting as a person naturalized in the state to which the husband belongs[1].

Loss of British nationality. § 25. The status of a British subject may be lost—

(1) by natural born British subjects of British origin:
 (i) through naturalization in a foreign state;
 (ii) by declaration of alienage, if born out of the British dominions of a father being a British subject;
 (iii) through marriage, in the case of a woman, with an alien.

(2) by natural born British subjects of foreign origin, and by naturalized persons—
 (i) by declaration of alienage;
 (ii) through marriage, in the case of a woman, with an alien.

British subjects, whether natural born or foreigners who

---

[1] Cf. Von Bar, pp. 173 and 175. It may also be noted, though the point is not perhaps very likely to be of much practical interest with reference to British natural born or naturalized subjects, that women permanently separated from their husbands by catholic ecclesiastical law do not in catholic countries follow their husband's naturalization, when he takes up a new national character.

have been naturalized, can only acquire a fresh nationality in conformity with the provisions of British law. It is for the state, which relieves or deprives a person of its nationality, to determine the conditions under which its national character is lost. The provisions of British law affecting the matter are simple and large [1]. But simple and large as they are, a certain amount of comment upon them is requisite.

§ 26. Voluntary naturalization occurs when a person of due capacity becomes a subject or citizen of a foreign state at his own request, or when, being also of due capacity, he becomes a citizen or subject by operation of law in such circumstances that his wish or consent may be presumed. Capacity being of course defined, like all other conditions of the loss of British nationality, by English law, persons below the age of twenty-one years, insane persons, and idiots are incapable of becoming naturalized in a foreign state, nor can married women be naturalized independently of their husbands.

Naturalization in a foreign state.

Into the conditions under which nationality can be acquired in foreign countries after the performance of formalities which clearly attest the will of the individual it is not worth while to enter. Great Britain has no wish to question the effects of naturalization intended by both parties to the contract. It would be more important, were it possible, to lay down general rules for the validity of naturalization by operation of law. But on this point it is

---

[1] Naturalization Act, 1870, Sects. 3, 4, 6, and 10. The Act is expressly retrospective in regard to naturalization abroad, it being applicable to 'any British subject' (presumably alive at the date of its enactment) 'who has, at any time before' it was passed, become naturalized in a foreign state. It was no doubt intended also to be retrospective in regard to marriage. 'A married woman shall be deemed to be a subject of the state of which her husband is for the time being a subject'; a woman, therefore, found at any time after the passing of the act to be married to a foreigner, is a subject of the state to which he belongs irrespectively of the date of her marriage.

PART II.
CHAP. I.

Naturalization by operation of law.

difficult to go beyond the statement, already made, that there must be sufficient presumption of consent.

A state has necessarily the right in virtue of its territorial jurisdiction to confer such privileges as it may choose to grant to foreigners residing within it; and when the status of subject or citizen is accepted by a foreigner according to the forms prescribed by the state legislation, he becomes in every respect, as between the state and himself, a member of the state community. But apart from the assent of the individual privileges alone can be conferred; a state has no right to impose the obligations of nationality, still less to insist that the foreign subject shall abandon in its favour his nationality of origin. Whether or not a fair presumption of consent has arisen must always be a matter of deduction from the facts of the case. Obviously a person entering Venezuela for the purposes of his commerce cannot be supposed to accept the position of a Venezuelan citizen simply because a decree of the President has invested every immigrant upon his arrival with Venezuelan nationality [1]; and far short of so extreme a case, it is at least questionable whether the nationality of a country in which a foreigner is living ought ever to be imputed to him until after the performance of some act on his part showing a desire to associate himself with the public life of the state. From acts not merely of a political, but of a municipal, nature he may be expected to refrain if he holds to his country of origin, and before doing them it is only reasonable that he should inquire whether their effect would be inconsistent with his wishes. But mere residence, marriage with a native, the acquisition of landed property, and other such acts, lie wholly within the range of the personal life; they may be the necessities of commercial or industrial business; they indicate no intention on the part of the

[1] Resolution of the Venezuelan Government of Dec. 1, 1865. Cogordan, Annexe H. H.

individual doing them to throw off his ancient allegiance; and so long as he confines himself to them, his national character may properly be considered to remain unaltered. The extent to which it may be reasonable or excusable for a country to impute its nationality to a foreigner, whether on the ground of residence or of the performance of acts without apparent significance in themselves, is no doubt favourably affected by permission being accorded to him to make a declaration of adherence to his nationality of origin before the expiration of some fixed period of residence ; but it cannot be admitted, so long as it is exceptional for states to impute their nationality to resident foreigners, that a provision to this effect can bind other countries to recognize the validity of imputed naturalization, unless the period is of considerable length, and unless the terms of the law are brought to the individual notice of all foreigners establishing themselves in the territory. The average person cannot be expected to inquire whether a trap is laid for him by the constitution of the state into which he enters, and ought not to be damnified by omission to take a precaution the necessity of which he could not fairly be supposed to divine [1].

[1] By the 69th article of the Brazilian Constitution of February 1891 'foreigners who, having been in Brazil on the 15th November 1889, shall not have declared within six months after the Constitution comes into force, their intention to retain their original nationality,' together with 'foreigners who possess real property in Brazil, and who have married Brazilian women or have Brazilian children, so long as they reside in the country, unless they announce their intention to retain their original nationality' are declared to be Brazilian citizens. In Bolivia every person who marries a Bolivian woman, or who buys landed property in the Republic becomes *ipso facto* naturalized; in Uruguay by the Constitutional Charter of 1829, persons who should marry an Uruguayan woman, or should buy landed property, or should exercise any industry, or being married should live three years in the country, were declared to be Uruguayan citizens. In 1853 a law was passed making it a condition of the enjoyment of the rights of a citizen by such person that a patent of naturalization should be asked for and delivered. It does not however appear certain that they are legally freed

PART II.
CHAP. I.

While in determining whether a given person is or is not a British subject it has to be inquired whether a foreign nation has unduly imposed its national character upon him, it has also to be inquired whether the foreign nation has admitted him to the full status of subject or citizen, or has contented itself with investing him with civil rights within its own boundaries. In the latter case it is of course possible, though not very probable, that the person enjoying such rights may be a British subject even within the state of which he has partially become a member; and he continues to be a British subject for all purposes in countries other than the state in question[1].

from the obligations of citizenship. Venezuela seems to appropriate every one who enters the country otherwise than as a passing traveller; and it appears probable that nationality may be unduly imputed in Colombia, the constitution of which declares foreigners to be Colombians by naturalization, if they have lived a year in the Republic and manifest their intention to acquire a domicile there (avecindarse). The language is wide and vague, but perhaps it may have been interpreted to mean that some positive declaration of intention shall be made; as in the analogous case of the Argentine Republic, where notwithstanding language in the Constitution which seems to confer nationality upon certain classes of persons automatically, it has been decided by the Supreme Court that Argentine national character is in no circumstances imposed upon a foreigner. Nationality and Naturalization, Parl. Papers, Miscell., No. 3, 1893. Cogordan, Annexe O. Calvo, Le Droit International, Liv. viii, Sect. 1.

[1] Perhaps the above may be the position occupied in Spain by an 'avecindado' who has not renounced his British nationality. 'Vecindad' is a sort of citizenship, which does not of itself confer naturalization, but which used to separate the persons enjoying it from passing strangers (transeuntes) by carrying with it the privileges of Spanish law, which were withheld from mere foreigners. It is acquired, amongst other ways, by marrying a Spanish woman and residing in the kingdom, by possession of real property, by exercising a profession, or by living ten years in a town or village. The precise difference between the legal situation of an avecindado and that of a full subject on the one hand, or of a simple foreigner on the other, is very obscure; but that he differs from both is certain. It is not in the least likely that an Englishman obtaining vecindad ceases, in doing so, to be a subject of Great Britain.

Where two grades of naturalization exist a question may possibly arise whether persons in possession of the lesser naturalization have been so

THE STATUS OF BRITISH SUBJECTS. 49

§ 27. It has already been remarked that by the laws of most states a foreign woman, on marrying a subject or citizen, acquires his nationality; and that by the law of Great Britain a woman is deemed to be a subject of the state of which her husband is for the time being a subject[1]. An Englishwoman, therefore, on marrying a foreigner, is absorbed into his nationality by British law, and as a general rule acquires his national character by the law of the state to which he belongs. As regards the latter point, however, one exceptional case occurs. In the Argentine Confederation, by a provision of the law, which is remarkable in a state where the general conditions of naturalization are unusually easy, a foreign woman does not become Argentine on marrying an Argentine citizen[2]. This peculiarity, as it will lead to an Englishwoman who marries an Argentine citizen having no nationality in contemplation of British law, may occasionally produce

PART II.
CHAP. I.
———
Marriage of a woman who is a British subject with an alien.

absorbed into the foreign community as to have lost their British nationality.

[1] Previously to 1870 this may not have been so. Upon the law, as it then was, the national character of a British woman married to a foreigner was open to some doubt; but for any practical purpose it is now most likely immaterial whether doubt upon the subject was well or ill founded. The first subsection of section 10 of the Naturalization Act seems to refer, especially if read in conjunction with Sect. 6, not to women married subsequently to its enactment, but to women married to persons of another nationality, irrespectively of the date of their marriage. If this view be correct an Englishwoman married to a foreigner may have been a British subject up to the date of the Act; so soon as it was passed she was transferred to her husband's nationality. This construction may perhaps at first sight seem to be inconsistent with the view previously taken (§ 18) as to the non-retroactive effect of the fifth paragraph of the same section; but the appearance of inconsistency is superficial. The paragraph in question is limited in its application by the words 'certificate of naturalization,' which can only refer to the certificate contemplated by the Act itself, since that which was granted under the Act of 1844 was given under different conditions and had different effects. There are no words expressing or implying a like limitation in the first paragraph.

[2] Von Bar, 172, note.

E.

inconvenient results; but it in no way modifies the effect of that law. In all cases the conditions of loss of nationality are regulated solely by the law of the state to which a person is subject.

Marriage with an alien possessed of no nationality.

If a British subject marries a foreigner possessed of no nationality, it is to be presumed that she retains her own nationality of origin. The Naturalization Act of 1870 does not declare that a British woman loses her national character by the fact of marriage with a person who is not a British subject, but that marriage with the subject of a foreign state carries with it absorption into the nationality of the husband; it seems therefore to be a fair inference that she only ceases to be a British subject and is regarded as an alien from the moment at which she acquires a new national character. A foreign marriage is, in effect, for a woman a form of naturalization in a foreign country; and it is simply because of the inconveniences of double nationality that a person naturalized abroad becomes an alien. Where no double nationality can exist, no object is served by depriving of her nationality a person who is guilty of no wrong against the State[1].

Marriage with a person who has lost the privileges but not the obligations of his nationality.

The distinction above noticed between complete absence of nationality and privation of the privileges of nationality must however be borne in mind. An Englishwoman, for example, marrying an Austrian who has emigrated with the permission of his government, and who has not yet acquired a fresh nationality, remains a British subject until her husband becomes the subject of another state; but if she marries an Austrian who is an unauthorized

[1] It is to be wished that such cases as that of an Englishwoman married to an Argentine citizen could be brought within the principle of the above paragraph; in view however of the extremely clear language of the 10th section of the Naturalization Act of 1870, which declares unreservedly that 'a married woman shall be deemed to be a subject of the state of which her husband is for the time being a subject,' it seems impossible that the wife of a foreigner possessed of a nationality can retain her British national character.

emigrant, living in a state with which Austria has no treaty of free emigration, she no doubt acquires an Austrian nationality, notwithstanding that her husband has lost his right of citizenship.

PART II. CHAP. I.

If an Englishwoman marries a foreigner who loses his nationality subsequently to her marriage, her situation, after he has ceased to have any national character, would seem to be regulated by different considerations. She has acquired a foreign nationality by her marriage; but the circumstances which have extruded her husband from the community of his state do not taint her; she is as separate a personality as a son who has reached his majority, and she continues for good or evil to be identified with the state into which she has been received.

Loss of nationality by the husband subsequently to marriage.

When a person, who has been a British subject by birth, and who is married to a foreigner, becomes a widow, the fact of widowhood does not import reversion to her nationality of origin; and analogously when a like person has obtained, or has suffered, a divorce, she preserves her acquired national character. The foreign nationality is not a mere incident of marriage, to be put on and taken off with it; it is a permanent alteration of status, obtained by marriage, but independent of marriage in its duration and results.

Widowhood and divorce.

§ 28. A declaration of alienage is a statement made before a competent authority, specified in the Act of 1870, that the declarant desires to be thenceforth an alien. From the date of the declaration the declarant ceases to be a British subject.

Declaration of alienage.

Persons who may make a declaration of alienage are:—

(1) Persons who, by reason of their having been born within the British dominions, are natural born British subjects, but who at the time of their birth have become under the law of a foreign state subjects of such state, provided that they are of full age and under no disability.

(2) Persons born out of the British dominions of a father being a British subject, if of full age, and under no disability.

(3) Persons naturalized as British subjects, provided that a convention shall have been entered into between Great Britain and the state of their origin, permitting them to divest themselves of their acquired nationality within a limit of time fixed by the convention.

On these provisions it is only necessary to remark that they must be read subject to the rule, already stated, that the conditions of release from a given nationality are solely determined by the state granting the release, and that therefore the words 'full age' and 'disability' must be taken in the sense affixed to them by British law.

§ 29. Persons who have lost their British nationality by naturalization in a foreign state, or by marriage with a foreign citizen or subject, can recover their nationality of origin, provided in the latter case that they are widows [1] or have been divorced, on the same conditions as those upon which an alien by birth becomes a British subject. The persons recovering their nationality thus stand in a position identical with that of a naturalized alien, and not with that occupied by themselves previously to naturalization abroad.

Minors who have become foreign subjects by residence abroad with a naturalized father, and minors who, being children of an Englishwoman by marriage with a British subject, have become naturalized abroad by residence with her after she has married a foreigner, recover British nationality on the resumption of it by their parent; and in their case the recovery is complete, they being 'deemed

---

[1] It is of course a consequence of the effect of the Act of 1870, as stated in a previous note (§ 27) that a British woman married before that date, and becoming a widow after it, must recover her nationality in the same manner as a woman married after the Act was passed.

to have resumed the position of a British subject to all intents.'

Children born to a British father during a period of naturalization abroad, and children born of a British mother during a foreign coverture, are not specifically mentioned in the Act of 1870, and it is a question whether the language of the Act can be strained to embrace them. Notwithstanding the very general terms of the fourth subsection of the tenth section, which speaks of 'every child of such father or mother who during infancy has become resident in the British dominions with such father or mother,' it is difficult to include them among the children there contemplated, because on the most liberal construction of the words they can hardly be 'deemed to have resumed' a national character which they never possessed; and they cannot be covered by the fifth subsection, because a certificate of readmission is carefully distinguished from a certificate of naturalization, and the subsection in question applies only to children of persons who have received the latter. If neither the fourth nor the fifth subsections apply to the class of infants under consideration, their position must apparently be determined by the governing fact of the nationality of their parent at the moment of their birth; they have been born subjects of a foreign power, and they must remain its subjects until they can be independently naturalized. This solution of the difficulty might often involve no inconsiderable hardship, but it perhaps responds quite as well to the policy of the Act, which sedulously endeavours to avoid all possibility of collision with foreign powers, as would that which a violent construction of the fourth subsection might furnish. It may also be observed that upon the terms of the Act there is no alternative between regarding such children as aliens, and placing them in a situation which is more advantageous than that occupied both by

PART II.
CHAP. I.

other natural born subjects of foreign powers, and by their own parents. Whether or not it be reasonable to assimilate the position of readmitted British subjects to that of naturalized foreigners, there seems to be no adequate ground for treating preferentially their foreign born children.

Recovery of foreign nationality by persons naturalized in Great Britain.

§ 30. In foreign countries recovery of nationality is not attended by the limited effects which it has in Great Britain; a person who resumes his or her nationality resumes it for all purposes. So far therefore as the effect of foreign legislation upon the individual is concerned there is nothing under this head which calls for notice. He is in no way left upon the hands of Great Britain.

From the point of view of British legislation the case is different. By the third section of the Act of 1870, it is provided that 'where Her Majesty has entered into a convention with any foreign state to the effect that the subjects or citizens of that state who have been naturalized as British subjects may divest themselves of their status as such subjects,' such subjects or citizens may make a declaration of alienage under conditions prescribed in the section, and from the date of the declaration they shall be regarded as aliens, and as subjects of the state to which they originally belonged. No mention is made of subjects of a state with which no convention has been entered into; they therefore remain subjects of Great Britain.

It is to be presumed that in the unlikely case of application being made by persons of the latter class for protection within the country allegiance to which they had resumed, no endeavour would be made to afford it. It is not probable therefore that their existence, especially as their numbers must always be very limited, will ever give rise to embarrassment.

Double nationality.

§ 31. The object of the foregoing sections has been to ascertain what classes of persons fall under the denomina-

THE STATUS OF BRITISH SUBJECTS.   55

tion of British subjects, irrespectively, so far as possible, of the complications which are introduced through the possession of a second nationality by certain of their members. This having been effected, it now becomes necessary to examine under what conditions double nationality can exist in persons to whom a British character is attributed.

PART II.
CHAP. I.

§ 32. By the Act of 1870 a British subject who, before the passing of the Act, had become naturalized in a foreign state, and who consequently was by the then law a subject both of that state and of Great Britain, was enabled to retain his British nationality on making a declaration of his wish to do so, subject to the qualification that he was not to be deemed a British subject within the limits of the foreign state in which he had been naturalized, unless he had ceased to be a subject of that state in pursuance of the laws thereof, or in pursuance of a treaty to that effect [1].

English law in relation to double nationality.

The same qualification applies to an alien who has been naturalized in Great Britain, and to a British subject who, having been voluntarily naturalized in a foreign state, is readmitted to his British nationality [2]. In these cases double nationality exists, but in ordinary circumstances its existence is in no way likely to give rise to practical difficulty. Except through the performance of certain kinds of voluntary acts by the individual, in doing which he would follow the law of the country which he preferred, his nationality would only come into play if he stood in need of protection, or if a demand were made for his extradition. In applying for a passport he would make choice between his two national characters, and upon the state thus chosen would lie the burden of any more active protection which might subsequently be required. If a question of extradition were to arise, it is not probable that a competitive demand would be made by the two

[1] Sect. 6.   [2] Sects. 7 and 8.

PART II. CHAP. I.

states to which he might be attributed; and supposing such a case to occur, it would evidently be for the Courts of the third power to decide to what country he should be surrendered.

Double nationality may also exist in persons born within the British dominions, but for some reason other than naturalization, claimed also as subject by another state, and in persons born in a foreign country to whom Great Britain attributes her own national character. In these instances the conflicting claims are brought into immediate presence of each other. From the present point of view the result is that the members of the above classes are British subjects, whose quality as such is absolute until they shall appear, on being confronted with the laws of another state, to have a foreign nationality which the British government recognizes as being legitimately dominant within the territory of that state over the national character asserted by itself, and whom consequently it refuses, either as a matter of international policy or in obedience to law which it has imposed upon itself by enactment, to shelter there with its protection, or to allow to do acts under its sanction which are permitted to its unquestionable subjects.

Foreign laws. French laws.

§ 33. In this relation French law calls for particular attention. Taking those provisions only which are pertinent to the subject in hand; in other words, taking those only which refer to persons who, in the absence of a claim on the part of France, would be considered to be British subjects; the laws of June 26, 1889, and July 23, 1893, determine to be French:—

(1) Persons who, not having reached their majority before the former date, are children born in France to a foreign father not himself born in France, and who are domiciled[1] there at the time of attaining their majority

---

[1] Le mot domicile a été employé dans toutes les dispositions de la loi

according to French law; unless in the year following the attainment of their majority, they shall have intimated their intention of preserving their foreign nationality in a certain prescribed manner, and proved the retention of their nationality of origin by producing a certificate in due form from the British Government. The above class of persons are regarded as French until the required formalities have been gone through, and may consequently be obliged to go through the usual service in the army[1].

(2) Persons who have been born in France at a later date than June 26, 1867, of a foreign parent not himself or herself born there, and who, not being domiciled at the date of their majority, shall have applied before the age of twenty-two years to fix their domicile in France, and having fixed it accordingly, have claimed French nationality within a year of the date of application. So long as such persons are minors they are not considered to be French unless they shall, if drawn for military service, obey the call without pleading alienage, or unless their father, mother, or guardian, shall in prescribed

de 1889, dans le sens le plus large de résidence, aussi décide-t-on que l'article 8, paragraphe 4, s'applique (1) aux individus qui nés en France y résident lors de leur majorité même si leurs parents ont leur domicile légal à l'étranger; (2) aux individus qui résident à l'étranger mais dont les parents sont domiciliés en France. Stemler in Rev. de Droit Int. Privé, xvii. 563.

[1] After the law of 1889 came into operation, a claim of exemption from military service was made by the son, born in France, of a British subject also born in France, on the ground that the law was not retroactive. It was decided that he was liable independently of the special provision with respect to sons of foreigners themselves born in France. In all cases in which option is permitted after attainment of majority, 'le droit de la nationalité étrangère n'est pas fixé sur la tête' so long as a person is a minor. The appellant was a Frenchman in the eye of the laws of 1851 and 1874 until he had exercised the right of repudiating his French nationality, and 'la faculté qui lui était laissée à cet égard n'avait pas le caractère d'une condition suspensive.' Trib. Civil de Bordeaux, Juillet 11, 1892, ap. Rev. de Droit Int. Privé, xix. 997.

circumstances have made a declaration on their behalf of intention to adopt French nationality.

(3) Persons who have been born in France later than the above date of a foreign parent, whether father or mother, who has also been born in France; except that if it be the mother who has been born in France, they shall be permitted, in the year following their majority, to declare for retention of their foreign nationality in the same manner as is prescribed for the first class of persons above mentioned [1]. Thus if an Englishman, born during a winter visit of his parents to Cannes, becomes a secretary of the British Embassy at Paris, the children born there during his residence on diplomatic duty are French irretrievably, liable to all the onerous incidents of French nationality, and without legal means of obtaining their freedom. In so extravagant a case no doubt some administrative means would be found to avoid the application of the law [2]; but instances of extreme hardship will assuredly take place long short of this point, for it is not every foreigner who thinks it a privilege to be a Frenchman. It has, for example, been decided by the Appeal Court of Pau that a person born of foreign parents, one of whom was born in France, cannot be allowed to escape the liabilities of his French nationality on the ground that he has been called upon in his own state for military service, failure to go through which would, of course,

---

[1] Nationality and Naturalization Reports, Parl. Papers, Miscell. No. 3, 1893; and Miscell. No. 4, 1893, in continuation of the foregoing. The laws of 1889 and 1893 apply to Algeria, Guadaloupe, Martinique, and Réunion. They can be extended to any other colonies by administrative decree, but until such decree be issued, colonies other than those mentioned remain under the previously existing law.

[2] MM. Le Sueur and Dreyfus, 'Attachés au Ministère de la Justice,' writing on the effect of the law of 1889, in the Revue de Droit International Privé (xix. 102), indicate means by which, in their opinion, the French government might be able to effect the exemption of children of diplomats and other persons in whose favour it might be wished to make an exception from the rigour of the law.

expose him to punishment far better deserved than that which would await him in France for disregard of his so-called duties there [1].

(4) Persons born in France before 1867 of a foreign parent, who was himself or herself born in France, provided that they have not exercised the right of option on attaining their majority; it having been decided that the law of 1889 is not retroactive [2].

(5) Persons who are born abroad of a French father, if legitimate; or who, if illegitimate, are there born of a French parent, and are subsequently recognized by such parent, or attributed to him or her by due process of French law, provided that, the other parent being of a different nationality, recognition by, or attribution to, him or her has not previously taken place [3]. It follows from this state of the law that persons born in wedlock of a French father, within the British dominions, have both French

---

[1] It may be useful to exhibit the effect of British law and of the French laws of 1889 and 1893 in a comparative table.
  A. British male subject born within the British dominions.
  B. Son born in France to A of British wife born within the British dominions.
    British subject by English law.
    British subject, if not domiciled on attaining majority, by French law.
    French subject, if domiciled on attaining majority, but with right of option; French, until option be exercised, by French law.
  C. Son born in France to B.
    British subject by English law.
    French subject by French law, without right of option.
  D. Son of C.
    British subject by English law if born in the British dominions.
    French subject by French law if born in the British dominions.
    French subject by both English and French law if born in France.
  F. Son born in France of E, daughter born in France of A, married to British subject born in the British dominion.
    British subject by English law.
    French subject by French law, with right of option.

[2] Trib. Civil de Lille, 1890; Journal de Droit Int. Privé, xix. 706.

[3] Cour d'Appel de Nancy, Mars 25, 1890; Journal de Droit Int. Privé, xviii. 539; Code Civil, Liv. i. Tit. i. § 10; Arts. 8 and 12 of the law of 1889.

and British nationality, and that among illegitimate children, all of whom have British nationality by being born on the soil, those who have been born either to a Frenchman or of a Frenchwoman, and have been recognized by, or attributed to, the French parent in accordance with French law, are themselves French.

(6) Children of French fathers, and presumably the other children above mentioned, together with like children born in France, retain their nationality notwithstanding the acquirement by their fathers or mothers of a foreign national character [1].

In other countries than France the law bearing on the subject in hand is invariably more simple than it there is, and the conditions under which a British subject may be affected by a second national character do not need a like distinct and minute investigation. It will be sufficient to separate the various states into groups corresponding with the principles which underlie their law [2].

States in which the children of foreigners, born within the state jurisdiction, are themselves foreigners. In the larger number of European countries, and in some American republics, the children of foreigners born within the state jurisdiction are themselves foreigners. This is the law in Austria, Hungary, Belgium, Denmark, Germany, Greece, Roumania, Russia [3], Servia, Spain, Sweden, Norway [4], Switzerland, Salvador, and Costa Rica. Italy adheres in principle to the rule, but makes the

---

[1] Von Bar, p. 175, note.

[2] Except when other reference is made, the legal facts stated in the remainder of this section are derived from the Reports of Her Majesty's Representatives abroad upon the Laws of Foreign Countries. Parl. Papers, Miscell. No. 3, 1893.

[3] Children of aliens, not Russian subjects, born and educated in Russia, acquire the right of being admitted to Russian allegiance, should they desire it, within one year after the date on which they shall have attained their majority. The law is merely permissive; and choice of Russian nationality must be evidenced by an oath of allegiance being taken before a Provincial Board.

[4] The law relating to Norwegian State Citizenship of April 21, 1888, contains no express statement to the above effect, but the fact is an inevitable deduction from the language of the first section.

exception that 'the child of an alien who has established a legal domicile by an uninterrupted residence of ten years, for other than commercial purposes, within the kingdom, is recognized as a citizen, power being reserved to him, on attaining his majority, to elect to become an alien by making a declaration to that effect [1].' A further temporary exception is caused by the Code of 1866, which is at present in force, not being retrospective; persons born in Italy of British parents before that date remain Italian subjects. Bulgaria, while also adhering in principle to the rule, arrests its operation at the children of foreigners who have been themselves born in the country; but it enables them to elect, during the year following the attainment of their majority, whether they will become Bulgarian or will preserve their foreign nationality. In the Netherlands children of foreigners not domiciled in the kingdom are themselves foreigners; those that are born of domiciled parents are prima facie Netherland subjects, but all claim to them is relinquished so soon as it is shown that, by the law of their country of origin, they remain its subjects. Thus the national character of children of British origin is determined by English law [2]. In Portugal and in Mexico the principle of the law is reversed, and the children of foreign parents are regarded as territorial subjects, unless they shall personally declare on reaching their majority, or in the former country while still minors through their parents or guardians, that they wish to retain their nationality of descent.

PART II. CHAP. I.

Modifications of the principle.

States in which the principle of law is reversed.

In states which unreservedly recognize the foreign character of the children of foreigners, there is of course no

Effect of the above laws.

[1] The exception assumes a certain importance in view of the fact that, while election is made at the age of twenty-one, it is the practice to call up conscripts at twenty. In the only two known cases, however, in which persons of the above class have been drawn by conscription, they have been discharged on production of a certificate attesting their British nationality.

[2] Law of December 12, 1892, Parl. Papers, Miscell. No. 5, 1893.

PART II.
CHAP. I.

States in which children of foreigners, born within the state jurisdiction, are subjects.

possibility that a British subject may find himself in unwilling possession of a second nationality. In those which, whatever the principle of their law, offer means of ready escape from the status of subject or citizen, there is little chance that embarrassment or difficulty will arise, except perhaps in the case of Italy, with reference to persons born before 1866. It is otherwise in the very considerable number of states which hold that nationality is conferred by birth within the territory. In the Argentine Confederation, Bolivia, Brazil[1], Chile, Guatemala, Paraguay, Peru, Uruguay, and Venezuela[2], all persons born within the state are its subjects or citizens, and in Ecuador all such persons are so if their fathers are 'resident' in the country at the moment of their children's birth. In all these cases, except the last, children born to a British father during the most transient passage through the country, are saddled with the territorial nationality, and in strict law remain subjected to all obligations and inconveniences arising from it, if at any subsequent time they re-enter the state.

The United States occupy a position apart. By the fourteenth amendment to the constitution 'all persons born in the United States and subject to the jurisdiction thereof, are citizens of the United States;' and by section 1992 of the Revised Statutes 'all persons born in the United States and not subject to any foreign power are declared to be citizens of the United States.' It might be somewhat difficult to seize the intended effect of these provisions if it were necessary to interpret them without external assistance. Happily an administrative gloss has been provided, which seems — if I rightly understand it — to afford a very reasonable and convenient sense. Starting from the judicially ascertained circumstance that Indians

---

[1] It appears that the sons of foreigners are administratively exempted in Brazil from the conscription, though in strict law they are subject to it. Cogordan, p. 45.   [2] Ib. p. 44.

are not citizens of the United States because they are not, in a full sense, 'subject to the jurisdiction' of the United States, it is considered that *à fortiori* the children of foreigners, in transient residence, are not citizens, their fathers being subject to the jurisdiction less completely than Indians. The children of foreigners, who are not naturalized, but who are in more prolonged residence, fall provisionally within the category of American citizens; but they lose their American character if they leave the United States during their minority. They are allowed to resume United States nationality on arriving at full age; and in connexion with this permission arises the only difficulty which, from the point of view of British practice, is offered by their situation. No specific mode of declaring election seems to be provided, so that in contentious cases it might perhaps be found that an inference of election had been made by the Government of the United States without warrant in the intention of the individual.[1]

Cases of imputed nationality, or of naturalization by operation of law, are not within the scope of the present section. If a British subject has acquired a foreign nationality in circumstances which raise a sufficient presumption of consent, his British character has been lost; if the imputation has been improperly made, he has never been clothed with a second nationality of international value[2].

Since Great Britain confers her nationality upon all persons born within her dominions, double nationality must exist in every case in which children are born in her territory to a foreign father whose state claims as its subjects the legitimate descendents, whether in the first or in a further degree, of home born parents. The states of which the laws make this claim are Austria, Hungary, Belgium[3],

Double nationality in the case of persons born in the British dominions.

---

[1] Wharton, Digest of the International Law of the United States, § 183.
[2] Comp. § 26.
[3] It has to be remembered, with respect to the probable legal position of children of a person prima facie Belgian, that Belgian nationality is lost by

PART II. Bulgaria, Germany, Greece, Italy, the Netherlands, Portu-
CHAP. I. gal [1], Roumania, Russia, Servia, Brazil, Guatemala [2], Costa
Rica, Chile [3], Mexico [4], Paraguay [5], Bolivia [6], the United
States [7], and Uruguay [8].

settlement in a foreign country 'sans esprit de retour.' It has at the same time to be remembered that Belgian law throws the burden of proof upon the person alleging that Belgian nationality has in this manner been lost.

A further complication is introduced into questions of Belgian nationality by the principle, affirmed in the Belgian courts, that 'l'enfant conçu est censé né, quand il s'agit de son intérêt.' If a Belgian acquires a fresh nationality between the conception and the birth of his child, the latter on attaining his majority may elect to declare himself Belgian.

[1] The claim is only made in the case of children of a Portuguese father, upon return to Portuguese territory and establishment of domicil in it. It does not appear in what domicil consists.

[2] Children of a Guatemalan father are not considered to be Guatemalans until 'the moment when they shall reside in the Republic.' Presumably this amounts to saying that they will not be protected abroad, but that they will be claimed on entering the state.

[3] On the translated text of the Chilean law there may be some doubt whether it is not a condition that both parents shall be Chilean. I have not had the advantage of seeing the original. On analogy and the probability of things I should suppose it more likely that a Chilean father would suffice.

[4] Inheritance of Mexican nationality is subject to the condition that the father shall not have forfeited it in certain specified manners.

[5] On condition of 'taking up residence.' It is not apparent whether this condition will be implied in certain circumstances, or whether it must be an evidently deliberate act intended to have legal effect.

[6] Upon acquisition of 'domicil.' It does not appear whether this is a voluntary act or not.

[7] 'All children heretofore born or hereafter born out of the limits and jurisdiction of the United States, whose fathers were or may be at the time of their birth citizens thereof, are declared to be citizens of the United States, but the rights of citizenship shall not descend to children whose fathers never resided in the United States.' Rev. Stat. § 1993, ap. Wharton, Digest, § 185. 'If, by the laws of the country of their birth, children of American citizens, born in such country, are subjects of its government, the legislation of the United States should not be construed so as to interfere with the allegiance which they owe to the country of their birth while they continue within its territory, or until they shall have relieved themselves of that allegiance and have assumed their rights of American citizenship in conformity with the laws and constitution of the country, and have brought themselves personally within its jurisdiction.' Mr. Frelinghuysen, Sec. of State, to Mr. Morton, Nov. 9, 1883, ib.

[8] The claim begins only 'from the moment' that 'establishment' in the States takes place.

In a certain number of countries illegitimate children born abroad of a native woman are considered to be subjects or citizens of the state, either absolutely, as in Germany, Greece, Hungary, Mexico, Spain, and Costa Rica, or conditionally upon taking up residence or becoming domiciled within the territory, as in Brazil, Ecuador, Guatemala, Paraguay, and Uruguay. In Portugal declaration of choice of Portuguese nationality, made during minority by the mother, or on attaining majority by themselves, forms an alternative to acquisition of domicil.

PART II. CHAP. I.

Illegitimate children.

§ 34. In their practical aspect questions of double nationality are less thorny than might in the abstract seem to be likely. The whole class of persons born during the passage of their parents through British territory, or during a purely temporary sojourn, and not subsequently resident, may be put out of consideration. They are not regarded as British subjects for any purpose external to the British dominions. Where the persons born to foreign parents upon British territory have themselves become identified with it by habitual residence, they will unquestionably be protected in countries other than their country of descent, and they would be claimed under an extradition treaty; but it may be doubted if circumstances could arise in which they would properly be held to be British subjects adversely to the state which also claims their allegiance. The general rule in such cases of double nationality is that the jurisdiction of the country in which the individual happens to be prevails over that of the competing state, notwithstanding that the nationality of the latter may evidently be the nationality of personal choice. All consequently that is open to Great Britain to do in favour of a subject by birth who has chosen to return to his country of descent is to use her good offices in circumstances which, if he were simply a British subject, would justify the exercise of diplomatic protection.

Questions of double nationality in their practical aspect. Persons of foreign origin born in the British dominions.

F

PART II.
CHAP. I.

Persons of British origin born abroad.

It is not, on the other hand, the practice to afford protection to British subjects born abroad if, by the laws of the state within which they are born, they are subjects of that state through the circumstance of birth within it. Practice was originally founded upon the principle of reciprocity; it is continued independently upon the ground of convenience. So long ago as 1843 the policy of the British government was laid down with great breadth and clearness. Lord Aberdeen having then had occasion to consult the Queen's Advocate with respect to the validity of a claim made by the government of Portugal to consider as Portuguese subjects all persons born in Portugal, notwithstanding that they might be the issue of foreigners residing in that country, wrote as follows to the British minister at Lisbon. 'The substance of' the Queen's Advocate's 'opinion is that although by the statute law of this country all children born out of the allegiance of the king, whose fathers and grandfathers, by the father's side, were natural born subjects, are themselves entitled to enjoy British rights and privileges while within British territory, yet the effect of British statute law cannot extend so far as to take away from the government of the country in which those persons may have been born, the right to claim them as natural born subjects, at least so long as they remain in that country. By the common law of England all persons born within the king's allegiance, whether the children of British subjects or foreigners, are deemed to be natural born subjects of the crown of England; and if the law of any foreign state upon this be the same as the English law, and if such foreign state places persons born within its territory upon the same footing as its own subjects or citizens, the government of that state has the right to exact the service of a subject from such persons, even if they may have been the children of foreigners, at least while such children remain in the country of their birth[1].' PART II. CHAP. I.

It has been observed, and will no doubt be remembered, that in time of peace between the countries interested, all disputable questions arising out of double nationality must be connected with the right of protecting subjects in a foreign state, or, since countries almost invariably refuse to surrender their own subjects accused of crime, with demands made for the extradition of particular persons under treaty of extradition. In other directions double nationality is without much practical importance. The quasi jurisdiction exercised by consuls, and the right to attach such value as a state may choose within its dominions, to acts done elsewhere by its subjects, remain unaffected by the fact that a person may have two national characters. In the former case the necessary connexion with a merchant ship of the

Actual range of disputable questions.

---

[1] Lord Aberdeen to Lord Howard de Walden, June 10, 1843. Naturalization Commission Report, 1869, Appendix, p. 72. See also Drummond's case, ii Knapp. 294.

On one occasion domicil was allowed to intrude itself for a moment into the law of nationality. Lord Russell, in dealing with the case of a Lieutenant Arguimban, who claimed exemption from military service in Spain, as being a British subject, wrote that it must be determined by the domicil of the parents at the time of the birth of the children within the territories of the crown of Spain. 'If, at the time of the birth of Lieutenant Arguimban, his father was not only a natural born British subject, but legally domiciled in the British dominions, I am of opinion that Lieutenant Arguimban himself was at the time of his birth a British subject, owing permanent allegiance to the British crown, and entitled to British protection. If, on the contrary, his father was then domiciled in the dominions of the Spanish crown, he became a Spanish subject, and is not entitled to claim British protection against any obligations resulting from his Spanish allegiance, although by an English statute he may be also entitled to the privileges of a natural born British subject in Great Britain.'

It is impossible to put too strongly that the domicil of a given person has nothing whatever to do with his national character; 'there is no authority,' said Chief Justice Cockburn in speaking of the case in question, 'for the introduction of domicil as an element in determining the question of nationality, according to the law of England.' Nationality, p. 112.

state fixes the momentary nationality of the individual for the purposes of consular jurisdiction. In the latter, whether ministerial acts be done by the agents of a state, or contracts or other acts be effected by its ordinary subjects, it is impossible that the sovereign rights of a country over the members of its community when within its territory, and its consequent right to give or refuse value there to acts wherever done, can be diminished by the existence of identical rights on the part of another state.

In time of war it is possible that attention might be called to a question which, whatever may be the solution that it must have received in foreign states, has not hitherto happened to become of practical importance to Great Britain. In countries where nationality is not lost by taking military service in another state—and English law contains no provision to that effect—what is the position of a subject who, in consequence of a claim made upon his allegiance elsewhere, appears in arms against his mother state or against a state to which he has voluntarily joined himself by naturalization? British law and practice would apparently give a simple answer. No doubt the practice of surrendering a British subject by birth to a state which also claims him, when he is within its territory, would be continued in time of war, and the individual would be regarded as a legitimate combatant; the claim of the enemy state would be reinforced by his own action, which whether really voluntary or not, would externally represent his own choice between the rival nationalities. The case of a naturalized subject is morally different; the person who voluntarily joins himself to a state community for his own advantage deprives himself of the right of fighting against it; but English law recognizes the superior legal claim of the country of origin by refusing to protect the naturalized subject within it; when a choice between the two allegiances becomes inevitable, she must, and no doubt would, give effect to the logical consequences of her own admission.

§ 35. Theoretically it is unnecessary, in view of possible occurrences it may be as well, to devote a few words to the legal situation of persons who are imperfect or inchoate subjects of foreign powers. When the conditions which have to be fulfilled for the acquisition of the nationality of a state include the performance of acts, which are separated from each other by a space of time, and of which the earlier express or imply a declaration of intention, the question has arisen, though in connexion only with the pretensions of a single government, whether a right accrues to the state to protect within foreign countries a person who has intimated his wish to become a subject or citizen, or whether that right comes into existence only at the moment when the full national character is imparted. By the law of the United States the conditions requiring to be fulfilled before admission to citizenship can take place are residence of five years in the country, and a declaration of intention to become a citizen made before a justice of the peace at least three years prior to application for admission. Under this law the government of the United States seems to consider that it has the right to extend its protection to persons who have made a declaration of intention to become citizens, but who have not yet been admitted to American nationality, and have not even fully satisfied the antecedent legal requirements. The attitude is one which it is not very easy to understand; but as more than one American Secretary of State has acknowledged that 'declaration of intention to become a citizen does not, in the absence of treaty stipulations, so clothe the individual with the nationality of this country as to enable him to return to his native land without being subject to all the laws thereof[1],' and as it is not very

PART II.
CHAP. I.

Imperfect nationality.

---

[1] Wharton's Digest of the International Law of the United States, § 175.

likely that questions will arise upon the point between Great Britain and the United States in third countries, the chances of collision are scarcely sufficient to render necessary an examination of the contention in detail. It is enough to say in relation to British law that the language of the enactment of 1870 contemplates perfected naturalization; the complete act alone is recognized. A British subject, while floating in the intermediate state, is a British subject still. From the point of view of international law the merits of the case are equally simple. A state may grant to a stranger the fullest privileges which a member of its community can possess as within its own territory, while refusing to undertake any responsibility for him abroad. By such action the interests and the rights of foreign states are untouched; to it they remain indifferent. But the action cannot be reversed. A state cannot hold out a stranger to foreign powers as having been received into its community, so long as he does not enjoy the rights which membership of the community involves. Substantially he must be in the same position as that occupied by born members of the state. It is solely because of that thorough association of a given individual with a nation, which is implied in the status of subject or citizen, that foreign governments refrain from asserting over him in certain respects the sovereignty which in strictness grasps every person on the soil of their territories. The association is fictitious abroad if it imports no correlative intimacy at home.

It is a further and different question whether the British government is bound, as between itself and subjects who are in the intermediate state, to afford in all cases the protection which it would extend to persons who had done nothing tending to separate them from their mother country. There would certainly seem to be occasions on which it is free to act according to its own convenience, or according to what it judges to be the equities of the case. During the American civil war various British subjects living in the United States appealed to the British government to obtain immunity for them from military service, and from other consequences of the state of war, to which they found themselves exposed. In some instances they had publicly declared their intention to become citizens as a condition of being admitted by anticipation to privileges of state citizenship; in others they had contrived, without their true status being known, to exercise political franchises to which none but full citizens in the particular state could be admitted. In such cases the British government considered the applicants to be morally estopped from denying the citizenship, the rights of which they had arrogated to themselves, or from repudiating obligations correlative to the privileges which, but for their formal expression of intention, they could not have enjoyed. Protection was refused. The adoption of preliminary steps towards naturalization, without possession or exercise of any privileges, stands on another footing. Up to the moment of completion of an act, the doing of which is spread over some time, a *locus paenitentiae* is always open, when the attitude of the person proposing to act remains one of mere intention. In cases where the applicants for protection were in this situation, protection seems to have been given. The difference in the merits of the cases, and the difference of conduct with respect to them, mark a distinction which may well constitute a foundation of general practice.

CHAPTER II.

GENERAL FUNCTIONS OF AGENTS OF THE BRITISH CROWN IN FOREIGN COUNTRIES.

<small>PART II.
CHAP. 2.

Classification of functions.</small>

§ 36. THE functions of agents of the British crown in foreign countries may be divided into three groups corresponding with their protective duties, with ministerial acts which they perform, and with the jurisdiction which they are permitted to exercise.

<small>Protective functions.</small>

§ 37. Speaking broadly, British subjects who enter a foreign country do so on the understanding that they must submit to the laws of that country. Apart from highly exceptional cases, in which the laws may be such as to constitute grievous oppression in themselves, all that strangers in a country can ask is that the protection of the state and the justice of its courts shall be afforded equally to them and to the territorial subjects, and so long as this fairness of administration is secured they cannot as a rule complain of the effects of the laws upon them, however great may be the practical injustice from which they suffer. If however the laws provide no remedy for obvious wrongs; if they are unjustly administered through corruption or prejudice; if administrative agents of the government maltreat a foreigner, and no means of obtaining legal redress through the tribunals exist, or such means as exist have been exhausted in vain; then the state to which the injured person belongs has the right to demand reparation, and to exact it if necessary by such means as it may find appropriate.

A reservation must also be made with regard to laws PART II. of a certain class. The foreigner resident in a country CHAP. 2. enjoys the advantages of public order; he not only therefore is bound to obey the laws which are enacted and enforced for its preservation, but may even be called upon to contribute in person to the support of the law. It is not beyond the rights of a state to enrol him in bodies of men used strictly for purposes of internal police, even if these bodies take the form of a militia. But at this point the rights of a state in this direction cease. In no case can a foreigner be employed, otherwise than voluntarily, against a foreign enemy, or against insurgents in possession of belligerent rights; so soon indeed as disturbances cease to be temporary in the fullest sense, and merge into civil war, the right of the state over a foreign subject falls to the ground. Being without political privileges, he cannot be obliged to identify himself with political action; and it is only so long as the action of a government can fairly be said to be police action against disorder or riot in contradistinction to political action against insurgents, that his duty to the state in which he resides for the time, survives.

When redress for any wrong is needed, request may be Redress of made in the first instance either by a diplomatic or consular wrongs. agent; consuls being empowered to make representations to the local officials. But if redress cannot be obtained from them, or if the subject of complaint be not within their jurisdiction, the case must be placed in the hands of the diplomatic representative; consuls not being permitted to act from the moment when the matter becomes international, and that direct appeal is made to the government of the country. If the diplomatic representative fails to arrive at a satisfactory settlement, the controversy naturally passes away from the immediate competence of the British agents, of whatever kind, resident in

PART II. the foreign state, and becomes a subject to be dealt with by
CHAP. 2. the two governments themselves.

Protective supervision of person and property.
Besides endeavouring to obtain redress for specific wrongs a consul exercises a general protective supervision in respect of both the persons and property of British subjects to guard them, so far as may be, from the likelihood of injury, and to afford them all reasonable assistance.

Passports.
Among the protective functions of consuls is that of issuing passports, if needed, to British subjects, and of affixing a visa to passports granted elsewhere, whenever local regulations require that foreigners passing through a place where a consul of their nationality is stationed shall have their passports countersigned by him. Before granting a passport it is the duty of a consul to satisfy himself by sufficient evidence that the person applying for one is a British subject; if he be an Indian or colonial subject the fact is noted by the insertion of his place of birth; if he be a naturalized subject the qualification that 'the bearer shall not, when within the limits of the foreign state of which he was a subject previously to obtaining his certificate of naturalization, be deemed to be a British subject, unless he has ceased to be a subject of that state in pursuance of the laws thereof, or in pursuance of a treaty to that effect' appears on the face of the document; and if he be naturalized in a British colony the consul is only enabled to grant a provisional passport, good for a limited time, so that the holder may return to his colony or to the United Kingdom [1].

[1] It may be worth noting that a new name cannot be added to an existing passport. If, therefore, for any reason a person becomes associated with another in a foreign country in such way as to affect the passport which may be held, the consul must either issue a fresh passport for the two, or a separate one for the person who needs British protection. Probably there is no scope for the application of the rule except in the sufficiently numerous cases of women marrying British subjects abroad.

It may also be worth noting that persons naturalized between 1850 and

In like manner it is among the protective duties of a consul, in cases of doubtful or disputed nationality, to transmit the evidence proving that a person is of British nationality to the local authorities, and if a certificate is required by them to supply one, provided that he is satisfied of the conclusive character of the evidence.

§ 38. Perhaps the most important of the functions having reference to individuals, which British agents in foreign countries are charged to perform, are those under which ministerial acts are embraced. Chief among ministerial acts is the celebration of marriage—a subject the largeness of which compels its treatment in a separate chapter; the minor categories include notarial acts, registration of births and deaths at consulates and diplomatic houses, and the protection of property belonging to deceased British subjects.

By the 6th Sect. of 52 Vic. ch. 10, 'every British Ambassador, Envoy, Minister, Chargé d'Affaires, and Secretary of Embassy or Legation, exercising his functions in any foreign country, and every British Consul-General, Consul, Vice-Consul, Acting Consul, Proconsul, and Consular Agent exercising his functions in any foreign place, may, in that country or place, administer any oath, and take any affidavit, and also do any notarial act which any Notary Public can do within the United Kingdom; and every oath, affidavit, and notarial act administered, sworn, or done by or before any such person, shall be as effectual as if duly administered, sworn, or done by or before any lawful authority in any part of the United Kingdom.'

PART II. CHAP. 2.

Ministerial functions.

Notarial Acts.

1870 under the Act of 1844, were only entitled to receive passports good for a limited time, and were obliged to obtain licences, also limited in duration, to reside abroad. There is no object in maintaining any distinction between this class of persons and the persons naturalized under the Act of 1870; and there is reason to believe that the practice of granting licences and limited passports must have in fact been dropped.

It is obligatory upon consular officers[1] to perform the functions with which they are thus invested, when required to do so by British subjects, in any case in which an oath, affidavit, or information may properly be required; and they are not entitled to decline to administer an oath or to attest a signature on the ground that they are ignorant of the correctness of the facts or of the contents of the document presented to them. They merely attest to the fact of an oath, affidavit, or information having been made, or of a document having been signed before them; they do not guarantee the correctness of the statements made, and they are not even permitted to insist on acquainting themselves with the contents of any document except so far as may be necessary to assure themselves that the matter is one as to which an oath can lawfully be administered, and that the notarial act, as performed by them, will not, in the circumstances, be an infraction of the territorial law[2].

There are, however, cases in which a consular officer is expressly asked to certify to the correctness of fact. On such occasions it is of course not necessary for him to accede to the request; it is on the contrary incumbent upon him to do so only when he is fully satisfied that his attestation can properly be given. Requests to attest the authenticity of the signature of a foreign official, or the validity of a document professing to be legally good in the country of residence of the consular officer, are instances of cases of this nature.

It is competent to a consular officer to perform any of the above functions at the instance of a foreigner, but whether he consents to do so or not is a matter for his discretion. It

---

[1] 5 & 6 William IV. cap. 62. sect. 13. It is believed that it is not obligatory upon a diplomatic officer to perform notarial acts when a consul is present in the place of residence of the former.

[2] Comp. § 41.

is not very easy to imagine a case in which he could properly so act if neither British subjects nor British interests were involved. PART II. CHAP. 2.

Diplomatic and consular agents keep registers for births, and for deaths, of British subjects occurring in the country to which they are accredited, or the district to which they are appointed. Consuls also keep a register of births and deaths which have occurred on board British ships touching at ports within their district. Registration of birth is of no legal value as regards the status of the child, and consequently implies no claim on the part of the state to the allegiance of the registered person, still less to his exclusive allegiance. There would seem, therefore, to be no objection to the registration of all persons of legitimate birth[1], whose parents can give *primâ facie* evidence that the child is a British subject. Registration of births and deaths.

Consular agents lie under the general duty of protecting to the best of their power the property of British subjects dying abroad, but unless more active functions are imposed upon them by treaty or the local law, they leave the management and realization of it to the persons succeeding or inheriting, except when there is no one on the spot able or legally competent to act. Property of British subjects dying abroad.

§ 39. The derivative jurisdiction, or quasi-jurisdiction, as it may perhaps be more accurately called, possessed by the British crown in foreign countries of the European type is limited as regards its objects to matters connected with British ships and their crews; ordinary travellers, commorants, or residents, being in all circumstances subjected completely to the local jurisdiction in respect of criminal and administrative law. The derivative jurisdiction in question is exercised in civil matters, and to a certain extent over persons, by consular officers; in the latter form more amply by courts called 'Naval Courts.' Functions of quasi-jurisdiction.

[1] Illegitimate children born abroad cannot be British subjects. Cf. § 16.

PART II.
CHAP. 2.

A consul having no magisterial power, and his powers altogether being extremely undefined, his position, whether in the assertion of discipline, the settlement of disputes, or any other of the minor subjects which come under his cognizance, is merely that of an arbitrator. He has no direct means of compelling obedience to any judgement that he may give. Indirectly, however, through his right to withhold his sanction to the discharge of a seaman, and his power to summon a naval court, which is possessed of coercive authority, he is able to use sufficient pressure; and minor offences can be restrained, and can be punished by arrangements, consented to by the parties to a dispute, to the effect that deduction shall be made from wages or sums be paid by way of compensation.

Crimes committed on board ship.

In the case of crimes committed on the high seas on board a British ship which subsequently comes into foreign territorial waters, and of offences against property or person committed anywhere in foreign territory by a person belonging to a British ship, or who has so belonged within three months previously, a consular officer may inquire into the circumstances on oath, and if there be in his view sufficient evidence against the accused person, he may send the latter home for trial; for this purpose he is in possession of coercive power.

Naval Courts.

When a consul is unable in light cases to act in the manner above indicated, because of the indisposition of the persons concerned to accept his judgement, or in more serious cases, is either desirous that a summary punishment shall be inflicted, or that he should be assisted by the opinion of other competent persons before determining to send home the accused for trial, any naval officer in command of a Queen's ship on a foreign station, or in the absence of such an officer the consul himself, may summon a naval court composed of a naval or consular officer as president, and not less than two or more than four other members, who must be either naval officers, a consular officer, masters of British merchant ships, or British merchants[1]. Naval courts are empowered to punish misdemeanours and other offences against the Merchant Shipping Acts, in respect of which two justices would, if the case were tried in the United Kingdom, have the power of summary conviction[2]. In cases of murder, piracy, slave trading, manslaughter, aggravated assault, wilful destruction of a ship, mutiny, and other serious offences, the accused person is sent home for trial, if there be a *primâ facie* case against him, at the public expense; and in cases of theft, insubordination, and like matters he is also sent home on an undertaking being given by the master or agent of the vessel, or other person concerned, that he will prosecute and pay the expenses of sending home the offender and the witnesses.

§ 40. The foregoing brief statement in outline of the jurisdiction exercised by consuls and naval courts shows that accused persons may be held in custody, may be tried and sentenced to imprisonment or lesser penalties, and may be sent in custody out of the territorial jurisdiction, either for the purpose of being tried or of undergoing a sentence. If these powers were regarded as ousting the local jurisdiction, still more if they were extended in any of their effects to the soil of the country[3], they would

Relation of the above powers to the local law.

---

[1] There are fixed rules as to the proportions in which the different elements may be combined.

[2] The most important misdemeanours are :—any breach of duty by which ship, or life, or limb is endangered; wrongfully forcing a seaman ashore, or leaving him behind; leaving seamen behind without the formal consent of a consul; and failing to render assistance, &c., in cases of collision. Merchant Shipping Act, 1854, sects. 206-8, and 239, and the Act of 1873, sect. 16. The list of misdemeanours is by no means exhausted by the above.

[3] Persons are no doubt frequently sent on shore from ships to a consulate in custody, but in such cases there is obviously at least tacit consent on the part of the territorial authorities. Adversely to such authorities it cannot be done.

PART II.
CHAP. 2.

constitute a serious derogation from the sovereignty of the foreign state. Great Britain, however, makes no such pretension. She fully admits the supremacy of the territorial law, not merely on land, but in the ports and harbours. She recognizes that every country has the right of enforcing its own criminal laws and police regulations, and that if any offence is committed against such laws or regulations on board a British merchant ship in territorial waters, or outside the ship by a person belonging to it, the offender is liable to be locally dealt with. In such cases Great Britain confines the duty of her consuls to seeing that the person accused is fairly tried, and that justice is properly administered, reserving to herself the protective rights which have been already mentioned.

But while the supremacy of the territorial law is admitted, subject to the qualifications introduced by custom and treaties, Great Britain has the right to demand not merely that the narrowest international custom shall be observed, but that a foreign state shall act upon the doctrine held by it, and usually applied, as to the due range within which it may assert its authority.

Usual practice in civil and criminal matters.

Probably no state would be anxious to mix itself up with questions of breach of contract or other civil disputes [1]. Were it even disposed to do so, occasions for the exercise of its jurisdiction would be few. Apart from miscellaneous disputes originating within its territory, questions arising out of contracts concluded there, and of contracts to which subjects of its own were parties, would alone be open to it. It is the usual course for the local authorities to permit the consul to settle these matters, and not to interfere without reference to him and reason for belief that he is unable to make a satisfactory arrangement.

In matters falling under the head of criminal jurisdiction

---

[1] Occasionally the consular officer finds it worth while to have matters of this sort adjudicated upon by the local courts by consent.

most states allow consuls to have exclusive charge of the purely internal order of the merchant vessels of their nation, and the local authorities intervene only when either the peace or public order of a port or its neighbourhood is disturbed [1], or when persons other than the officers and crew of a ship are mixed up in the breach of order which is committed. The usage is sufficiently established in its broad lines to render it a fair subject for international complaint if local authorities interfere in questions of discipline which involve offences criminal by British law; and generally abstention from interference goes considerably further. On one important point custom is decisively settled. If a person on board a British ship commits a crime on the high seas and is brought in custody into a foreign port, the territorial authorities will not interfere with his being kept in custody on board, nor with his being transferred to another vessel for conveyance to England [2]. But if a crime is committed in a port, the

[1] For example, in 1849 a murder took place on board an American vessel lying in the port of Havre, which excited so much feeling among the crews of other American vessels in the port that there was some talk of lynching the murderer. The local authorities stepped in, arrested, and tried the criminal. On the other hand, in 1889 a murder took place on board a British steamer at San Ramon Manzanillo in Cuba. No external disturbance seems to have taken place, and the Spanish authorities refused to take cognizance of the case, holding it to be one for the exercise of British jurisdiction. Ortolan, Diplomatie de la Mer, vol. i, Annexe J.; Rev. de Droit Int. Privé, xvii. 96.

[2] Of course the local authorities have no jurisdiction enabling them to try the offender, even if he be landed, unless he is a subject of their state. In the latter case, however, it is the view of Great Britain that concurrent jurisdiction on their part is permissible. Under a misapprehension of the law, the High Court at Calcutta tried an English sailor, who had stabbed the mate of an American vessel, and who had been brought into the port and handed to the local authorities for safe custody. The American minister in London complained of the exercise of jurisdiction by the High Court, alleging that as regards common crimes committed on board merchant vessels on the high seas the competent tribunals of the vessel's nation have exclusive jurisdiction. While surrendering the man on the ground that he had been tried under an erroneous view of the

PART II.
CHAP. 2.

authorities of different countries would no doubt take different views as to what amount or kind of disturbance to the peace or order of the port should attract their notice; their right to determine for themselves in what circumstances their jurisdiction should be exercised cannot be gainsaid.

Cases in which a consul has to call in the aid of the local authorities.

There are occasions on which it may become the duty, or be at least advisable, for a British consular officer to invoke the action of the local authorities. If an offence has been committed which is punishable both by British and by local law, and the territorial authorities are willing to take cognizance of the matter, reasons of convenience to the ship and the witnesses, or considerations based on promptness or certainty of justice being done, may prompt him to send a case before the courts of the country, if their practice can be trusted, and their modes of punishment are in harmony with English ideas. It is a matter for his discretion whether this course be adopted or not [1].

Since a British agent has no power of acting on the soil of a foreign state he must apply to the local authorities for the apprehension and surrender of an escaped criminal, or of a deserter, if they are willing to lend assistance, or if

municipal law, the British government recorded its dissent from the general proposition laid down by the American minister. It was not prepared to admit that a statute conferring jurisdiction on the British courts, in the case of offences committed by a British subject on the high seas on board a foreign vessel, or in places within foreign jurisdiction, would violate any principle of international law or comity; on the contrary, it was of opinion that there were many cases in which the assumption of such jurisdiction would subserve the purposes of justice. The British government did not intend to suggest that in ordinary circumstances it would be convenient or advisable to supplant the jurisdiction of the state which actually had a right at the place and time when the criminal act was committed.

[1] There are a certain number of consular functions in connexion with wrecks, salvage, &c., upon which it is unnecessary to touch, the jurisdictional elements in them being very slight. There are others connected with the engagement of seamen, &c., which are distinctly jurisdictional, but which do not call for any remarks.

a treaty or convention exists under which they are bound to do so. Agreements, in various forms, have been entered into between Great Britain and most foreign countries for the mutual surrender of seamen, other than slaves or subjects of the local territorial power, who desert from merchant ships of one of the contracting parties at ports belonging to the other [1].

§ 41. It is scarcely necessary to point out that as British consuls have no extra-territorial jurisdiction within states of purely European type, they cannot do any jurisdictional act in a foreign country of that type which is inconsistent with the local laws; so that if any act permitted or enjoined by the British government were found to be locally forbidden, it would be the duty of the consul to refrain from performing it until an arrangement had been come to between the two states. *Limitation by territorial law of consular powers given by British law.*

With regard to ministerial acts the case would seem at first sight to be different, The duties of a consul in the more important particulars, such as the celebration of marriage and the performance of notarial functions, are prescribed by statutes which confer benefits upon the subject. It is not for the official, as between himself and a British subject, to accord or withhold these benefits at his discretion or caprice. The subject has a right to demand that they shall be given. But the official and the subject do not stand alone, face to face. Territorial sovereignty has a higher right than the foreign law; and if the municipal law of the country forbids the act which the foreign law appears to prescribe, it must be supposed that the latter has been enacted in ignorance of the former,

---

[1] Agreements of the above kind have been entered into with Austria, Belgium, Chile, Colombia, Denmark, Ecuador, France, Germany, Greece, Italy, Madagascar, Morocco, Netherlands, Nicaragua, Paraguay, Peru, Portugal, Russia, Salvador, Sandwich Islands, Siam, Spain, Sweden and Norway, Tunis, Turkey, and Uruguay.

and that it does not intentionally clash with it. In other words, it is contrary to the comity of nations to allow a consul to do anything inconsistent with the law of the country in which he resides; there is consequently an absolute presumption that legislation enjoining acts, which are there unlawful, is invalid and nugatory to the extent of the unlawful acts. To take an example; the celebration of a marriage or the administration of an oath within the German Empire by any one who is not a duly qualified official of the German state, is punishable by fine and imprisonment. Before these territorial prohibitions the positive injunctions of British enactments become valueless, and the right of the British subject to demand the performance of acts for his benefit disappears. The right, therefore, of a British subject to require that any ministerial act shall be done for him by a British consul must always be tested and limited by reference to the municipal law of the territorial state[1].

[1] Though the precise point has never been decided in an English court, there can be no question what, if it were to present itself, the decision would be. 'If the meaning of an Act is doubtful,' said Mr. Justice Maule, in Leroux v. Brown, ' it is a reason for not putting a particular interpretation upon it, that that interpretation would violate the comity of nations' (xxii Law Journal, C. P., 3) ; and in Atkinson v. the Newcastle Waterworks Lord Cairns expressed the opinion that ' it must depend on the purview of the legislature in the particular statute, and the language which they have there employed,' whether, 'wherever a statutory duty is created, any person who can show that he has sustained injuries from the non-performance of that duty, can bring an action for damages against the person on whom the duty is imposed' ii. Ex. D. 448.

CHAPTER III.

CELEBRATION OF MARRIAGE BY BRITISH AGENTS IN FOREIGN STATES.

§ 42. It follows from the principles laid down in the first chapter that Great Britain can enable agents in foreign countries, duly empowered by itself, to celebrate marriages between British subjects, or between a British subject and a foreigner, which shall be good within the British dominions[1]. Such marriages were in fact formerly celebrated at diplomatic missions under supposed diplomatic privilege[2]; since the year 1823 they have been performed at diplomatic missions, under an Act of 4 Geo. IV. c. 91; by consuls since 1849 under an Act of 12 & 13 Vict. c. 68; and from an early period under implied authority on board ships of war lying in foreign waters, and within the lines of an army on foreign soil. It equally follows from what has been already said, that no marriages thus contracted under British authority, are necessarily valid out of the British dominions. Unless they are sanctioned by law, by treaty, by competent permission,

PART. II
CHAP. 3.

Summary of principles.

---

[1] In a bare legal sense Great Britain can also validate marriages as within its dominions, which are contracted in like manner to the above, between two persons neither of whom are British subjects. Legislation to this effect would, however, be clearly beyond its moral competence.

[2] It is not known to what date the practice goes back. Previously to the year 1816 marriages solemnized at British Embassies and Legations were registered only by the chaplains of the Missions, who kept the registers in their personal custody. They are now no doubt irrecoverable. In 1849 a notice was published in the London Gazette requesting persons in possession of such registers to send them in for deposit in the London Registry Office. Not one was forthcoming in answer to the appeal.

or as occasionally happens by privilege, they are not good within the state where they take place; and third states, if the question of validity came before them, would usually, and probably always, be guided by the *lex loci contractus*. Marriages, therefore, which are celebrated abroad by British officials, must be regarded from two points of view;—from that of the conditions of their validity within the British dominions, and from that of their relation to the law of the territory in which they are entered upon.

Provisions of the Marriage Act of 1892.

§ 43. The conditions precedent to the solemnization of a marriage abroad under the authority of a British agent, the forms to be observed and other conditions of the actual marriage, and the mode in which registration is to be effected, are now prescribed by an Act passed in 1892, entitled, 'an Act to consolidate enactments relating to the marriage of British subjects outside the United Kingdom' (55 & 56 Vict. cap. 23), and by an Order in Council, made in the same year, in pursuance of certain provisions contained in the Act [1].

Ambassadors, Consuls, Consular or other officers [2], and other persons appointed in manner specified, are empowered, when provided with a 'marriage warrant' signed by

---

[1] The Act of 1892 introduced no new principles. It merely substituted order for confusion and certainty for doubt. It is therefore superfluous, it might also be inadvisable, to review the circumstances in which marriages were previously contracted abroad under the actual or supposed sanction of British law. It is certain that some of the marriages thus contracted were invalid in the British dominions; it is possible, notwithstanding section 26 of the Act of 1892, that the validity of some of them may still be open to argument; but the defects of any which are not already validated by the section in question, can at any moment be cured by legislation, and would no doubt be at once remedied if sufficient reason should appear.

[2] In view of the very limited range of the functions of a Pro-consul it may be worth while to notice that by sections 11 and 24 of the Foreign Marriage Act, 1892, Pro-consuls are included among the persons capable of being marriage officers; although in no case, it is believed, has the necessary authorization been hitherto given.

a Secretary of State, or when duly authorized to act without a marriage warrant, to solemnize marriages in specified places, or to legalize them there by their presence [1].

Marriages may be solemnized between British subjects or between persons of whom one is a British subject. In every case each of the parties must appear before the officer appointed to perform or legalize marriages, and make oath that he or she believes that there is not any impediment to the marriage by reason of kindred or alliance or otherwise; that both of the parties have had for three weeks immediately preceding had their usual residence within the district in which the officer is authorized to act; and that where either of the parties, not being a widower or widow, is under the age of twenty-one years, the consent of the person or persons, whose consent to the marriage, is required by law, has been obtained, or, as the case may be, that there is no person having authority to give such consent. It is further required by the Act that a notice of the intended marriage, containing certain particulars, and especially stating that both parties have had their usual residence for three weeks and their residences [2] for not less than one week then preceding within the district, shall be delivered to the

---

[1] Sects. 8, 11, and 21.

It is believed that on some occasions English chaplains abroad, and even English clergymen temporarily appointed to officiate at the churches in places frequented by tourists on the Continent, have independently celebrated marriages, under the impression, it would seem, that the powers possessed by ambassadors, ministers, and consuls are shared by persons in orders, and that any marriage celebrated in due religious form must necessarily be valid. In view of a possible repetition of like irregularities it may not be superfluous to say that under the Act of 1892 no marriage is legal which is not performed in the manner and under all the conditions prescribed by the Act, except in places where no duly qualified marriage-officer is accessible (comp. § 55), or unless it be valid by the *lex loci*.

[2] It is to be presumed that the word 'residence' in this place means continuous residence, since the expressions 'residence' and 'usual residences' can hardly be intended to have the same signification.

officer in question. After the expiration of fourteen days from the date of the notice, the marriage may be solemnized if no lawful impediment has in the meantime been brought to the attention of the officer, and if the marriage has not been forbidden in manner provided by the Act [1]. These provisions are however modified by the Order in Council so as to permit that persons, one of whom only has dwelt within the district of the marriage officer, shall be married upon certain information as to residence being afforded under due guarantees, and upon notice of the intended marriage being given in the place of residence of the party not living within the district of the marriage office. A Secretary of State can also authorize the celebration of a marriage on being satisfied that it is not clandestine and that adequate notice has been given [2]; it is however understood that this power is rarely exercised, and only in cases of emergency or urgency.

The formal conditions of the actual marriage are that it shall be solemnized at the official house of the officer, with open doors, within the hours of eight in the forenoon and three in the afternoon, in the presence of two or more witnesses, and may be solemnized by another person in the presence of the officer, according to the rites of the Church of England, or such other form and ceremony as the parties thereto see fit to adopt, or may, where the parties so desire, be solemnized by the officer, provision being made that, when the rites of the Church of England are not followed, certain words shall be employed in some part of the ceremony [3].

Perpetuation of evidence of the marriage is secured by provision for the maintenance of a register, a copy of the entries in which for each year must be sent to a Secretary of State for transmission by him to the Registrar General [4].

---

[1] Sects. 1, 2, 4, 7, 8.
[2] Art. 6 of the Order in Council.
[3] Art. 8.
[4] Arts. 9 and 10.

While the largest possible range of persons is thus included within the marriage powers which are taken by the Act, and great elasticity in point of forms is accorded, power is given to the Queen in Council to obviate the risk, which might otherwise be sufficiently serious, of collision with the local jurisdiction, by 'prohibiting or restricting the exercise by marriage officers of their powers under the Act in cases where the exercise of those powers appears to Her Majesty to be inconsistent with international law or the comity of nations, or in places where sufficient facilities appear to Her Majesty to exist without the exercise of those powers, for the solemnization of marriages to which a British subject is a party,' and apart from any regulations a marriage officer is not 'required to solemnize a marriage, or to allow a marriage to be solemnized in his presence, if in his opinion the solemnization thereof would be inconsistent with international law or the comity of nations[1].'

§ 44. The act is so clearly drawn, and has evidently been framed after so exhaustive a consideration of all circumstances likely to occur, that very few remarks are needed upon its provisions, apart from the large subject of its relation to foreign laws. Those which appear to be required are the following.

Restrictions upon the operation of the Act with reference to

§ 45. By the first section a person called a marriage-officer is authorized to solemnize or to legalize marriages in a foreign country between parties one of whom at least is a British subject. Upon this point it has to be kept in mind that, while naturalized persons are British subjects to every intent in all countries other than their country of origin,

1. persons naturalized in Great Britain.

---

[1] Sects. 19 and 21. The meaning of the words 'inconsistent with international law' is not very obvious. It is hard to conceive in what way the performance of a marriage not claiming to be valid, except by consent of the due local authority within the *locus contractus*, can be an infringement of international law otherwise than by violating the comity of nations, if indeed violation of comity constitutes a violation of international law in its proper sense.

within it they are not so unless by the laws of that state, or by treaty, they have ceased to belong to it before, or upon, becoming naturalized. Subject therefore to the exceptions thus caused naturalized persons are, in view of British law, aliens for the purposes of marriage in their country of origin.

2. persons naturalized in a colony.

It has also to be kept in mind that as the effects of colonial naturalization do not extend beyond the territory of the colony where a person has been naturalized, he cannot be married as a British subject in any foreign state, even if that character be attributed to him in the state of his origin [1].

3. persons of double nationality.

On the other hand, the words 'British subject' are used without qualification, so that the fact that a natural born British subject is claimed also as a subject by the territorial sovereign is, in strictness, no bar to his marriage under the authority of the Act with a foreign person, also a subject of the territorial sovereign, or belonging to a third state. The Order in Council, however, directs a marriage-officer not to celebrate a marriage between a British subject and a subject or citizen of the territorial state, unless he is satisfied that sufficient facilities do not exist for its solemnization in accordance with the law of the country. In the case supposed, both the persons are British subjects, but one is also a local subject, and as it is the policy of the Act and Order so far as is reasonably possible to discourage acts which ignore the territorial law, the foreign national character of the person clothed with a double nationality must be allowed more weight than his or her quality of British subject. Supposing, for example, that a British subject born and domiciled in a foreign country, the son of a British subject also born and domiciled there, were to present himself in that country to the marriage officer, for the purpose of being married to a woman of the local nationality, he being

---

[1] Comp. § 20.

himself considered to possess that nationality by the territorial authorities, it would in ordinary circumstances be the duty of the marriage-officer to refuse to solemnize the proposed marriage.

Where a large English mercantile community exists a curious case might not inconceivably occur, in which two persons desiring to marry are possessed of the same double nationality, each being a British subject, and each being a subject or citizen of the local state. As a general rule it would be judicious on their part to marry in accordance with the law of the country, and it may even be an open question whether their case was contemplated when the Order in Council was drawn; but as they are both British subjects they fall within a class of persons whom the marriage officer is permitted by the Order to unite irrespectively of the facilities offered by the local marriage law; and it cannot be alleged that their marriage is within the scope of the 15th section of the Act as being inconsistent with the comity of nations. It would seem therefore that a marriage-officer, if asked to solemnize a union of this sort, would not be justified in declining to act.

§ 46. It is necessarily an implied condition precedent of the celebration of a marriage between two persons *primâ facie* authorized by the Act to marry, that they shall not by the law of England be under any incapacity to contract, and it is expressly enacted that they shall be provided with the like consent to that which is required for marriages solemnized in England. Thus insane persons and idiots are naturally unable to marry. Minors can only do so if duly permitted with the consent of parent, of guardian, or of the Court of Chancery, as may be needed in the particular case. Divorced persons cannot enter into a second marriage until a decree absolute has been made; persons who have obtained a divorce abroad which is not valid in England

Conditions precedent of a valid marriage.

PART II.
CHAP. 3.

labour under a permanent incapacity; and a marriage between a man and his deceased wife's sister or his niece cannot be celebrated.

By these limitations foreigners are bound as amply as are subjects of the United Kingdom. In order that a marriage performed under the sanction of British authority shall be good in the British dominions it must conform in all respects to English law; to the liberties and restrictions of foreign laws the Act is indifferent. Hence when a foreigner above the age of twenty-one years marries a British subject at an embassy or consulate it is immaterial, so far as the validity of the marriage within the British dominions is concerned, whether by his national law the date of majority for the purpose of marrying without consent, is fixed at twenty-one or twenty-five years; and a person tied under the law of his country by religious vows of celibacy is still fully capable of entering into a marriage good within the British dominions [1]. On the other hand, that the forms of foreign law may differ somewhat from those exacted by English law is unimportant, provided that they cover the demands of the latter, or meet them in essence. A divorce, for example, if it be in itself valid, which is definitively pronounced at the time of the hearing of the matrimonial suit, is the equivalent of a decree nisi which has been made absolute after an interval.

Marriage warrants.

§ 47. It is to be observed that the Act contemplates the issue of a marriage warrant or other enabling warrant, either to a particular officer named in it, or to the holder of a particular office, and that in the latter case a person

---

[1] Bare legality, however, it must always be remembered, is not enough to justify the celebration of a marriage by the marriage-officer. To sanction the marriage of an Englishman with a nun, or of a Catholic priest with an Englishwoman, in a country where the binding force of religious vows is legally recognized, would be an act of flagrant disobedience to the spirit and intention of the 19th section of the Act.

temporarily acting for the holder of the office has the same powers as are possessed by the former. Like powers do not seem, however, to be given in the case of a person acting for an officer indicated by name, so that whenever the name of any person is mentioned in the warrant, as being the recipient of its powers a temporary occupant of his post is unable, without himself receiving a warrant, to perform or legalize a marriage; and unless this warrant is so worded as expressly to continue the temporary powers until they are revoked, or until the return of the old, or appointment of a new, permanent official, they fall through upon the resignation or death of the person named in the original warrant.

It is also to be observed that when a warrant is issued to a person named in it, he is appointed not simply as an individual of a certain name, but as an individual so named who is the holder of a certain office. Hence if a consul or other marriage-officer is transferred to a fresh post, he ceases to have a right to celebrate or legalize marriages at his old post from the date at which his new appointment is conferred.

The same effect is produced by a transference when the marriage warrant refers to the office without designating by name the person holding it. Although in his new post the occupant may possess marriage powers, they extend only to the district associated with that post; from the moment of his formal appointment those with which he was invested in his original district pass to his successor or the person acting for the time being.

§ 48. In the 8th section the words 'official house' as explained in the 24th section and the 2nd and 7th articles of the Order in Council, comprehend both the 'official house of residence' of the marriage officer, if there be such a house, and the office at which his business is transacted, if there be a separate office. Marriages can be solemnized

The official house.

PART II.
CHAP. 3.

in either place. The official house of a consul being any 'house in which the consul is for the time being resident'[1] no room for error exists in the case of consular marriages; in that of embassies and legations the room is not really greater, but it may not be useless to note that the definition of the official house of an ambassador given in the 24th section of the Act is controlled by the terms of the Order in Council, and that consequently any house occupied by an ambassador or minister as his place of abode, even though it be not officially provided, is the official house for marriage purposes, together with the Chancery, if the latter happens to be separate from it. It might easily occur at Bern, for example, where no official house is provided by the British government, that the minister lived in the suburbs, or a few miles away in the country, while the business of the legation was conducted in the town; in such a case both the minister's residence and the chancery of the legation would be available for the solemnization of marriage; and in the same way where, as at Constantinople, both town and country residences are officially provided, marriages may be performed at either.

Temporary residence of a diplomatic agent.

It is, however, to be pointed out that when a minister is accredited to two Courts, but officially resides at one of them, as in the case of Hesse Darmstadt and Baden, and analogously in the republics of Central America, a house temporarily occupied by him in the second state cannot usually be his official house within the intention of the Act, notwithstanding that he may transact official business in it. It is conceivable that in exceptional cir-

---

[1] The term house, of course, means either house or such portion of a house as is in the occupation of a consul. If he has an apartment in a house occupied by several families, that apartment only is his official house; if for temporary reasons he is living in an hotel—while, for example, his consulate is being rebuilt—the whole hotel is not his official residence; those parts only are so which are in his actual exclusive occupation.

cumstances a house temporarily hired by a minister in a state other than that of official residence, might be so clearly 'occupied for the purposes of his Embassy[1],' that marriages could be duly celebrated within it; but there would be a very strong presumption in the opposite direction and it would as a general rule be unsafe to act adversely to the presumption.

It is provided by the Order in Council that the official house of an Ambassador or other diplomatic agent, shall be held to include 'every place within the precincts or curtilage of any such house, and any church or chapel annexed to such house, or for the time being used with the consent of the government to which the ambassador is accredited as the chapel thereof. Except as regards a chapel outside the embassy enclosure, the diplomatic character of which is dependent upon the consent of the territorial government, the above definition merely repeats the language of international law. By well-ascertained custom the immunities of a diplomatic building extend to the whole enclosure which surrounds it, and it is impossible for any purpose to look upon one part of the included space as distinct from the remainder.

Area included in the 'official house' of Diplomatic Agents.

The description of the official house of a consul is a matter of course, and the language of the Order is more fruitful of consequences. The house is declared to comprise, like the ambassador's residence, every place within its curtilage or precincts; and every place within the house so defined, to which the public have ordinary access, is considered to be part of the consular office. It seems to result from this, that any room which is habitually used for religious services, any chapel which forms part of the same block of building with the consulate and is connected with it by a door, or which opens out of its garden, and even any chapel detached from the building

of consuls.

---

[1] Foreign Marriages Order in Council, sect. 2.

PART II. but within its garden, and opening from the latter, must
CHAP. 3. be part of the office of the marriage-officer, and a legitimate place for the celebration of marriages.

Before dismissing the subject of the consular house one point must be noted similar to that which has already offered ground for remark in the case of the ambassadorial house. The official house of a consul is that only which is occupied by himself as his official home, precisely as the official home of a minister is the only official house for the purposes of the Act. Hence a consul cannot solemnize marriages or legalize them by his presence in the official house of a subordinate consular officer within his district.

Incapacity of marriage-officers to use the marriage service of the Church of England.

§ 49. Some consuls, when the parties to a marriage have wished the ceremony to be performed according to the rites of the Church of England, appear to have read the marriage service, in the absence of a clergyman. Something more than doubt has been felt by competent authorities as to the legal permissibility of this course. Curiously enough, the language of the Act might almost seem to leave the question open. In subsection 2 of section 8 it is stated that a marriage may be solemnized by another person in presence of the marriage-officer, according to the rites of the Church of England, or otherwise; or it may be solemnized by the marriage-officer, no forms being forbidden or prescribed in the latter case. It may perhaps be surmised that the incapacity of consuls, or of any one not in priest's or deacon's orders of the Church of England, to use the marriage service, appeared to the draftsman of the Act to be too evident to render legislative precautions needful. In any case not merely is it the unquestionable intention of the section that the particular form of words prescribed for use, when a marriage is celebrated by a marriage-officer, shall always be employed; it is also by these words alone that the legal contract is entered into, and whatever service may be read by the officer it is valueless to effect a marriage unless the words are somewhere PART II. introduced. CHAP. 3.

§ 50. Where British chapels detached from the consulate Order of exist, instances may readily occur in which persons will precedence when desire to go through the marriage ceremony in them as civil and religious well as at the legally appointed place. In such cases the ceremonies question may arise whether the religious ceremony should are both precede or follow the civil marriage. The point is of no performed. great importance in view of English law, since, as the former ceremony has no legal effect [1], persons married at the chapel will appear at the consulate unmarried; and once married it is immaterial what ceremony they go through afterwards. But it would seem to be more correct that the legal ceremony should take place first; and it is always possible that in some countries the law and the local authorities might refuse to look beyond the ceremony first performed, and might withhold a recognition from the religious service which they would accord to the marriage celebrated before the consul; or they might regard the civil marriage as vitiated by a previous marriage according to the rites of a religion locally unrecognized. In any case, the civil marriage being alone legal, registration cannot take place till after its performance.

§ 51. The preservation of evidence of marriages duly Registration of contracted abroad between British subjects, or between marriages. a British subject and a foreigner, is secured by the 9th, 10th, 16th, and 18th sections of the Act, and by the 8th article of the Order in Council. The 9th section provides for the compulsory registration of marriages celebrated by or before an ambassadorial or consular marriage officer.

---

[1] Obviously what is above said has no reference to places where a religious marriage is alone recognised, and where marriage according to the rites of the Church of England or of a dissenting community is valid by the *lex loci*. Such a marriage is good in the British dominions, and a subsequent consular marriage is superfluous.

H

Neither it, nor the three following sections, stand in need of any further comment than the simple remark that registration being purely for purposes of record, it has no effect in validating, and its absence has no effect in invalidating, a marriage which is good or bad in other respects. The 18th section of the Act and the 8th article of the Order in Council perhaps require some elucidation.

The main object of the Act is an enabling one; it provides a machinery for the celebration of marriages. But it is not intended to provide an exclusive machinery. It does not prescribe that British subjects shall enter into the marriage contract in no other manner than through the agency of the marriage-officer; on the contrary, it contemplates that marriages shall also be entered into in accordance with the local law of the country where they take place; and if one of the parties is a territorial subject, the Order in Council, through which the policy of the Act receives fuller effect than is obtained from the Act itself, exacts as a condition precedent to the performance of the ceremony by a marriage-officer, that sufficient facilities shall not exist for its solemnization by means of the local law. In thus recognizing that marriages, to which its subjects are parties, are valid when performed in accordance with the law of a foreign state, Great Britain only follows a universal custom, and obeys what may be termed the common law of nations. Every country admits that marriages contracted by its subjects in another country have been solemnized in due form if the local law has been satisfied in respect of the forms and ceremonies required by it.

Marriages solemnized in accordance with the local law.

Such being the attitude of Great Britain towards marriages solemnized abroad in accordance with the local law, it is obviously advisable that means should be afforded for perpetuating evidence within the British dominions of their due celebration. This is effected by the sections of the Act and the article of the Order in Council now under consideration. It is permitted to consular officers, acting in their capacity of consuls, and not as marriage-officers, to attend marriages solemnized under the local law within their district, for the purpose of seeing that due solemnization has occurred; and if the marriage is celebrated at the place where the consul is appointed to reside, he is required to attend, provided that certain fees shall have been paid beforehand. On being satisfied that the marriage has been duly solemnized, he is required to register it in a manner prescribed by the marriage regulations, and to transmit copies of the register, and ultimately the book containing the original register, to a Secretary of State.

PART II.
CHAP. 3.

Upon these provisions the questions arise:—

(1) To what extent is the consul bound to satisfy himself that the marriage is in accordance with the local law?

Duties of a marriage-officer with respect to them.

(2) Is he required to attend and to register a marriage which in his view is illegal, or of doubtful legality by the English law?

It has not been thought proper to embody any directions upon these points in the Marriage Regulations; it is only possible, therefore, to make suggestions, for what they are worth, as to the view which it may be reasonable to take with respect to them.

On the first head, it will be observed that the consul is only required to assure himself that the marriage is duly solemnized. He is consequently not obliged, nor ought he, to go behind the forms of marriage, and inquire into the capacity of the parties under the law of the state which is the scene of the contract. In the larger number of cases indeed, the local law in this respect is immaterial. In the eye of English law capacity is governed by the law of the country in which a person is domiciled, and usually the domicil of British subjects marrying abroad would be that of some part of the British Empire. In any case, to throw upon the consul the duty of entering into questions of domicil, would be to load him with an impossible burden.

On the second head, it is to be noted that the 18th section of the Act not only refers to marriages solemnized in accordance with the local law solely in their relation to that law, but expressly declares that nothing in the Act shall affect the validity or the invalidity of marriages so solemnized. The provision that they may be registered, the injunction in the Marriage Regulations that they shall be registered, are therefore made in full view of the possibility that marriages, registration of which is ordered, may not be valid in the British dominions. Moreover, as the consul is only required to satisfy himself that the formal conditions of the local law have been obeyed, he travels beyond his prescribed duties in instituting further inquiries. Registration is merely evidence that a certain ceremony has been duly gone through; whether the persons who have gone through it had the right to do so, is left for the courts, if necessary, to determine. It may be added, that however much it might be wished that those marriages only should be registered which are good in the British dominions, a consul is necessarily incompetent to judge of the validity of marriages. Without more knowledge of the law than every consul can reasonably be expected to possess, without authority to declare it, and without knowledge of facts which the parties to a marriage may ignorantly omit to place before him, he might easily refuse to register a marriage the validity of which was unquestionable. If, for example, an Englishman, domiciled in Denmark, were to require a British consul in Denmark to register his marriage, performed according to the local law, with his deceased wife's sister, it is quite possible that the consul, knowing marriage between a man and his sister-in-law to be invalid by English law, might refuse registration on the ground of invalidity; though in the particular case the marriage would be perfectly valid within the British dominions[1]. The policy of the Act is therefore as satisfactory as it is clear. The function of the consul ought to be, as it is, merely ministerial. At the same time it may be suggested that, if there is nothing to the contrary in instructions issued to consuls, it would be permissible, and might be of advantage, that a consul, who is aware of circumstances constituting, or supposed by him to constitute, an impediment to marriage in the eyes of English law, such as a prohibited degree of affinity or consanguinity, should append a note to the entry in the register, drawing attention to the fact.

PART II. CHAP. 3.

§ 52. It remains to consider the relation of the Act to the laws of foreign states. Its policy is again clear. On the one hand wide powers are given, so that the utmost freedom of marriage which is compatible with the local laws may be enjoyed; on the other, means are preserved for narrowing the exercise of those powers within any limits that the comity of nations may demand, or of suppressing them altogether where adequate facilities for marriage exist. The Order in Council has already supplemented the Act in this direction, and so far as words necessarily general in scope, and definite in form, can go, accommodates practice to the circumstances which are likely to arise and which ought to be regarded. Extended comment upon the terms of the Act and of the Order in Council in this relation is therefore superfluous. It may, however, conduce to their due understanding if a slight and very general sketch be given of the

Points to be considered with reference to the laws of foreign states.

---

[1] Comp. the dicta of Lords Campbell, Cranworth, and Wensleydale, in Brooke v. Brooke (ix House of Lords' Cases, 213-222) on the effect of such a marriage in a conquered colony where it is permitted by the local law.

considerations, with respect to marriages celebrated by British agents in foreign states, which flow from the principles of comity and of territorial sovereignty in their operation on one another. Some guidance may thus be incidentally given to marriage-officers, upon whom is thrown the duty of interpreting specific injunctions and, in so far as these do not afford a distinct rule of conduct, of considering whether proposed marriages are consistent with the comity of nations. It may also be useful to place the sections of the Act and the articles of the Order in Council which indicate the range, or narrow the exercise, of the discretion confided to marriage-officers, in immediate juxtaposition with the survey in question; and, finally, to state so far as possible what the laws of foreign countries are which affect marriages contemplated by the Act.

The right of a state to sanction the performance of marriages abroad in relation to the duties of comity.

§ 53. The foundation of comity may be said to be a recognition on the part of a state of the propriety and the practical necessity of doing towards a foreign country as it would be done by in various matters which are not strictly within the scope of international law. No state would willingly see planted within it the agents of a foreign power, employed in doing or sanctioning acts, not in conformity with the local laws, to which subjects of the territorial sovereign are parties. Even when the laws of the two powers are in harmony with each other, a state may reasonably think that undue interference with its sovereign functions takes place, if acts are legalized by an external authority, for the performance of which its domestic laws offer adequate facilities. It may therefore not merely deem such acts to be null as within its own territories for all purposes of their intended effect, when done independently of its own law, but may refuse to let them become valid on compliance with the conditions precedent or collateral to the performance of such acts, which are demanded by its own legislation; and if they are in grave opposition to the national policy or institutions it cannot be said to travel outside its rights in visiting them with penalties. Conversely, a state has not the right to direct or enable its agents to do acts elsewhere of like kind to those the performance of which it resents at home.

If these principles be applied to marriages in foreign countries, it becomes at once evident that the legalization by one state of mixed marriages upon the territory of another state is often inconsistent with comity when one of the parties is a territorial subject, especially if the laws of the former country are not in full harmony with those of the latter. The interests of the territorial sovereign are inevitably affected by whatever touches the relations of his subjects to himself, and marriages between subjects and foreigners can never, in their immediate or remote consequences, lie far away from questions of allegiance. Upon such points a state is necessarily sensitive.

But there are occasions when comity yields to higher considerations. While a state may in all cases decline to recognize marriages contracted within its territory under the sanction of agents of a foreign power, the latter is not morally compelled to respect legislation which prescribes the performance of acts violating the consciences of its subjects, or which is fundamentally opposed to its own marriage institutions. If, for example, a British agent is permitted to celebrate a marriage between a British Protestant and the subject of a foreign state, of which the law allows marriage only according to Catholic rites, the obligations of comity are not violated; however little judicious it may be for other reasons that a marriage of the kind should be sanctioned [1].

---

[1] Disagreeable international consequences may easily follow upon an indiscreet performance of mixed marriages. In Spain, in 1850, a Roman Catholic Spanish woman was married to a British subject in a British consulate. The Spanish authorities were courteous with regard to the particular marriage, and offered to facilitate by all means at their

PART II. A state is more bound to protect the religious convictions
CHAP. 3. of its subjects than to be neighbourly to its fellow states.
But again, a limitation must be placed on the exception.
When a marriage, which is consonant with British institutions, profoundly shocks the moral sense of a community, the obligations of comity regain the upper hand,
unless it can fairly be alleged that the moral objections
entertained are wholly unreasonable. A marriage law
which forbids the union of Catholics with Protestants,
except upon conditions implying a practical abandonment
of their religion by the latter, offends both by its intolerance
and by the impolicy of debarring whole sections of human
kind from contracting alliances with each other. But
a marriage law which declares that a person who has
taken vows of celibacy, with the sanction of the laws of
his country, shall not be permitted to repudiate his
voluntary and deliberate act, can neither be accused of
unreasonableness nor of impolicy. If it is not inconsistent
with the duties of comity to refuse that the disabilities of
a law of the former type shall affect marriages to which
a British subject is a party, to the extent of their effects
within British territory; it must always be improper to
encourage violation of a law which, though not in harmony
with British legislation, is in itself reasonable from the
point of view of English ideas.

When both parties to a marriage are British subjects, the
matter assumes a different aspect. The interests of the
territorial sovereign are not involved. It is of no moment
to him whether or not two foreigners are married, or by

disposal the procurement of a dispensation to legalize it, in order to put
a stop to action on the part of the ecclesiastical authorities, which otherwise could not be arrested. But they at the same time intimated that in
their view the celebration of a mixed marriage was an assumption of
foreign jurisdiction, and a contravention of the laws, which would compel
them to at once withdraw the consul's exequatur in case of any repetition
of the offence.

what ceremonial they are united. The duties of comity fall rather upon his shoulders than upon those of the sovereign of Great Britain, and he may be expected to throw no unnecessary difficulties in the way of the celebration of the marriage. It is at the same time to be remembered that as he cannot be required to make special laws for the benefit of foreigners, marriages in so far as their recognition and effects within his dominions are concerned must be subject, if the local law neither itself makes exceptions nor permits of administrative exceptions, to the necessary formal conditions prescribed for domestic purposes, and also, with a like qualification, to the essential conditions of capacity.

In what has been above said with reference to mixed marriages, those only have been contemplated in which the foreign party to the contract is a subject of the state where the marriage is performed. Frequently however he, or she, is a subject of a third state. In this case the law which has primarily to be considered in addition to British law, is that of the state to which the foreign party to the contract belongs; by it the validity of the marriage in the third state will be tested as regards all questions of capacity; but the formal conditions, for the due observance of which that state looks, will no doubt be always those exacted, or at least expressly consented to, by the local law of the country where the marriage has been celebrated.

In every instance, it is at least prudent, if it be of any importance that a marriage shall be valid outside the British dominions, that the requirements of the marriage law of the country where it is contracted shall, if possible, be satisfied in addition to those of British law [1]. The courts

[1] The inadvisability in any circumstances, of neglecting to satisfy the requirements of the local law is well illustrated by a case which occurred in 1886, of the marriage of two British subjects to Swiss wives at the Embassy at Paris. It had been the practice there, in the case of mixed marriages, to obtain from the representative of the nation to which the foreigner belonged a certificate that the marriage at the British Embassy

of all nations, in examining into the validity of a marriage, are guided on the question of forms by the law of the state where it has been celebrated; and though there may be good ground for holding that when marriages have been contracted at a consulate according to prescribed British forms under due authority, to the knowledge of the state within which the consulate is situated, and without objection being made, the territorial state ought to be held so far to have sanctioned by implication the use of those forms upon its soil, that a third state would be justified in considering a marriage performed in this manner to comply with the territorial law; there is no certainty, and indeed, it is improbable, as has been already said, that this view would generally be taken by the courts.

Directions given by Orders in Council in restraint of the discretion of marriage-officers.

§ 54. By the fourth article of the Order in Council, a marriage-officer is directed to satisfy himself upon certain matters before consenting to solemnize an intended marriage, unless a marriage contracted according to the local law is invalid by English law. The qualification refers only to Mohammedan and other eastern countries of a civilization so far removed from that of Europe, that no likeness generally exists between the incidents of marriage in them and in the states which share in the civilization of the west. For the purposes of the present chapter therefore the qualification may be set aside; all foreign countries of European civilization are countries in which marriages entered into under the local law are valid in England; they all are countries in which the marriage officer is bound to satisfy himself before solemnizing a marriage either—

would be deemed valid by the law of his or her country. A certificate to that effect had been obtained on the occasion of the two marriages in question; their validity consequently seemed to be beyond the reach of doubt. They were however afterwards declared to be null in Switzerland under Article 54, paragraph 3, of the Federal Constitution, it having been discovered that the validity of mixed marriages celebrated at the British Embassy at Paris was not recognized by French law.

(*a*) that both the parties are British subjects; or

(*b*) if only one of the parties is a British subject, that the other is not a subject or citizen of the country; or

(*c*) if one of the parties is a British subject, and the other a subject or citizen of the country, that sufficient facilities do not exist for the solemnization of the marriage in the foreign country in accordance with the law of that country.

Thus if both the parties are British subjects, or one of the parties is a British subject, and the other a foreigner who is not a subject of the local sovereign, the marriage-officer may at once proceed to solemnize the marriage; the territorial sovereign has no concern with the private relations of two foreigners who happen to reside or to sojourn within his dominions, and it is for those foreigners to consider whether it is of any importance to them that the marriage shall be recognized as valid within the *locus contractus*. If, however, one of the parties is a subject of the state in which the marriage is to be performed, that state has an interest in its member which it would be discourteous to ignore, and the private interests of the persons themselves, or of their children, will commonly be prejudiced by the illegality of their union. The marriage-officer therefore is only permitted to celebrate the marriage where sufficient facilities do not exist for its solemnization in accordance with the local law.

The term 'sufficient facilities' is nowhere defined; until therefore explanatory instructions are issued, it can only be read by the light of such external considerations as may be applicable. Unfortunately these considerations lead rather to probable than to inevitable conclusions. It cannot be supposed that the word 'facility' has reference to the adequacy of the means available for performing the ceremony in due conformity with the local law; in all towns important enough to be furnished with a British consul there must be proper officers and proper places for the due carrying out of a marriage under the sanction of the territorial law. Obviously the word refers to something else; it must therefore be presumed to point rather to legal than to material opportunities. A further element of doubt as to the exact intention of the term is introduced by the fact that its meaning evidently varies in different cases. If a woman who is a British subject is about to marry a territorial subject, the marriage-officer is required to satisfy himself before performing the ceremony that its validity will be recognized by the local law[1]. In this instance the deficiency of legal facilities, contemplated in the fourth article, can only have to do with formal conditions precedent, or forms of contract, which are enjoined by the local law, but are not absolutely necessary to validity, while compliance with them is extremely difficult or impossible. But the marriage-officer is not under a like obligation when a man who is a British subject is about to marry a foreign woman, whether she be a subject of the territorial sovereign or of a third state, or when a woman who is a British subject is about to marry a foreigner not owning the local allegiance. In these cases then, the performance of marriages, which may be radically in conflict with the local law, must be contemplated and intended; and the word 'facilities' must be construed to mean facilities for contracting marriage in such manner as not to violate the consciencious scruples of British subjects. On the whole it seems tolerably clear that the provision prohibiting marriage-officers to perform or legalize marriages, unless sufficient facilities are not offered by the local law, neither adds to nor explains the duties imposed by the injunction to observe the comity of nations.

The reason for the special precautions taken in the case of the marriage of a British woman with a territorial

---

[1] Foreign Marriages Order in Council, art. 5.

subject is evident, and has no bearing upon the extent to which the British crown feels itself bound to respect the marriage institutions of foreign states. A like precaution is enjoined when a British woman marries a foreigner belonging to a country other than that in which the ceremony is performed; but in this instance the marriage-officer must satisfy himself that the marriage will be recognized in the country of which the husband is a subject. The essential point is that the woman shall not be allowed to enter into a connexion, which may be terminated at will in the country where she probably has to live[1], and where the legitimacy of her children is of capital importance. The preliminary condition that her marriage shall be recognized in the appropriate state is exacted, not as a concession to the laws of that state, but as a safeguard to the woman herself. No similar risk to that run by a woman is encountered by a man, and British law guarantees the safety of his wife within the British dominions; there is no reason therefore for refusing liberty to a man to contract under British sanction wherever difficulties exist, which the comity of nations does not declare to be insufficient to justify independent action. The value of such difficulties as may be found in any given case are left, save to the extent provided for by the Order in Council, to the marriage-officer to appreciate[2].

§ 55. The conditions under which a marriage, valid by English law, may be contracted in a foreign country have hitherto been looked at solely from the point of view of the Foreign Marriage Act of 1892. It remains to inquire whether two British subjects can in any circumstances enter into wedlock in a country of European

Marriages per verba de praesenti before persons in episcopal orders.

---

[1] It would always be advisable, when the husband is domiciled in a country other than his own, especially if he has property in it and the marriage is performed there, that its validity by the local law, as well as by the law of his state, should be assured.

[2] Foreign Marriage Act, 1892, sect. 19.

civilization under the mere sanction of English law by means other than those prescribed by the Act in question.

By the law of England as it stood antecedently to the Act known as Lord Hardwicke's Act[1], marriages were valid if contracted *per verba de praesenti* before a clergyman in episcopal orders; and as that Act confined the changes which it introduced to the United Kingdom, British subjects, if the Act stood alone, would still carry with them the ancient law into foreign countries where they might travel or reside. But even at that early period it was fully established that as between England and countries in which the marriage of British subjects by the *lex loci* could be contemplated, that is to say as between England and states with which a jural intercommunion was possible, marriages were to be governed in their formal conditions by the *lex loci contractus*. In 1752 Sir Edward Simpson laid down that 'this question being in substance this, whether by the law of this country, marriage contracts are not to be deemed good or bad, according to the laws of the country in which they are formed ... there can be no doubt whatever but that both the parties in this cause, though they are British subjects, obtained a forum by virtue of the contracts in France. By entering into the marriage contract there they subjected themselves to have the validity of it determined by the laws of that country. ... As there is no positive law of this country which prohibits the court from taking notice of the *jus gentium*, and as the law of the country where the contract is made seems to me according to the law of nations to be the only rule of determining in these cases, I cannot pronounce for the marriage'[2].

---

[1] 26 Geo. II. cap. 33 (1753).

[2] Scrimshire *v.* Scrimshire, Haggard, Consist. Rep. ii. 395. A few years later (1756) the principle was reaffirmed by Lord Hardwicke, who said of a marriage of minors at Antwerp, 'It is said by Medwin that he saw them married according to the rites and ceremonies of the Church of England.

With reference to the general rule, and to its applicability in all ordinary circumstances, there can be no question. But it is not quite so certain whether there are no exceptional circumstances in which a marriage may be valid, that is contracted according to the ancient law of England within a state of European civilization. Underlying many judicial utterances may be discerned the feeling that there is a natural right to marriage, and that though in the interests of society it is well to surround the contract, whenever it be practicable, with compulsory formal conditions, these conditions ought not to be regarded as indispensable when there is a moral or material impossibility of satisfying them. Although, therefore, most decisions upon questions of validity have been, as it happens, in restraint of laxity, there are some, and there are also expressions of judicial opinion, which without clearly showing when informal marriages may be safely concluded, indicate that there are circumstances of necessity or even falling short of sheer necessity, in which marriages entered into *per verba de praesenti* before a person in episcopal orders would be held to be good.

The only case in which a marriage so contracted in a civilised state has been declared to be good is that of Ruding *v.* Smith[1]. In 1796 a young man of two-and-twenty, an officer in the British force which had conquered the Cape in the previous year, was married there by an

---

But it will not be valid here, unless it is so by the laws of the country where it was had; and so it was said by Murray, Attorney-General, to have been determined lately by the Delegates.' Butler *v.* Freeman, Ambler, 303. See also Middleton *v.* Janverin, Haggard, Consist. Rep. ii. 446 (1802); Dalrymple *v.* Dalrymple, ib. 59 (1811); Lacon *v.* Higgins, iii Starkie, 183 (1822); and Kent *v.* Burgess, xi Simon, 367 (1840).

[1] Haggard, Consistory Reports, ii. 371 (1821). I do not refer to cases in which marriages contracted in the above manner have been held to be invalid, because they have almost all been in fraud of the law, and have all been destitute of the conditions of necessity or quasi necessity.

army chaplain to a young girl of nineteen, also a British subject. By the local Dutch law the marriage was invalid, because it was had without consent of the parents or guardians, which under that law was required for the marriage of all persons below the age of thirty. The father of the young man was in England; in view of the length of time then needed for communication and of the circumstance of war, it was impossible to obtain his consent. The father of the girl was dead; her mother had married again, and was in India; no guardian had been appointed; the required consents were in her case still more unobtainable. The marriage was held to be good by Sir W. Scott (Lord Stowell) upon several grounds. In the portion of his judgement which is material to the present subject he said, 'it is true that English decisions have established this rule, that a foreign marriage valid according to the law of the place where celebrated is good everywhere else; but they have not *e converso* established that marriages of British subjects, not good according to the general law of the place where celebrated, are universally and under all possible circumstances to be regarded as invalid in England... The libel here states a case of marriage as nearly entitled to the privilege of strict necessity as can be.' He then after stating the facts adds, 'it would puzzle the person most versed in that most difficult chapter of general law, the *conflictus legum*, to say how a marriage could be effected under such circumstances in a manner satisfactory to the Dutch requisitions,' and finally in resuming the grounds of his judgement gives a prominent place to 'the insuperable difficulties of obtaining any marriage conformable to the Dutch law.' The decision is one of particular importance, in that it is free from the disturbing elements which affect questions of the validity of irregular marriages in an eastern country. It raises the clean issue of the possibility of the existence of such necessity in a civilized country as to overweigh the obligation of conforming to the local law, and determines that the necessity may exist[1]. From this point, however, to a general statement of the conditions under which the stage of necessity is reached, there is evidently a very long step. The courts have not spoken, and it would not be prudent for a mere writer to undertake the task. It will be enough to indicate the sort of occasion upon which it would at least be convenient that a settled rule should be at hand upon which action could unhesitatingly be taken. Doubtless there are remote parts of Peru, or of other countries under like laws, in which a considerable English mining population lives, far away from a British Consul, and for all practical purposes incapable of being married under the provisions of the Act of 1892. If Protestants, they cannot be married in accordance with the *lex loci*, because by Peruvian law legal marriage can only be contracted by persons who acknowledge the authority of the Council of Trent. If a chaplain is kept on the spot by the mining company, or if a person in episcopal orders, whether a Protestant or a Catholic not tied by Peruvian law, were to pass that way, would marriages performed by him be invalid? In the particular case the principle of Ruding *v.* Smith would seem to apply with certainty. Necessity could not be carried further. But a more complicated case might present itself, for example, in Brazil. In that country, consular marriages, in common with all other forms of civil marriage, are invalid, but duly performed religious marriages, under the sanction of any recognized Church, are held to be valid. To persons resident in a foreign place the local legitimacy of

---

[1] On marriages, *per verba de praesenti*, in Eastern and barbarous countries, see §§ 87, 88, 105. It is conceivable that the considerations which very probably may be held to validate marriages *per verba de praesenti* before witnesses, without the presence of a clergyman in episcopal orders, in Eastern countries, may also be found to be applicable to extremely remote places in civilized countries.

their marriage may be both socially and legally important. They choose to be married by a person in orders, and a consul being distant and accessible with some difficulty they neglect to be married also by him. Is there any amount of mere difficulty the presence of which would enable the marriage to be regarded as valid in contemplation of English law, or must there be a practical impossibility of contracting under the Act, and a moral impossibility of marrying in conformity with the *lex loci*? It might quite possibly be found that the marriage by a clergyman was not locally good, and that consequently, unless good as a marriage of necessity, it would be good nowhere. If the question were to arise whether the marriage had been duly performed, to whom could the Brazilian government address itself except to the British minister? He would be unable to say that the marriage was good by the laws of the Church of England, because the laws of the state are the laws of the Church of England, and there is no law which validates a religious marriage in a foreign country of European civilization. Thus the marriage would be invalid by the *lex loci*; and therefore, unless rendered good by sufficient conformity to the principle under discussion, it would be bad also in the British dominions.

Diplomatic and consular marriages in their relation to the laws of foreign states.

§ 56. It is unfortunately not possible to give a complete, or even an approximate account of the position taken up by foreign powers towards diplomatic and consular marriages celebrated within their territories between two persons who are not territorial subjects, and towards marriages contracted by such persons in other ways independently of the means locally provided. Very few if any countries have legislated with express reference to such marriages, and either the Courts have not had frequent occasion to adjudicate on their validity or the judgements have not generally become known. All that can be done is to present a few observations upon the different attitudes which it is open to foreign countries to take up.

In states, such as Austria and Italy, which recognize the validity of consular and diplomatic marriages, the situation of British subjects is affected by few possibilities of complication. Generally there can be little doubt that if a consular marriage is recognized at all, it will be recognized subject to the attendant conditions prescribed by the foreign state under the law of which it has been solemnized; the territorial law will accept the marriage as it finds it. But recognition does not everywhere mean quite the same thing; and in one direction its effects may not in consequence be always identical. In some countries, as in Switzerland, persons married by a British marriage officer are in the same position as if they had been married in England; the marriage is regarded as a foreign marriage, recognized because it is officially held forth as a valid contract according to English law[1]. In such cases, it would seem that the courts of a third state might refuse to consider the contract good, because it is not in itself good by the *lex loci*; it is not a marriage contracted under the local law; and British legations and consulates have no such extraterritoriality that marriages celebrated in them have the character of English *lex loci* marriages in virtue of the place where they are solemnized. In other countries recognition appears to convert the ceremony performed according to English law into a *lex loci* marriage, which is necessarily good, not only in the state where it is contracted, but in all places. In Italy, for example, the civil code permits contracts to be made by foreigners according to the forms enjoined by their national law, provided that one law is common to both parties[2]. A

[1] As regards Switzerland, ex relat. M. Rivier.
[2] Fiore, on the Italian law concerning marriages contracted abroad, in the Rev. de Droit Int. Privé, xiii. 303, citing the 9th art. of the Titolo Preliminario of the Civil Code.

marriage entered into by two British subjects before a marriage officer is thus a contract duly concluded in accordance with Italian law. Again, the probability that a consular marriage, if recognized at all, will be taken as it is found, must not be too absolutely relied upon. The bare fulfilment of the requirements of the Foreign Marriage Act may not always be enough to secure recognition. In the instance of Switzerland conformity to English law is obviously sufficient; and where, as in Austria, the law contents itself with a prohibitory injunction, which in that case is merely that banns must not be published outside the precincts of the consular office, no complication can well arise. But if a consular or diplomatic marriage is recognized as a *lex loci* marriage, the territorial law may prescribe conditions precedent or collateral, neglect to observe which may affect the local validity of the contract. In a country, for example, where foreigners are allowed to make contracts according to the forms of their own law, it cannot be quite certain that the courts would hold that they were absolved from complying with all the conditions laid down by the local law as compulsorily precedent to the making of any contract, or of a contract of a particular kind.

Many states refuse in any circumstances to recognize the validity of consular marriages performed within their territory by the agents of foreign powers; in some countries marriages performed in a diplomatic residence between persons who are not members of the ambassador's official suite or entourage will unquestionably not be recognized, and it is doubtful whether absolute certainty can even be felt as to the view which may be taken of marriages performed between persons who are covered by diplomatic immunities. In at least one case, viz. that of Germany, the extreme step is taken of rendering the solemnization of a marriage in a diplomatic house by any one not possessed of diplomatic privileges, a punishable offence. Sometimes in these countries the means of effecting a civil marriage is provided; sometimes the prohibition is founded upon the exclusive recognition by the territorial law of marriages contracted either under the sanction of a particular religion or at any rate of some religion. Laws only of this last-mentioned kind need a few words of comment. Where the list of religions contemplated by the law is sufficiently comprehensive to include the Church of England, the question presents itself whether a marriage solemnized by a clergyman in orders of the English or American Episcopal Church is a good marriage by the *lex loci*, and consequently whether an alternative to marriage before a minister or a consul is open to British subjects, who are unwilling to be joined to each other by the usual local religious forms, but to whom the local validity of their connexion is important. The answer depends upon the test which the territorial sovereign chooses to apply in order to ascertain whether a given religious marriage is good as such. If he requires that it shall be valid by the laws of the Church of England the difficulty occurs which was adverted to at the end of the last section. The marriage is only valid by English law if it is good by the *lex loci*; it is only valid by the *lex loci* if it is good by English law. Out of the vicious circle there is no issue. If, on the other hand, the territorial sovereign refrains from inquiry whether all laws regulating the Church of England are satisfied, and is content with the assurance that a marriage has been performed according to the rites of the Church of England in the sense that the prescribed religious ceremony has been used by a properly ordained person, the marriage becomes a marriage by the *lex loci*, as being a duly contracted religious marriage Again, the territorial sovereign may take the implied sanction afforded by the performance of a marriage in an ambassadorial chapel as evidence of sufficient compliance

PART II. with the laws of the Church, and may thus convert a religious marriage according to English forms into a valid *lex loci* marriage[1].

The foregoing remarks, though very likely not exhausting all the varieties of circumstance by which the effects of consular or religious marriages in foreign countries may be modified, are enough to show by what delicate legal considerations the validity of such marriages is determined, and what caution must therefore be exercised in forming and acting upon views with respect to them in the absence of judicial decisions, or of express general or particular recognition by a qualified organ of a foreign government.

Marriages on board vessels of war in foreign ports.

§ 57. Previously to 1890, when an Act was passed identical as regards the following subject with that of 1892, marriages were occasionally celebrated on board vessels of war in foreign ports. Performed in a certain manner these marriages were unquestionably valid. It has been seen that before Lord Hardwicke's Act was passed in 1753, marriages contracted *per verba de praesenti* in the presence of a clergyman of the Church of England, or of a priest of the Church of Rome, were valid wherever within British jurisdiction they were performed; and from the operation of that Act marriages beyond the seas were excluded. Assuming, therefore, that a ship of war lying in a foreign port is to be considered extraterritorial, in the full sense of the word, a marriage celebrated on board must have been good in law, provided that the one condition of validity above mentioned was observed. Marriages appear however to have been sanctioned by the presence of com-

---

[1] This appears to be what takes place in Russia, where marriages before a civil marriage officer are not recognized. All Church of England chapels in the Empire, in which a duly licensed clergyman officiates, are regarded as being under the protection of the British ambassador; and marriages solemnized in them are as certainly valid by the *lex loci* as marriages in such circumstances can be, upon which the courts have not pronounced. They have always been recognized as good by the administrative authorities.

manding officers, in the absence, it is to be supposed, of a chaplain; and it consequently became necessary in 1879 to validate by Act of Parliament such as might have been irregularly celebrated before that date [1].

Practice has now been placed upon a sounder footing. By the Act of 1892 [2] it is provided that marriages may be solemnized on board a Queen's ship on a foreign station; and the provisions of the Act have been supplemented and modified by the Foreign Marriages Order in Council. The remarks already made upon the conditions under which marriages may be celebrated in foreign territory cover all the points which can arise with reference to marriages on board ship in their relation to British law.

The very open question remains of the relation of such marriages to the law of the territory within which the ship is lying. So far as it has been possible to ascertain, no foreign country has legislated upon the matter, and no foreign courts have had occasion to adjudicate upon it. What view might be taken in the different foreign countries of the value within their territory of a marriage, performed on a British public vessel of the state, must remain a subject of mere speculation. It can only be said that the doctrine of the exterritoriality of vessels of war is held in so large a sense by almost every foreign state, that recognition of marriages contracted on them between two British subjects, in accordance with British law, may perhaps be looked for with some confidence. Logically, if the ship is a portion of British territory, foreign courts might be expected to go further, and to regard the effects of a marriage ceremony duly performed on board between a British subject and a subject of the state within the waters of which the vessel is lying, as being identical with those of a like ceremony performed on the soil of England. Whether, if the question came before them, this view would

---

[1] 42 & 43 Vict. cap. 29.   [2] Sect. 12.

be taken or whether those states which refuse to recognize an Embassy marriage, to which one of their own subjects is a party, would refuse also to recognize the marriage of a subject on board a British ship, is at least so far doubtful that it would hardly be prudent, without full assurance upon the point, to celebrate a marriage between an Englishwoman and a territorial subject, or if property in the country were involved, between an English man and a woman of local origin.

Marriages within the lines of a British army in foreign territory.

§ 58. The Act further declares that all marriages solemnized within the lines of a British army serving abroad, by any chaplain or officer or other person officiating under the orders of the commanding officer, shall be as valid in law as if it had been duly solemnized within the United Kingdom[1]. The enactment is no doubt sufficient to provide for an occurrence which will always be exceptional. The only point which calls for remark is the relation of such marriages to the territorial law.

Where a British force is quartered in, or passing through, a friendly state, comity would demand that some means be found of validating marriages between British subjects, and the reasons which might lead foreign courts to recognize them are stronger than would usually, or at least frequently, exist in the case of vessels of war. The force would be in the territory by express consent; and the exigencies of military service would prevent its being

---

[1] Sect. 22. Presumably, the words 'officiating under the orders' means officiating for the purpose of effecting the marriage by order of the commanding officer; but as the section is simply declaratory, and the twenty-third section provides that nothing in the Act 'shall confirm or impair or in anywise affect the validity in law of any marriage solemnized beyond the seas, otherwise than as herein provided,' it would seem that the decision in the Waldegrave Peerage Case (iv Clark and Finnelly, 649), still holds good, and that a marriage is valid which is celebrated by a chaplain of the British army within the lines of an army when serving abroad, without authority for performance of the ceremony having been obtained from the commanding officer.

reasonable to expect that recourse should be had to the facilities for marriages locally afforded, even where they were in themselves ample. Whether however this recognition would be extended to mixed marriages within the lines of an army is even more dubious than in the case of similar marriages on board a man of war. An army actually treads the soil of the country. The place, in which it is, has not even the potential extraterritoriality of fact which is enjoyed by the moveable vessels. To recognize as valid an act, done under the sanction of a foreign law, to which a subject of the country is a party, is a much larger concession when the act is done within the lines of a foreign army than when its scene is the quarter deck of a foreign national vessel.

When, on the other hand, the British force is in hostile territory it is needless to point out that if the validity of a marriage, whether between British subjects, or between a British subject and a native, were to be in question before the local courts after the termination of the war, it would be irrational to expect that they should hold it to be good, unless by the law of the country any promise before witnesses, or habit and repute, were sufficient in all circumstances to constitute or evidence a marriage. An army has no extraterritoriality as against its enemy.

PART III.

CHAPTER I.

THE PERSONS WHO ARE REGARDED AS BRITISH SUBJECTS IN EASTERN STATES.

PART III.
CHAP. I.

The two classes of Eastern countries.

§ 59. THE independent countries that, in contradistinction to states of European civilization, may be roughly designated Eastern countries, are divisible for international purposes into two great classes[1]. The members of one of these, though showing a very varying amount of capacity or of will to bring their conduct into harmony with western ideas, are all at least sufficiently developed to render the maintenance of permanent diplomatic intercourse with them both practicable and useful; some of them, apart from the effects of one or two radical differences of social organization, are not distinguishable internationally from their European neighbours. The other class consists of barbarous communities, destitute of almost every mark, other than independence, which is characteristic of a true state; with them treaties for specific objects may be made, but no such community of ideas with reference to the conception of a state, and to the rights and duties springing from it, unites them to civilized

---

[1] Japan may be left out of consideration. As it is a monogamous country, and as exterritorial jurisdiction within it will no doubt before long be abolished, there will soon be no difference between it and a European state.

countries, that habitual intercourse can be kept up with them on the basis of a common understanding in these respects. The existence of diplomatic relations in the one case, their non-existence in the other, correspond to, and are symptomatic of, differences between the two groups which necessarily modify the position of British subjects within them, and even affect the question of what persons make up the aggregate of British subjects. It will be convenient therefore to treat of the two classes separately.

§ 60. In countries which cannot be fully admitted to the community of Western states, because of the unlikeness of their social organization to that of the European peoples, it is evident that the list of persons who are British subjects can hardly be smaller than that which is elsewhere accepted, and that there may be good reason for endeavouring to embrace a certain number of individuals who would not be regarded as British subjects in Europe or America. As a matter of fact the claims of Great Britain in Oriental states, although gradually diminishing, are still somewhat wider than those which she puts forth in the West. Except in so far as various enactments operate adversely, whoever is a British subject in British territory is a British subject in every Eastern state, irrespectively of his character by the laws of the country. The principle was laid down, and its reason was suggested, by Lord Palmerston in 1850. 'In Europe,' he said, 'children born in England of parents subjects of a foreign state would be entitled to be considered as British subjects everywhere but in the country to which their parents belong, always assuming that the law of that country considers children, born to native subjects while out of the country, to be as much native subjects as if they had been born in the country. But though that would be the international rule in Europe, yet, considering the different and peculiar habits and practices of Asia, it seems to me that, considering that all persons born in British India, of whatever parents, are entitled to be regarded as British subjects, so far as concerns any privileges and advantages which attach to that character within the British dominions, it would be fair and right to extend to such persons, even in Persia, the benefits of being placed under British protection; and especially if they had resided in British India for any time, so as to have been practically domiciled therein.' Ten years later Lord John Russell, in giving instructions of like effect to the British minister in Persia, pointed out 'the impracticability of following out strictly, in relation to Persia or any other Mohammedan power, the principles of international law prevailing between Christian powers, so far as regards nationality and the right to protection [1].' To the extent, in other words, that it is possible, consistently with the sovereignty of the Eastern state, and with British law, to bring persons associated with British dominion under the protection of the British Empire, it is right, as it is politic, to do so. The methods of Oriental administration can nowhere be wholly trusted. Persons born in British territory can therefore be, and usually are, protected everywhere, whatever be their parentage, and against even their country of origin. A certain amount of discrimination is however shown; and if they behave so as morally to forfeit their right to protection in the judgement of the British government, or act in such manner as to show that they have elected the nationality of their father, they are not permitted, if subsequently the need arises, to avail themselves of their nationality of birth [2].

[1] Naturalization Laws Report, 1869, pp. 71-2.
[2] By a Turkish law of January 19, 1869, children of Turkish subjects, born without the Ottoman dominions subsequently to that date, were declared to be Turkish subjects. Questions do not seem to have as yet arisen, but it is evident that they might easily arise under this enactment with regard to a certain number of British Indian subjects, and subjects of British pro-

§ 61. From this point British statutes begin to speak. The Acts of George II and George III[1] stop the descent of British nationality at the grandchild of a person born within the British dominions. While therefore, for example, the child of Persian parents, born during their temporary sojourn in India, and their grandchild in turn, are British subjects, notwithstanding continuous residence in Persia, the great-grandchild ceases to be British, and in the case supposed reverts to a Persian nationality.

<small>PART III.
CHAP. I.

Effect of the Statutes and Orders in Council which are applicable.

Acts of George II & George III.

Naturalization Act of 1870.</small>

As the Naturalization Act of 1870 applies to all foreign states without reserve, a woman who is a British subject, marrying a subject of an Eastern state, acquires his nationality, provided that the marriage is valid according to the British law which is applicable in the case[2].

For the same reason, where, as in the instance of Turkey, an Oriental country possesses a naturalization law, a British subject duly naturalized in it loses his British national character, and carries with him his wife, and subject to the same qualifications as in Europe, his children also. Where no naturalization law exists, it would generally be difficult for a British subject to divest himself of his nationality of origin. A renunciation of allegiance on his part, and a declaration that he had become subject to an Eastern state, if coupled with express acceptance of him by the state, would no doubt be enough, however unusual the form might be, to prove an intention on both

---

tected states. It must be a question of policy whether such persons shall in the particular case be protected in their country of descent, or whether the European rule of not protecting a subject by birth within a state which claims him by descent shall be applied. It may be presumed that Turkish subjects in India, or in protected countries such as Zanzibar, are in the main a somewhat floating mercantile class, and that the birth of their children in British territory, or in a British protectorate, would often be in a sense accidental. It may, perhaps, be possible to exercise a wholesome discrimination between individuals.

[1] 4 Geo. II. c. 21; and 13 Geo. III. c. 21.
[2] Comp. §§ 87–88.

sides, which might reasonably, though not necessarily, be respected by Great Britain. But it would evidently be required that a transfer of allegiance, effected in so irregular a manner, should take place at a time when there could be no ground for suspicion that it was made in order to escape from obligations or onerous consequences of British nationality. Less than this would probably not suffice; and it is certain that no intimacy of association with, or length of service under, an Oriental government ought to be admitted, in view of the conditions on which Europeans frequently undertake employments in the East, as affording a presumption that a British subject had intended to abandon his nationality at an earlier period, if a motive of the kind above mentioned were found to exist at the time when a claim to have lost British nationality is set up[1].

Foreign Jurisdiction Acts.

Under powers given by a succession of Acts[2], Orders in Council have been issued, specifying explicitly as regards Turkey with Egypt and Tripoli, Japan, China, Morocco, and by implication as regards Persia and Siam, that persons naturalized in the British dominions shall be considered to be British subjects for all purposes of protection and jurisdiction. With reference to this provision it has to be remembered that the Orders in Council are incapable of overriding the sixth article of the Naturalization Act of 1870. The naturalized persons therefore who will be protected as such in the above countries do not include

---

[1] Some efforts have been made to escape from the obligations of British nationality by claiming to have adopted an Eastern national character; e.g. an English official, employed by an Oriental government, which has no naturalization law, and which had not previously recognized him as a subject, endeavoured a few years ago to avoid the consequences of a judgement which had been delivered against him in the consular court, by setting up a claim to the nationality of the state of which he was an official.

[2] These have been consolidated by the Foreign Jurisdiction Act, 1890.

natives of the country in which the question of protection arises[1].

It has also to be remembered that the difficulties, which have been already noticed as presenting themselves in connexion with colonially naturalized persons in European states[2], reappear with additions in Oriental countries. In accordance with the practice elsewhere they would no doubt be diplomatically protected, except in their country of origin, and it is not likely that the right to afford them diplomatic protection would be gainsaid. But would they be given the protection of the Consular Courts; would their civil disputes, or would criminal charges in which they were involved, be withdrawn from the local jurisdiction; would for example a Dutchman naturalized in Australia in circumstances which deprived him of his nationality of origin be obliged to submit himself and his causes to the territorial laws of Persia or Morocco? It is impossible to suppose the deliberate intention of the legislature in 1870 to have been to bring about such a result as that a European without any other than a British nationality should find himself ruled in life, and his property disposed of on death, by Mohammedan law. Upon the terms of the Act, however, it seems hard to avoid the conclusion that this is the situation in which he is placed.

Some difficulty in making sure of the meaning which is in certain cases to be attached to the term 'British subject,' would be introduced by the varying phraseology of the Orders in Council, were they not controlled by an Act of 1876 which declares that for the purposes of the Orders in question ' all subjects of the several princes and states in India in alliance with Her Majesty residing and being

Subjects of Indian native states.

---

[1] There is, however, nothing in the Act of 1870 to prevent naturalized natives of Turkey with Egypt, or of Persia, Morocco, Tripoli, or Siam from receiving protection in their country of origin under a usage which will be noticed later, § 66.

[2] § 20.

in the several dominions comprised in such Orders, are and shall be deemed to be, persons enjoying Her Majesty's protection therein [1].' In accordance with this Act passports are issued to the subjects of native states when they proceed on foreign travel; and when vessels from Cutch or other maritime states trade to foreign ports they are entitled to consular assistance and subjected to consular jurisdiction in the same manner as English and Colonial vessels. The Act must of course be read into the Chinese and Japanese Order, which on its own terms would seem to include natives of British India born in the provinces under the direct administration of the crown, and to exclude subjects of the protected states. The later Orders are not all identical in their language, but the differences between them are of no importance. In the Persia [2] and Siam Orders 'subjects of the several princes and states in India in alliance with Her Majesty' are classed as subjects; in the Persian Coasts and Islands Order and in the Morocco Order a British subject is so defined as to exclude them, and they are placed under the head of 'British protected persons.' As protected persons are in the same position with subjects of the crown, and are as fully exempted as they from the operation of the local laws, the effect of these Orders is identical. The future is now afresh provided for by the fifteenth section of the Foreign Jurisdiction Act, 1890, which enacts that where in future an Order in Council is made, which 'extends to persons enjoying Her Majesty's

---

[1] 39 & 40 Vic. c. 46.

[2] A difficulty in comprehending the exact scope of this term 'British subject' in the Persian Order is caused by the inclusion under it of persons 'enjoying Her Majesty's protection in so far as Her Majesty has jurisdiction in respect of any such person.' Possibly some light may be thrown on its meaning by the Morocco Order, which says that a British protected person is 'a person properly enjoying Her Majesty's protection in Morocco.' This seems to suggest that the persons described may in both cases be such as the British government can take under its protection consistently with custom and its own laws.

protection, that expression shall include all subjects of the several princes and states in India.'

PART III.
CHAP. I.

§ 62. The identification of British subjects as such is provided for in Eastern countries by a system of registration at the consulates, which in its essentials is everywhere the same. Every British subject, as defined in the Orders in Council providing for registration, is obliged, if he or she be over twenty-one years of age, or if married, or a widower or widow, though under that age, to register him or herself, under penalty of a fine for failure to do so, within a month after arriving in the country and thenceforward once in each year, reckoned from January 1. Omission to register, unless an excuse satisfactory to the British consular officer is offered, entails liability to nonrecognition as a British subject, and to refusal of protection.

Registration of British subjects.

In Turkey, Egypt, and Tripoli, by exception to the above regulations, it is not compulsory upon a native Indian subject of Great Britain to register himself, but until he does so he has not the advantage of the civil or criminal jurisdiction exercised by the consul; so that if accused of crime he is tried by the local tribunals without the support or protection of the consul being afforded; and he cannot sue in the Consular Court, though he remains liable to be sued there.

It is to be remarked that if a British subject fails or refuses to register, he is not exempted from the consular jurisdiction, even though the consular authorities may have declined to recognize him, and he may have thus lost the advantages of his British national character. The right to protection may be forfeited by neglect or misconduct; but there is no correlative immunity from the consequences of illegal acts. If a criminal charge is made, or an action is brought, against an unregistered person, the Consular Courts may impose their jurisdiction. He remains a British

Effect of failure or refusal to register.

K

subject in fact, no new nationality having been acquired, and he cannot escape from the obligations, under which as such he lies, by the simple process of repudiating connexion with his country.

It is also to be remarked that exercise of jurisdiction as against the individual neither seems to necessitate previous registration without his consent, nor to imply recognition in itself. In some cases the Order in Council enables the consular officer to levy a fine while refusing recognition; in other words, he exercises jurisdiction over a person who for protective purposes is not a British subject [1].

Impossibility of British subjects divesting themselves of their nationality in barbarous countries.

§ 63. In countries of a less civilized type than the least developed of those which have been under consideration in the foregoing sections, the list of persons who fall into the category of British subjects is identical with that which has been given for Eastern states; but their position in one important respect is widely different. It has been seen that, whatever practical difficulties may intervene, there is theoretically no bar to the naturalization of a British subject in an Eastern state; in barbarous and wholly uncivilized countries it is probably impossible for him to divest himself of his British character and to acquire a local nationality. The Naturalization Act of 1870 permitted British subjects to assume the nationality of a 'foreign state.' The term 'state' is not defined; but it must unquestionably be taken to apply only to those permanently established independent communities, formed with political objects, possessing a definite political organization, and guided by a sense of moral obligation towards other communities, which are generally denomin-

---

[1] As nationality and domicil are sometimes confused with one another, it may not be superfluous to note that acquisition of an Oriental domicil could not release a British subject from the effects of his British nationality, even if it be supposed possible for him to acquire such domicil where jurisdiction is exercised under an Order in Council, without having previously obtained local naturalization.

ated by the word. It is impossible to regard an island in the South Sea, or a kingdom in the interior of Africa as having the necessary marks of a state, even if they happen to be controlled by European adventurers. They are not therefore covered by the enactment which provides for foreign naturalization; and a British subject within them is incapable of ridding himself of his native allegiance. Nor does the fact of recognizing a native government to the extent of concluding treaties with it amount to such recognition that Great Britain is bound to admit the validity of naturalization granted by it. A community may be capable of understanding that it ought to adhere to a bargain, without being able to comprehend the general international responsibilities of a state; and a country is neither obliged, nor can it be asked consistently with its duty towards other states, to allow a subject to slip from its control without reasonable assurance that he is transferred to a state community which will be properly responsible for his actions. Hence British subjects remain amenable to British laws, both in respect to person and property, notwithstanding any attempted adoption of an uncivilized or barbarous nationality, and even though such adoption may be evidenced by letters of naturalization in due form[1].

[1] Several attempts have been made by British subjects to free themselves from the control of law by assuming the nationality of an irresponsible community. Some cases occurred in Fiji before its annexation, and some years later in Samoa, before it received its present organization.

CHAPTER II.

POWERS AND JURISDICTION OF THE CROWN IN EASTERN STATES.

PART III.
CHAP. 2.

Origin and growth of consular powers in the East.

§ 64. On passing from Europe to the East, a region is entered in which custom and necessity have set up relations between Western and Oriental countries differing widely from anything which now exists among the former group of states. On the one hand are extensive jurisdictional privileges; on the other are correlative derogations from sovereignty. Curiously at first sight, though naturally enough in reality, seeing what the conditions of life in a foreign state were in the middle ages, the consular powers, in which these privileges and derogations are embodied, were modelled in their earliest forms upon precedents supplied by the European nations; but while in these the authority of consuls has shrunk within the modest limits which have been already described, in the East it continuously grew and hardened. In early times a consul in a European port habitually exercised quasi-judicial functions as between the merchants of his own country; he, at least in some places, composed differences between his own people and the local traders, and caused satisfaction to be made in cases of injury and even of violence done to the latter. Sometimes the powers with which consuls were invested appear to have been assumed independently of the territorial sovereignty. The Letters Patent given to Lorenzo Strozzi, by Richard III in 1485, seem to rest rather upon the general usage of nations than upon any antecedent grant of privileges from Pisa, where the consulate was to be established; they moreover contain a direct creation of a royal magistracy, and put under it not merchants only, but all subjects of the crown in those parts[1]. When the position of consuls in the Ottoman Empire came to be regulated by capitulations, more extensive powers were readily accorded than the largest of those which had been enjoyed in European countries. To the Oriental mind a personal law is more familiar and appears more natural than a territorial law. There was no difficulty in subjecting Europeans of various nations to the jurisdiction of their respective consuls. The decision of all differences between persons of the same nationality were accordingly left to the consul or the ambassador, and the Turkish authorities were forbidden to interfere. But at first the consular powers were strictly confined within these limits; in mixed suits and in criminal cases the local jurisdiction was maintained; it was merely checked by the provision, as a safeguard against arbitrary conduct on the part of Turkish judges, that a consular interpreter should always be present during trial and upon judgement being given. Insensibly the privileges specifically granted were enlarged by custom, until at last in part by continued sufferance, in part by treaty confirmatory of custom, they reached the dimensions which will be indicated in the following sections[2].

[1] Rymer's Foedera, xii. 270.
[2] British jurisdiction in the Turkish dominions is originally founded upon the Capitulations of 1675, which confirmed and extended previous concessions. Their terms, as above intimated, are quite inadequate of themselves to support the extent of jurisdiction now possessed; but the 18th Art. (Hertslet, Treaties and Tariffs, Turkey, p. 13), placed Great Britain on the same footing as that of the most favoured powers, and enabled her to have the advantage of privileges which had been obtained by other countries. The article was always interpreted in practice to cover a right on the part of Great Britain to have the benefit of any definition or enlargement of privileges subsequently obtained by other states, and the privileges so acquired were confirmed by the Treaty of the Dardanelles of January 5, 1809 (Hertslet, ib. p. 38), in language which

PART III.
CHAP. 2

In other Eastern countries than the Turkish dominions jurisdictional privileges have been acquired later; and as the circumstances which have induced European states to press for immunities on behalf of their subjects in Turkey were essentially the same as those which have been met with elsewhere, the treaties by which powers have been conferred correspond in their main lines, and generally in the larger details, with the results which agreement and custom have brought about in the Ottoman Empire.

Protective rights.

§ 65. Following the same order that has been previously adopted in treating of the functions of agents of the British crown in foreign countries, protective duties are the first to offer themselves for examination.

Necessarily whatever forms of protection exist in Europe must exist also in the East. Less than the amount of protective supervision which is needed in countries of the same kind and degree of civilization, cannot suffice in countries of a civilization different in itself, and, from the point of view of the Western nations, of inferior quality. In saying this all has been said which for practical purposes is required. Whatever protective duties there are which go beyond the above range, and are imposed upon British agents in Eastern states, take a jurisdictional shape, and will be noticed in their jurisdictional aspect.

At the same time it is worth while to remember, in the

---

implies that the benefit had accrued as of right. The meaning assigned to the 18th Article must therefore be supposed to extend to privileges obtained by any state subsequently, as well as previously, to the Treaty of the Dardanelles, and the rights of which Great Britain is thus in possession have probably rendered it unnecessary to rely upon custom for the justification of any important practice, though details must of course be greatly regulated by usage. Exclusive criminal and police jurisdiction, except when British subjects alone were concerned, was not secured till after the Treaty of Adrianople in 1829 (De Martens, Recueil, viii. 147), by which Russia, and consequently Great Britain, obtained that their subjects 'demeureront sous la juridiction et police exclusive du ministre et des consuls.'

interest alike of historical and of theoretical accuracy, how largely the element of protection has determined the extent to which jurisdiction has been delegated, and how largely it is present in the jurisdiction which is actually exercised. Superficially, when a British consul tries an English prisoner, or adjudicates in a case between two British subjects, he is merely the agent of a state to which the territorial sovereign has granted authority to enforce the duties that are owed by its subjects. In fact, he protects those subjects from the operation of unfit or unequal laws, and from the danger of corrupt, or biassed, or ignorant courts. European states have only troubled themselves to obtain, and they only care to preserve, their delegated jurisdiction in Oriental countries as a form of their protective rights.

PART III.
CHAP. 2.

The protective element in jurisdiction.

Essential as the protective element is seen to be on analysing the facts, it is not of course to be denied that the jurisdiction exercised by a British consul is in something besides its formal aspect a delegation from the local sovereign. It is subjected to the incidents of delegation; that is to say, if there be doubt whether certain powers have or have not been conferred by the territorial sovereign, the doubt must be solved in his favour. Were custom less solid the circumstance might be important. But for the purposes at present in hand, considerations of this nature are immaterial. Whenever Acts of Parliament or Orders in Council exist, they suffice for the English lawyer, to whom they must be supposed to communicate the unquestionable effect of treaties or of established custom, or of the two in combination. Questions as to the right interpretation of international treaties or usages can only be entertained when their authoritative exponents are mute or fail to convey a sense which can be clearly understood. From the practical, as well as from the theoretical side therefore, the protective element remains, if not the most

PART III.
CHAP. 2.

Protected persons who are not British subjects.

obvious, yet certainly the most important factor in the powers exercised by the crown in foreign countries.

§ 66. A particular kind of protection which used to be extensively accorded in certain countries of the East, and which is still given, though more restrictedly, needs separate notice. It does not rest upon the principle of the right to protect subjects of the state; it rests indeed upon no principle whatever. It is simply a practice of extending the privileges of subjects to persons who are not subjects, and of investing them either temporarily or permanently with a British character, as against Oriental governments, and to a certain extent for other purposes. The protected person is removed from the jurisdiction of the native courts, and is placed under that of the British consular courts; in the more direct modes of protection he shares the rights of a natural born British subject. It follows from being in this position that not only is he diplomatically protected, but that for purposes of jurisdiction he becomes a British subject. He is not however wholly identified with Great Britain. While to the extent mentioned he is governed by English law, he still retains his personal statute. Thus in the case of a Chaldean Catholic born within the Ottoman dominions, who had been taken under the protection of the British government, probate of his will was granted by the Consular Court at Constantinople; but succession to his moveable property was held to be regulated by the laws which govern the successions in Turkey of his civil society, viz. the Chaldean Catholics[1]. The British courts exercise jurisdiction, but administer the law appropriate to the national character of the persons concerned.

Of late years the number of persons for whom responsibility has been taken in this way, and over whom jurisdiction has correlatively been exercised has been largely reduced.

[1] Abd-ul-Messih v. Farra, Law Rep. 13 App. Cases, 431.

Formerly it was the habit of every European legation in the Eastern states, where the custom existed at all, to scatter protection freely; natives of the country as well as foreigners were gathered in considerable numbers under the ambassadorial wing, and their privileges were continued from father to son. Great Britain at least has in this respect completely altered her policy. As a general rule protection is freshly given only to persons in the service of a British consulate, and to their wives and minor children; they and their families moreover cease, also as a general rule, to receive protection upon the cessation of their employment; *cessante ratione, cessat et ipsa lex*. Outside this class the surviving members of the miscellaneous crowd upon whom the immunities of British subjects were in past times conferred, are the only persons withdrawn from the ordinary jurisdiction; those who have once received protection must of course for the most part continue to receive it, but no addition is lightly made to their number[1].

<small>Persons to whom protection is now given.</small>

The countries in which it has been customary to give protection to natives of the territory or other persons not British subjects, and in which the Orders in Council applicable to the several cases contemplate the continued

---

[1] A case in point is that of the descendants of Russian Jews who in 1849 were placed under the protection of the British consular officers in Syria, and who are probably somewhat numerous. Measures have been taken to gradually extinguish claims to protection under this head. Persons of certain ages, and registered before certain dates, and the children of some of them until the age of twenty or marriage, continue to receive protection; those who do not fall within the categories indicated have ceased to be protected since 1885, and upon the death of persons now protected, the whole class will have passed out of British protection, unless the British ambassador shall have seen fit to allow a fresh grant in a particular instance. The case is a fair illustration of the actual policy of Great Britain. The old customary right of admitting subjects of an Oriental state to the advantages of British protection is not abandoned; but care is taken that it shall be used only for special and exceptional reasons.

PART III. existence of the class, are the Ottoman dominions [1],
CHAP. 2. Persia [2], Morocco [3], Muscat [4], Tripoli and Siam. It has not

[1] Turkish regulations of the years 1863 and 1865 limit the number of dragomans and cavasses in foreign consulates, and, while giving them the same rights as persons to whom protection has been granted by a foreign power, confine the duration of their immunities to the term of their employment (Hertslet, Com. Treaties, xv. 1061). These regulations do not of course override the right of the state employing the persons in question to grant permanent protection in individual cases.

So far as treaties rule, Roumania and Bulgaria are still in the same position as if they were part of the Ottoman dominions. By the Treaty of Berlin (Art. 49) Roumania was given 'power to make conventions to determine the privileges and attributes of consuls in regard to protection within the Principality. Existing rights shall remain in force so long as they shall not have been modified by the mutual consent of the Principality and the parties oncerned.' But it has not been found possible to use the power to the extent intended; and nominally, except with some of the powers as regards protection, the Capitulations remain in force, so far as they could by the local customs be exercised at the date of the treaty. What these customs permitted seems to be by no means clear, and between Roumania and Great Britain at least, they have in great part dropped into desuetude. Great Britain, says M. Djurara (Secrétaire Général du Ministère des Affaires Etrangères, writing in the Rev. de Droit Int. xix. 1120), has never made any difficulties upon the subject of protection; and even in disputes which unquestionably fall within the cognizance of the Consular Courts, suits are frequently taken by consent before the courts of the country.

The 8th Article of the Treaty of Berlin reserved in Bulgaria 'the immunities and privileges of foreigners, as well as the rights of consular jurisdiction and protection as established by the Capitulations and usages . . . so long as they shall not have been modified with the consent of the parties concerned'; and in Eastern Roumelia they were reserved without qualification. In neither of the two provinces of the present Bulgaria has any modification of the Capitulations or usages been introduced by convention or other agreement.

[2] By the Treaty of Paris in 1857, between Great Britain and Persia, the former renounced the right of protecting Persian subjects not actually in the employment of the British Legation or of the consuls general, consuls, &c., subject, however, to the condition that no more general protection should be exercised by other powers. Hertslet's Persian Treaties, pp. 19, 20.

[3] A Convention, to which Great Britain was a party, was signed at Madrid, July 3, 1880, between most of the European states and Morocco, for the regulation of the practice of protection in the latter country. State Papers, lxxi. 639.

[4] By a Convention of May 31, 1839, it is agreed that subjects of the

been the practice to give protection in China and Japan, and in the Order in Council affecting those countries, no mention is made of protected persons; jurisdiction is restricted to British subjects[1].

§ 67. Questions arising out of double nationality or of double claim to right of protective jurisdiction may present themselves with reference both to British subjects, and to protected persons who, for purposes of protection and jurisdiction, occupy an identical position with them.

Double nationality.

A natural born subject of Great Britain, for example, who is also by the law of another state invested with its nationality, may be claimed by either of the two countries. In Europe no difficulty would be likely to make itself felt in a third country. Neither state would have any interest in opposing the choice of the individual; he would obtain protection from the country of his preference. But so soon as jurisdiction is delegated by the territorial state, the aspect of the case is changed. The individual by placing himself under one jurisdiction rather than another, may obtain a personal advantage, to the disadvantage of one of the two states to which he may be ascribed, or to

In the case of natural born subjects of Great Britain.

Sultan of Muscat actually in the service of any British subject in his dominions, shall have protection as if they were themselves British subjects; but it is provided that if they are convicted of any crime or 'infraction of the law needing punishment,' they shall be discharged from their British service and handed over to the authorities of the Sultan. State Papers, xxviii. 1080.

[1] Comp. §§ 60 and 61.

Although in China and Japan it has been the rule to restrict protection and consequently jurisdiction to British subjects, there seem to have been exceptional cases, at any rate in the latter country, in which protection has been given in peculiar circumstances, and with the consent of the Japanese government, to persons who were Japanese in view of English law, and in which the persons in question have been registered as 'British subjects' under the Order in Council. The proceeding could evidently have no effect on nationality, and was merely of the nature of an administrative arrangement between the two countries.

PART III.
CHAP. 2.
the disadvantage of persons who are its subjects. Both countries may have a strong interest in urging their claim to his allegiance. In such circumstances no legal solution of the difficulty seems possible. In third states the right to him of each country is equal to that of the other. There is no such reason on either hand for yielding as proffers itself when a claim based upon origin is met by a like claim strengthened by the presence of the individual on the territory of one of the claimants. Unless diplomatic arrangement be possible, there is no escape from a flat conflict of jurisdiction [1]. A similar difficulty evidently occurs when a person of double nationality is accused of crime.

In the case of naturalized and protected persons.

The situation would no doubt be modified if a person were claimed by his state of origin or birth, who is only British by naturalization or protection. Unless he were associated with Great Britain by official employment, it is evident that the tie connecting him with his natural state is closer and more intimate than that linking him with his state of personal choice; and though theoretically he must almost certainly be regarded in the one case, and possibly might be looked upon rightly in the other, as being entitled from the bare legal point of view to the

[1] An exceptional state of things would appear to exist in Morocco, where Spain has a treaty, which seems to have been admitted to override the privileges granted to other countries; so that if a native of Gibraltar, born of Spanish parents, and therefore having a double nationality, be claimed as Spanish, his British character cannot be adversely asserted. The case is a curious one, and not easily explicable. The treaties between Great Britain and Morocco of 1728 and 1760 (De Martens, Recueil, Supp. i. 182 and Rec. i. 42) remove British subjects from the ordinary jurisdiction of the country; and the earliest treaty between Morocco and Spain appears to have been concluded in 1767 (Riquelme, Elem. de Derecho Publico Internacional, i. 392). It is unintelligible, whatever be the terms of a treaty between two foreign powers, concluded without the privity of Great Britain, that it should be held to deprive a person claimed as a British subject of advantages previously conceded to British subjects.

protection of Great Britain in a third state even against his country of origin, and as being as much subject to her jurisdiction as to that of the latter, it is highly improbable, save in very exceptional cases, that his British character would be contentiously supported or insisted on. Although the Naturalization Act of 1870 is satisfied with declaring that a naturalized foreigner shall not be deemed to be a British subject in his former state unless he has ceased to be its subject, the spirit of the enactment obviously is that acquired nationality has a lower claim to recognition than nationality of origin. The object of protection, on its part, as given to persons who are not British subjects, is to secure them against the risks incident to ordinary Eastern administration; it has no reference to the circumstances of European nationality. There are however some occasions on which the right of granting protection in an Eastern country might be valuable, and might be legitimately used adversely to a European power. It is not possible to naturalize a foreigner resident abroad, were it even desirable to do so; it would be undesirable to accord too freely the privileges of denization; unless protection were at least understood to withdraw persons, while employed in the British service, from the jurisdiction of a government claiming them, a state of things would be set up which, though affecting almost entirely persons in very subordinate employment, might nevertheless be inconvenient and disagreeable.

§ 68. It may be worth while to notice the limitations upon an outlying instance of protection temporarily accorded to persons, not on their own account, but because of their association with British property. Persons forming part of the crew of a British vessel, whatever may be their nationality, are protected while in an Oriental port, not merely to the point up to which the customs of Europe allow members of a crew to be subjected to British jurisdiction,

PART III.
CHAP. 2.

Protection to foreign members of crews of British vessels.

PART III. but to the full range, whether with respect to acts done on
CHAP. 2. the vessel or on shore, that merely protective jurisdiction stretches in an Eastern state. Punitive jurisdiction does not however go with protective jurisdiction in this instance. British courts can only exercise criminal jurisdiction over British subjects, and persons to whom the privileges of subjects have been regularly extended; they consequently have no power to try a foreign seaman belonging to a British ship for any offence committed within or without the territorial jurisdiction. He must be handed over to the consular authority of the nation of which he is a subject [1].

[1] In time of war, or if a European power has no agents of its own in an Eastern country, its subjects are sometimes placed temporarily or permanently under the protection of another European state. Some uncertainty seems to exist as to the effect of this arrangement; and different powers appear to have taken different views upon the matter. In one instance some foreigners having been placed under the protection of Great Britain in a district where their country had no consul, an action was brought against one of them in the British Consular Court. His ambassador at Constantinople objected to the exercise of jurisdiction, contending that though the national interests had been placed under British protection, the intention of the measure was only that protection should be afforded against the local authorities. On another occasion a British subject and a foreigner, both of whom were Protestants, wished to be married at a British Legation. The interests of the state to which the foreigner belonged were at the time in charge of a third power, the minister accredited by which was doubtful as to the right course to pursue. On the question being referred to the government of the state to which the foreign party to the intended marriage was subject, it was decided that the third power had taken over charge of the national interests for all purposes, and that therefore the parties must be married at its legation, and according to the forms prescribed by its law.

The views of different governments being so markedly different from one another, it would be well that inquiry should be made, before consenting to accept charge of foreign subjects in the East, in what position it is intended that they shall be placed; and if it could be done consistently with comity, it might be judicious to refuse to undertake the office of protection unless jurisdiction were permitted. A British consul would find himself in an embarrassing situation relatively to the local authorities, if while pushing claims on behalf of one foreigner, or while shielding him from wrong, he were obliged to confess that he was totally unable to punish the crime of another person of the same nation-

§ 69. In addition to the right of protecting British subjects and other persons in a general manner, which has been discussed in the foregoing sections, Great Britain possesses in some Eastern states specific privileges which have been yielded to her in order that her subjects and other persons under her protection shall not be exposed to illtreatment or injustice at the hands of the local authorities.

PART III.
CHAP. 2.

Special protective privileges,

In some countries a certain degree of protection is formally conceded to things and places as well as to persons. In the Ottoman Empire, and in the territories to which the Capitulations extend, the local police are forbidden to enter by force a house inhabited by a British subject without giving notice to the ambassador or consul, if either be within reach, so that an agent of the British government may be present to see that no irregularity is committed[1]; where a criminal is caught *flagrante delicto*, or necessity of some kind interferes with previous notice, a consul must be made acquainted with the fact of arrest within four and twenty hours after its occurrence. In Persia formal authorization from the minister or consul is required[2]. Ships and their boats are assimilated to houses. No arrest for example can be made on board a British vessel in Turkish waters by Turkish officials without the presence or sanction of a British consul[3]. The treaties with China and Corea secure a larger immunity than that stipulated in Turkey. By the former it is implied that in no circumstances can Chinese officials

in respect of houses and ships.

---

ality, or to afford the civil justice of his court against him. The practical result of refusal on the part of a foreign power to submit its subjects to British jurisdiction would be to withdraw them from the operation of all jurisdiction.

[1] Protocol of July 28, 1868; Hertslet, Com. Treaties, xii. 1211.

[2] Treaty of Tourkmantchai, between Russia and Persia, 1828, Hertslet's Persian Treaties, p. 127.

[3] When it is desired to arrest the subject of a third power on board a British vessel, it is believed to be the practice to give notice to the consul of the power in question before the arrest is permitted.

PART III.
CHAP. 2.
enter the houses or the vessels of British subjects at the open ports; and by the latter it is expressly stated that no Corean officer shall do so without consent of the British consular authorities[1]. By the Morocco and Siam Orders in Council and by the Africa Order in Council, 1890, except probably within the Congo Free State[2], the British crown is declared to possess identical powers and jurisdiction over the property of its subjects on land and over their vessels in Moroccan and Siamese waters with those which it has with respect to British subjects themselves; it may therefore be assumed that usage and sufferance in these cases free the houses and ships of British subjects from all interference on the part of the local authorities as fully as their persons are freed from the local jurisdiction[3].

[1] Treaty of Tientsin, June 26, 1858, Art. 21, and Treaty of Hanyang, Nov. 26, 1883, Art. 3; Hertslet's Commercial Treaties, xi. 90; State Papers, lxxiv. 86, 93. The Chinese treaty only directly contemplates immunity from search for Chinese offenders; immunity for other purposes is an inference *a fortiori*. As the article of the treaty applies only to the open ports, it is possible that the houses of British subjects in the interior may be liable to invasion by the Chinese authorities.

[2] By the Convention of December 16, 1884, between Great Britain and the King of the Belgians, it is agreed that British consular officers shall exercise exclusive jurisdiction over British subjects and their property, but it is expressly said that the latter are not relieved from the obligation to observe the laws of the Free State applicable to foreigners; it is simply provided that infractions are to be justiciable only by a British Consular Court. This does not seem to exclude the possibility of police action by the local authorities.

[3] By the treaty with Siam, the British consul is bound to apprehend, and on conviction to punish, British subjects who commit any grave infractions of the laws, or who have injured 'Siamese subjects, their persons, houses, property or premises of any kind'; by that with Corea the consul is bound to arrest Corean subjects charged with crimes who have taken refuge in the houses or ships of British subjects. These provisions are merely a partial embodiment of a duty which is correlative to the privileges and immunities enjoyed by Great Britain. To the extent that British subjects, and their houses or ships, are withdrawn from the native jurisdiction, the British government is under a moral obligation to make such regulations, and take such measures, as will prevent the territorial state or its subjects from suffering wrong through the existence of the privileges that it has conceded.

In other cases Treaties and Orders in Council are alike mute upon the point; but it is in the highest degree unlikely that the native authorities in Muscat or on the Persian coasts and islands would endeavour to assert jurisdiction in any manner over a British house or ship.

The significance of this privilege must not however be exaggerated. It constitutes a safeguard; it does not confer an immunity. It is not intended that asylum shall be afforded to persons who have violated the ordinary territorial law. The usual course seems to be—making allowance perhaps for some variation of custom in places of inferior civilization—always to permit the arrest of persons accused by the competent local authorities of having committed a specific offence against the law. After arrest they are either retained by the authorities if territorial subjects, or are handed over, if British or other foreign subjects, to the appropriate consular jurisdiction.

At the same time it is not to be forgotten that in Oriental countries the administration of law tends to confuse itself with executive measures which are often arbitrary and oppressive, and which it may be neither just nor politic to sanction. It would be highly inexpedient that a certain margin of indefiniteness, favourable to the Western state, should not, where possible, surround the application of its rights. In the East questions of law and policy melt into one another; and it would not be well to allow a too rigid interpretation of the conventional or customary rights of the British crown to narrow its powers, or to give the local government an opportunity of gradually restricting them. The usual course adopted where territorial subjects are the accused persons, may not be that which policy will dictate, or which is absolutely needful in law, when the alleged offences are of a certain character, or when the motives for arrest are open to suspicion. It is difficult to reclaim a person who has once

PART III.
CHAP. 2.

in respect of trials.

been surrendered; it may be possible altogether to avoid surrender if delay is interposed until diplomacy has had time to act.

By some treaties, precautions of more or less value are taken that cases triable by the local courts shall be conducted without patent injustice, or that at least the consul shall have a knowledge of what takes place which will enable him if necessary to cause diplomatic representations to be made. The Corean treaty provides that 'in all cases, whether civil or criminal, tried in Corean courts, a properly authorized British official shall be allowed to attend the hearing and shall be treated with the courtesy due to his position. He shall be allowed, whenever he thinks necessary, to call, examine and cross-examine witnesses, and to protest against the proceedings or decision.' In Siam the British consul is at liberty to attend at, and listen to, the investigation of the case; and copies of the proceedings are to be furnished from time to time, whenever desired, until the case is concluded[1]. In Morocco the governor of the town or district, or the kadi, judges all criminal and civil cases in which a Moorish subject is the accused or the defendant, but the British consul general or his deputy has a right to be present in court during the whole trial[2]. In like manner in Turkey, and the countries subject to the Capitulations, 'the judge shall not hear nor decide' cases in which he has jurisdiction 'until the ambassador, consul, or interpreter shall be present[3].'

Scope and limits of

§ 70. On approaching the jurisdictional powers of the

[1] Commercial Agreement of May 13, 1856, Hertslet, Com. Treaties, x. 567.
[2] Treaty of December 9, 1856, Art. 9, Hertslet, Com. Treaties, x. 907. In civil cases there is an appeal to the British Chargé d'Affaires and Consul General, and by the defendant to the Moorish Commissioner for Foreign Affairs.
[3] Art. 24 of the Capitulations as confirmed by the Treaty of the Dardanelles of January 5, 1809; Hertslet, Com. Treaties, ii. 352.

British crown in Eastern states they are seen to divide themselves into heads which correspond with the persons affected, with the laws which are applied, and with the machinery for the application of law.

The first head offers little difficulty, and may be quickly dismissed. It is everywhere conceded that the British Consular Courts shall judge in both civil and criminal matters where British subjects alone are concerned[1]. It

<small>PART III. CHAP. 2.

British jurisdiction.

Exclusive jurisdiction when British subjects are alone concerned.</small>

---

[1] There is an important exceptional case in Turkey, where foreigners, including British subjects, are assimilated to Ottoman subjects whenever the ownership of real property is concerned, and are solely amenable to the Ottoman civil courts, even when both parties to a case are British; reservation only being made of the immunities attached to their persons and their personal property as prescribed by the treaties. (Protocol relative to the admission of British subjects in Turkey to the right of holding real property of July 28, 1868. Hertslet, Com. Treaties, xx. 1214.) In this instance conflicting claims of jurisdiction have arisen. The Ottoman government has claimed on behalf of the Turkish courts that disputes between landlord and tenant in relation to rent, or damages arising out of contract with reference to land, fall under their exclusive competence. The view of the British government, and, it is believed, of the European governments in general, is that the jurisdiction of the Turkish tribunals is confined to questions regarding the title to the land itself or the right to its possession or occupation. It has been decided on appeal from the Supreme Consular Court at Constantinople (Abbott v. Abbott, L. R. 6 P. C. 220) that an order made by that court for the sale by a receiver in a partnership suit of lands, held by the partner in the name of a Turkish subject, was valid. '*A fortiori* it would seem that an order for sale of lands held by British subjects in their own name would be valid.' Tarring, British Consular Jurisdiction in the East, p. 92. See also Pitts v. La-Fontaine, L. R. v. App. Cases, 564.

By the convention signed at Madrid in July 1880 (State Papers, lxxi. 639) between Morocco and Great Britain and other powers, the right of all foreigners to hold real property was recognized. It was provided by this convention that any question which might occur respecting such right should be decided 'according to Moorish law,' and the proviso has been interpreted to mean that all questions relating to the title and tenure of real property shall be heard and determined not only according to Moorish law, but in a Moorish court, whoever the parties in the case may be.

There is also a slight exception in Egypt, incidentally consequent upon the existence of the international tribunals. Certain criminal acts done by British subjects against British judges or British jurymen, and police offences, are or can be dealt with by the tribunals. Comp. note, p. 152.

PART III.
CHAP. 2.

Jurisdiction in mixed cases.

is admitted almost as universally in principle that where a British subject on the one hand, and a native of the territory or a subject of a third power on the other, are concerned, the proper forum is that of the party against whom pursuit is directed, so that in criminal cases the offender is tried by his own courts, and in civil matters the action is brought in the court of the defendant. That cases involving none but British subjects, and no interests other than British interests, should be judged solely by British courts follows almost inevitably from a recognition of the fact that Eastern conceptions of law differ too widely from those of the West to render it possible to subordinate persons belonging to the nations of European civilization to the full local jurisdiction; and if the subjects of a European state will settle their quarrels among themselves, and punish their own crimes efficiently, the Eastern state has no adequate motive for exercising in any point an authority which it has already surrendered in principle. That in mixed cases the court of jurisdiction should be the court of the defendant is at least natural. An accused person is taken to be innocent until he is shown to be guilty; the allegations in an action have to be proved against the defendant. As between the territorial state and a foreign country, the former can no more be expected to abandon subjects presumably guiltless of wrong doing to a law of alien ideas and foreign in administration, than the European state can be supposed willing to hand over its members to the laws and the courts of the East. As between two foreign countries, since the territorial law is acceptable to neither, and the territorial state is disinterested, the consideration that wrong doing has to be proved again operates, and preference is given to the courts of the person against whom proceedings are taken.

Ground of

§ 71. It has been mentioned that the British Consular

Courts have everywhere sole jurisdiction in both civil and criminal matters where British subjects alone are concerned. It might be expected that this delegation would in all cases be made by treaty. But it is not so. The powers exercised by Great Britain are expressly given by treaty with Morocco, the Congo Free State, Madagascar, Siam, China, Corea, and Japan[1]. With Persia there is no treaty in which the question of jurisdiction is touched directly; but by that of March 4, 1857, the most favoured nation treatment was obtained, and as France and Russia had previously secured jurisdiction, both civil and criminal, over their own subjects, identical advantages are now enjoyed by Great Britain[2]. So far then Great Britain rests safely upon treaty. But in the large range of territories which are subject to the Turkish capitulations, and in the exceptional instance of Muscat, the treaties in force convey no more than civil jurisdiction. Criminal jurisdiction is founded upon custom only. Nevertheless as between the Levant Company and the Ottoman Empire, whilst the former existed, and after its dissolution as between Great Britain and the Empire, the ground was firm and undisputed; but until legislation took place questions as to whether it was open to the crown to exercise jurisdiction, and as to the extent to which usage and sufferance had placed jurisdiction in its hands, might have given rise to grave legal difficulties in relation to its own subjects[3].

PART III.
CHAP. 2.

Jurisdiction as between Great Britain and the various Eastern states.

---

[1] No reference is made by name in the treaty with Japan to British subjects who commit crimes against their fellow subjects. Jurisdiction over them is obtained by the provision that 'British subjects who may commit any crime against Japanese subjects or the subjects or citizens of any other country, shall be tried and punished by the consul or other public functionary, authorized thereto, according to the laws of Great Britain.'

[2] Hertslet's Persian Treaties, pp. 19, 82, 128, and 129.

[3] By a charter of James I, confirmed by Charles II, and recognized by various Acts of Parliament, the Levant Company was invested with a general power of making bye-laws, and appointing consuls with judicial and regulatory functions. It did not receive power to exercise either

PART III. A series of Foreign Jurisdiction Acts, and the Orders in
CHAP. 2.   Council authorized by them, have now cleared away all
possibility of doubt, and have settled the jurisdiction in
this respect also upon a solid foundation.

As between Great Britain and its subjects.

At the same time, though the foundation is solid, it cannot be assumed that the superstructure will always be adequate in its details. Difficulties may present themselves in the construction of the Acts and Orders. The Foreign Jurisdiction Act of 1890 therefore provides means for determining what the true extent of any jurisdiction shall be held to be. 'If in any proceeding, civil or criminal, in a court in Her Majesty's dominions or held under the authority of Her Majesty, any question arises as to the existence or extent of any jurisdiction of Her Majesty in a foreign country a Secretary of State shall, on the application of the court, send to the court within a reasonable time his decision on the question, and his decision shall for the purposes of the proceeding be final[1].' Usually it is for a court to itself determine the scope of its jurisdiction, subject to such appeal or revision by a higher court as may be provided; and it is to be presumed that

criminal jurisdiction, properly so called, or civil jurisdiction in mixed suits; these branches of jurisdiction were probably not pretended to in those times, and were of subsequent and gradual acquisition; usage and sufferance confirmed them. When the Company ceased to exist in 1825 a new state of things arose. A necessity presented itself of testing the powers vested in the consuls by the recognized principles of the Constitution, which had not been felt while the authority of the Company stood between the crown and its subjects in the countries of the Levant. In 1826 the Law Officers threw the doubts, of which mention has been made, upon the legality of the general powers of fine and imprisonment, and of the power in certain cases of sending back His Majesty's subjects to this country, which had previously been thought to be possessed by the consuls; it became necessary to relieve the latter from the inconvenience and danger of their situation; and in 1836 an Act was passed, followed in 1843 by the more efficient Foreign Jurisdiction Act of that date, and later by various Amending Acts, which have all been now consolidated in the Foreign Jurisdiction Act of 1890.

[1] Sect. iv.

in this instance it is not intended to deprive the courts of all power in this respect. The somewhat imperative language of the section is so far modified by the words, 'on the application of the court,' as to render it probable that a certain discretion is meant to be left, and that in spite of the use of the phrase 'any question,' they are only required to apply to the Secretary of State when doubts occur as to the intention of the Act or Orders, as to whether a customary practice is authoritative, as to the compatibility of an Order in Council with a treaty, or as to the relation of a treaty to usage, which they do not feel themselves competent to solve upon the knowledge at their command[1].

British subjects in ordinary civil employment under the British

[1] It has been suggested (Piggott, Exterritoriality, p. 58) that to interfere with the capacity of a court to determine the limits of its own jurisdiction is so very unusual a proceeding that the 4th section of the Act ought to be construed as excluding reference to a Secretary of State upon such a matter as the compatibility of an Order in Council with a treaty, and as bearing only upon questions of simple fact; such, for example, as were referred in Harvey v. Fitzpatrick (23 Law Journal Rep. Chancery, 564, cited *ad loc.*), in which a question was put by the court to the Secretary of State for the Colonies, 'whether Her Majesty has at any time exercised any jurisdiction with respect to the administration of personal estates of persons dying intestate in Cape Coast Town; and if so, to what extent and in what manner and through what court or officer such jurisdiction has been exercised.' In support of this contention are adduced the language of the Act of 1843, which treats the answer of the Secretary of State as material for the 'due determination of the issue or question,' and a statement of the Attorney-General in the House of Commons that the Bill introduced in 1890 made no changes in the law. Notwithstanding the latter fact, which moreover does not seem to be incapable of explanation, it is hard to see why the language of the Act should have been changed if no change were intended in the effect of a reference to the Secretary of State; and it is easy to understand that reasons of policy may have rendered an alteration desirable. To give to the Secretary of State, when appealed to, the power of authoritatively determining the 'existence or extent' of jurisdiction in an Oriental country, may afford him the opportunity of avoiding an inconvenient conflict of jurisdictional claims, and may also enable him to prevent the views of the various Consular Courts from gradually becoming divergent from each other, and so giving rise to differing practice in identical circumstances.

PART III.
CHAP. 2.

Subjects in the employment of an Eastern state.

government of an Eastern state remain in principle under the jurisdiction of the British courts; but when the employment, though civil, is such that the persons engaged in it are placed under disciplinary rules, it would manifestly be unwise, and indeed unfair, to insist upon taking jurisdiction out of the hands of the native authorities in respect of breaches of those rules; and when the employment is military or naval the necessary conditions of service are such that persons entering it must be supposed to submit themselves voluntarily to the territorial authorities. Without saying that there are no circumstances in which it would be proper for British jurisdiction to be asserted, it is at least evident that the circumstances would be rare and exceptional in their nature.

Criminal jurisdiction in mixed cases.

§ 72. In criminal cases in which the accused person is a British subject, while the other person concerned is a territorial subject or other foreigner, the almost universal rule is that exclusive jurisdiction shall be exercised by the British courts. This for instance is the case in Egypt[1].

---

[1] Although Egypt is a part of the Ottoman Empire, and is therefore nominally affected by the Capitulations and by Turkish laws, various circumstances, amongst others the impossibility of having recourse to the Porte in the more serious cases, whether criminal or civil, has long caused both sources of authority to be displaced by customary practices differing from those existing in Turkey. In a report on judicial reform, presented by Nubar Pasha to the Khedive in 1867, it could be accurately said, 'de ces capitulations, il n'existe plus que le nom; elles ont été remplacées par une législation coutumière arbitraire, résultat du caractère de chaque chef d'agence, législation basée sur des antécédents plus ou moins abusifs, que la force des choses, la pression d'un côté, le désir de faciliter l'établissement des étrangers de l'autre, ont introduite en Égypte.' Quoted by Lawrence, Commentaire sur les Éléments du Droit International, iv. 183.

In respect of criminal cases in which British subjects are the accused persons, usage in Egypt has arrived by another road at the point where practice in Turkey would be if the treaties were fully carried out (see notes, pp. 133 and 153).

A quasi exception exists through the possession, by the International Tribunals organized under the Réglement d'Organisation Judiciaire of 1874, of jurisdiction in respect of 'contraventions de simple police,' and of 'crimes et délits commis directement contre les magistrats, les jurés et

China, Japan, the Congo State, Morocco, Madagascar, and Muscat[1]. In Corea, while the jurisdiction is not disturbed, it is provided that a Corean official may be present at the trial, with power to call, examine, and cross-examine witnesses, and to protest against the proceedings or decision.

In the Ottoman dominions, criminal charges brought by a Turkish subject against a British subject are as a matter of practice submitted to the Turkish tribunals. 'But the presence of a dragoman from the British consulate is necessary to the validity of the proceedings; and (in Constantinople at least) if he refuses to sign the sentence, it can only be carried into effect after negotiations between the higher authorities[2];' the criminal is in all

officiers de justice des Tribunaux Egyptiens dans l'exercice ou à l'occasion de l'exercice de leurs fonctions ; commis directement contre l'exécution des sentences et des mandats de justice des mêmes Tribunaux ; imputés aux juges, jurés, et officiers de justice des Tribunaux comme commis dans l'exercice de leurs fonctions ou par suite d'un abus de ces fonctions' (Hertslet, Com. Treaties, xiv. 310, 311). The International Tribunals are not Egyptian courts, but courts established, under international sanction, by agreement between Egypt and the body of civilized nations having interests in the country, for the purpose of taking cognizance of civil cases between persons of different nationalities. Their criminal jurisdiction is incidental, and in the main merely self-protective.

[1] The exceptional provision contained in the Africa Order, 1889 (Art. 17), that crimes and offences affecting natives of Africa or other foreigners, committed by British subjects or protected persons, shall with the consent of such natives or foreigners, be punishable as if they were committed against British subjects, must presumably have been inserted because the Order does, or may, extend to places where no treaty confers jurisdiction, and where no sufficient usage justifies the British government in assuming jurisdiction. In such places justice can be offered ; it cannot be imposed. The Congo State and Madagascar, however, which are the only territories falling within the scope of the present chapter that are affected by the Order, are excepted from it in this particular by their treaties with Great Britain.

[2] Tarring, British Consular Jurisdiction in the East, p. 91. Notwithstanding the actual practice, it may be worth while to repeat, what has already been stated in a previous note, that though the Capitulations, in the countries to which they extend, only themselves cover crimes perpetrated by one British subject upon another, an article of the Treaty of the Dardanelles obtains for Great Britain the benefit of the

154   POWERS AND JURISDICTION OF THE

PART III. cases handed over to the British authorities to undergo his
CHAP. 2. punishment. Charges brought by foreigners other than Turkish subjects are adjudicated upon in the British courts. In Persia crimes and offences committed by one British subject against a Persian subject or a foreigner are tried by a Persian judge in presence of a British consular official [1].

Police Powers.   § 73. In intimate connexion with criminal jurisdiction is the police power of arrest. No Oriental states have surrendered the right of apprehending persons accused of crime or minor offences, and it is obvious that in none would it be possible to forego the right in practice. British subjects and protected persons can therefore be arrested by the local authorities, subject to the safeguards which have been

Treaty of Adrianople between Russia and Turkey, and consequently secures in the amplest manner that her subjects 'demeureront sous la juridiction et police exclusive du Ministre et des consuls.' A later treaty of the year 1839, between Belgium and Turkey (de Martens, Nouv. Rec. xvi. 961), and another of the same year between the Porte and the Hanseatic towns (ib. 888), stipulate in practically identical terms that Belgian or Hanseatic subjects 'vaquant honnêtement et paisiblement à leurs occupations ou à leur commerce, ne pourront jamais être arrêtés ni molestés par les autorités locales; mais en cas de crime ou de délit, l'affaire sera remise à leur ministre, chargé d'affaires, ou consul ou vice-consul; les accusés seront jugés par lui et punis suivant l'usage observé à l'égard des Francs.'

[1] By the most favoured nation clause, upon the Russo-Persian Treaty of 1828. Hertslet, Persian Treaties, p. 129.

It may be useful to note, though no question of British jurisdiction is involved, that in criminal cases where the accused person is a native of the territory, or a foreigner belonging to a third power, the principle that an accused person must be judged by the laws of his territory almost universally holds. It is not derogated from in Morocco by the provision that the British consul general or his deputy shall be allowed to be present during the trial of the case, that being a safeguard for due render of justice, which is based upon the right of protection; nor in Muscat by the accidental fact that, as no subjects of European states are settled there, the only consul, other than the British consul, who has established his right of jurisdiction over persons of his own nationality is the American. The only real exception is in China, where in Shanghai there is a mixed court, presided over by a Chinese magistrate assisted by a British consular official.

mentioned in a previous section as being provided in some countries against oppressive action on the part of those authorities. At the same time British consular officers have a concurrent power; they are even, as has been seen, under a treaty obligation in some cases to exercise it. In addition they are furnished by English legislation with the means of laying hands upon persons accused of offences of a certain gravity who have escaped into a British possession or into any place in which British extraterritorial jurisdiction exists. The Foreign Jurisdiction Act of 1890 enables the Queen in Council to extend the operation of the Fugitive Offenders Act[1] to any country in which the crown has such jurisdiction; and the latter has accordingly been applied with some necessary modifications within the spheres of the various Orders in Council[2].

§ 74. Practice in civil cases is far from being so uniform as is practice in criminal matters. It is compulsory by treaty in Morocco, the Congo State, Muscat, Corea[3], and Siam[4] that a native shall bring his suit

Civil jurisdiction in mixed cases.

---

[1] 44 & 45 Vict. c. 69.

[2] On at least one occasion a practical difficulty is believed to have declared itself in connexion with the functions of police, which was not without importance in itself, and which was of far reaching interest, because, while it could only be solved in one way, the solution which it might have received was susceptible of general application. An Eastern state was anxious that certain police regulations should be enforced by the Consular Courts within its territory. It was met in the case of Great Britain by the incapacity of British Consular Courts to administer any but British laws; they could not be made auxiliary to the local courts for the purpose of administering local law. It was however possible for the competent British authority to issue identical regulations binding on British subjects; and it is to be presumed that this would have been done, had not collateral circumstances prevented an arrangement of which acceptance of the proposed police laws would have been a part.

[3] Corean officials have the same rights in civil that they have in criminal cases.

[4] The Siamese authorities are at liberty 'to attend at the investigation of the case; and copies of the proceedings will be furnished from time to time' of them.

By the Order in Council 'wrongs, and breaches of contracts affecting

PART III.
CHAP. 2.

against a British subject in the British Consular Court. Somewhat curiously the Orders in Council do not always take the full powers the assumption of which the treaties would allow. By the Africa Order in Council, 1889, which extends to the Congo State, foreigners, among whom are included subjects of that state, are permitted to 'institute or take a suit or proceeding of a civil nature against a British subject,' provided that 'the foreigner (i) first files in the court his consent to the jurisdiction of the court, and (ii) also, if required by the court, obtains and files a certificate in writing from a competent authority of his own government to the effect that no objection is made by that government to the foreigner submitting the particular cause or matter to the jurisdiction of the court; and (iii) also, if required by the court, gives security to the satisfaction of the court, to such reasonable amount as the court directs, by deposit of money or otherwise, to pay fees, costs . . . and expenses, and to abide by and perform the decision to be given by the court or on appeal.' It may probably be assumed without undue rashness that the second of these requirements contemplates only foreigners who are not

Congo Free State.

the property or rights of natives of Siam, committed by persons subject to this Order, are cognizable under the provisions of this Order, with the consent of such natives.' The intention of this clause is not evident. The power of entertaining a suit takes with it as of course, either the power of giving effect to the judgment given, or the right of demanding that the territorial authority shall enforce it. The treaty suffices; consent by the individual is superfluous.

It may be noted here that in the remoter parts of Siam, viz. Chiengmai, Lakon, and Lampoonchi, Siamese judges may exercise civil and criminal jurisdiction between British subjects or between British and Siamese subjects, but the British consul or vice-consul is entitled to be present, to be furnished with copies of the proceedings, and to make suggestions to the judge in the interests of justice, and at any time before judgement to signify his desire to the judge in writing that any case in which both parties are British subjects, or the accused or defendant is a British subject, be transferred for adjudication to the British Consular Court at Chiengmai; whereupon the case shall be transferred (Hertslet, Com. Treaties, x. 565).

subjects of the Congo State[1]; the third is obviously necessary in a country of rudimentary organization, where the local authorities might not always find it easy to recover on behalf of the court, or of a successful British litigant, such sums as might have become due by way of fees or costs and expenses; the first requirement, which is absolute and not at the discretion of the court, is in its present form somewhat difficult to understand. It certainly appears unnecessary upon the terms of a treaty which declares that 'every British consul ... who shall be thereunto duly authorized by Her Britannic Majesty's government, may hold a Consular Court for the district assigned to him, and shall exercise sole and exclusive jurisdiction, both civil and criminal, over the persons and property of British subjects within the same, in accordance with British law.' The agreement that the Consular Court shall be the sole court for certain purposes places automatically under its jurisdiction every Congo subject who brings his suit in it, and saddles the state with an obligation to take any action with regard to its own subjects which may become necessary for giving effect to the judgements rendered. The Siam Order in Council is identically framed.

Siam.

The Morocco Order in Council on the other hand corresponds exactly with the agreements between that country and Great Britain. It recites the language of the treaty by which powers are conferred, and gives such jurisdiction as may be necessary for carrying them into effect. The Muscat Order enables Her Majesty's consul to do all acts which British consuls are entitled to perform in any other state, by law, usage, or sufferance; and in Corea it is ordered that jurisdiction shall be exercised in accordance

Morocco.

Muscat.

Corea.

---

[1] It will be seen later that there are cases in which a certificate to the above effect is required from subjects of the territorial state, but in these no such definite treaty exists as that between Great Britain and the Congo State.

PART III. with the provisions of the China and Japan Order in
CHAP. 2. Council, which enables the Consular Courts to take
cognizance of any suit or proceeding of a civil nature
brought against a British subject by a native.

China and   It is remarkable that the Order in Council applicable to
Japan.
China and Japan goes further than the treaties in force
with those countries would seem to warrant. It is agreed
by the XVIIth Article of the Treaty of Tientsin, of
June 26, 1858, that 'if a Chinese have reason to complain
of a British subject, the consul shall listen to his complaint,
and endeavour to settle it in a friendly manner. If disputes
take place of such a nature that the consul cannot arrange
them amicably, then he shall request the assistance of the
Chinese authorities that they may together examine into
the merits of the case and decide it equitably.' The
treaty concluded in the same year with Japan is similar
in its terms. No later agreement appears to have been
entered into with either nation; the courts, therefore, have
no delegated jurisdiction. They are nevertheless enabled
by Order in Council[1] to take cognizance of all suits or
proceedings of a civil nature instituted or taken by
a Chinese or a Japanese against a British subject, provided
that the conditions before quoted from the Africa Order
of 1889 are complied with. At this point the question
suggests itself:—of what nature are the functions of the
court; does it exercise jurisdiction or does it carry out an
arbitration[2]? The answer, in relation to a Chinese or
Japanese plaintiff, must be found in the attitude of the
local government. If it be willing, on need being shown,

---

[1] China and Japan Order in Council, 1881, and China, Japan, and Corea
Order in Council, August 6, 1886.

[2] So far as the Chinese or Japanese plaintiff is individually concerned
the function of the court is necessarily arbitral. He is incapable of
consenting to exercise of jurisdiction in the true sense of the word, for he
cannot make a submission which implies surrender of a sovereign right
of his country.

to enforce upon him any liabilities arising out of the decision of the court, it must be supposed to consider that it has allowed true jurisdiction to grow up upon usage and sufferance. If it stands aside, then the court must obviously be understood to act with reference to the native as an arbitral tribunal. At the same time as the institution of proceedings takes place by the joint will of the plaintiff and the court, and is compulsory on the British defendant, the court with reference to him must be in exercise of its ordinary jurisdiction[1]. A like state of things exists in Madagascar. The British consul 'aided by an officer duly authorized by Her Majesty the Queen of Madagascar' is there empowered by treaty 'to hear and decide' all 'disputes or differences' between Malagasy and British subjects. The presence of the native official is the condition of the exercise of jurisdiction. The Africa Order in Council, however, which applies to Madagascar[2], authorizes the Consular Court to take cognizance of suits against a British subject irrespectively of any native official, upon conditions identical only with those observance of which is required in China and Japan. The situation thus created in the three countries, though not without interest, is of little practical import, since the court can always see that sufficient security is exacted to render ulterior measures unnecessary.

In the cases of the Ottoman Empire[3] and Persia, Great

---

[1] Art. 47 of the China and Japan Order in Council, 1881. The British government has changed its views as to the conditions under which it is proper that a court shall entertain a suit brought by a native plaintiff against a British defendant. By the Order in Council of 1881 he was required to produce 'the consent in writing of the competent authority of his own nation to his submitting to the jurisdiction of the court'; by the Order of 1886 it is merely laid down that 'if required by the court' he shall obtain a certificate to the effect that 'no objection is made by his own government to the foreigner submitting in the particular cause or matter to the jurisdiction of the court.'

[2] Africa Order in Council, 1889, Art. 4.

[3] Egypt is excepted so long as the International Tribunals, established by the Réglement of November 10, 1874, continue to exist. 'Ces

Britain enables its courts to adjudicate upon all suits brought by a native against a British subject, but exacts as a preliminary that the intending plaintiff shall produce and file in court the consent in writing of the competent authority on behalf of the Ottoman Porte or of the Persian government to his submission to the jurisdiction of the court, and give security if required to pay costs and expenses, and to abide by and perform such decision as shall be given by the court originally or on appeal[1]. It is at least open to argument whether the express consent of the territorial sovereign, if given, would not constitute a delegation of powers to the Consular Court and give it compulsory jurisdiction, so that if necessary it could take measures to carry out or enforce its decisions. Express consent on the part of the sovereign to the exercise of a foreign jurisdiction, is a much more positive act than a statement, that in the particular instance no objection will be made to justice being sought by a subject in a certain manner. The latter is perfectly consistent with the court being regarded as a mere arbitral tribunal; the state simply refrains from interesting itself, and leaves the individual to make his private arrangements. The former recognizes the courts as jurisdictional tribunals, and by

tribunaux connaîtront souls de toutes les contestations en matière civile et commerciale, entre indigènes et étrangers, et entre étrangers de nationalités différentes en dehors du statut personnel. Ils connaîtront aussi de toutes les actions réelles immobilières entre toutes personnes, même appartenant à la même nationalité.' Tit. I. Art. ix. (Hertslet, Com. Treaties, xiv. 306). British jurisdiction to the extent of the competence of the International Courts was suspended by Order in Council of February 5, 1876.

[1] The Russian treaty with Persia of 1828, of which Great Britain has the benefit, provides that suits between Russian subjects shall be adjudicated upon by Russian consuls, that suits between Russians and the subjects of third powers shall also be so decided with the consent of the parties, and that suits between Russian and Persian subjects shall be heard by the Hakim or Governor, in presence of the dragoman of the Mission or Consulate. Hertslet, Persian Treaties, p. 128.

doing so, either gives them the power of enforcing their jurisdiction, or if not, assumes the obligation of enforcing it for them [1].

Finally the Persian Coasts and Islands supply an instance in which unconditional British jurisdiction can be, and is, exercised upon the basis of usage and sufferance alone. No treaty exists, and the Persian Coasts and Islands Order, 1889, directs that 'Every suit in which a British subject is a defendant, and a Persian subject is a plaintiff, shall within the Persian Coasts and Islands be heard by a court established under' the Order, the court so established being assimilated in jurisdiction and organization ' to the courts of the Bombay Presidency.'

Persian Coasts and Islands.

§ 75. The courts are usually permitted by the various Orders in Council to adjudicate in civil suits or proceedings, when the plaintiff is a British subject, and the defendant is a native or subject of a third state; provided that the same consents are obtained that have been mentioned as necessary in the inverse case of the defendant being a British subject. In such instances, unless the Eastern or foreign European state be bound by its form of consent to give effect to the judgement rendered, the character of the proceedings is necessarily arbitral in relation to the foreigner; although as they are sanctioned by the appropriate Order in Council, any onerous results which may happen, can be enforced against the British plaintiff.

Civil suits in which the plaintiff is a British subject.

---

[1] Practically it would seem that in the Ottoman dominions the British courts have no opportunity of exercising the jurisdiction between British and Turkish subjects which is conferred on them by their government. The necessary consent must be always wanting, since the Turkish government regard the ordinary Turkish tribunals as alone competent in most cases in which British are concerned together with Turkish subjects, whether as plaintiffs or defendants. The only exception made is one in favour of commercial cases, technically so called; of these a special court called the Tidjaret takes cognizance, and in it a British subject has a right to the attendance of two assessors of his own nationality on the bench. Tarring, Brit. Cons. Jurisd. p. 92.

PART III.
CHAP. 2.

Often, however, practice does not conform altogether to the capacities of the British courts. Civil actions in Japan brought by British subjects against Japanese, 'are taken into the Japanese courts of first instance, which, when necessary, call in experts to assist them [1].' In China 'civil claims by British subjects against Chinese in Shanghai go before the mixed court, and in other ports are preferred to the local authorities through the British consulate [2].' In Madagascar and Muscat the cause is decided, as provided by treaty, by the native authorities, under the check of the presence of a British consular official.

Applicability of English law.

§ 76. If a sovereign delegates to a foreign state, of different civilization from his own, and of fundamentally different laws, exclusive or partial jurisdiction within his territories over the subjects of the latter, the delegation carries with it as of course power to administer the foreign law, to the extent of the jurisdiction delegated, unless express reservation upon the point be made. The jurisdiction which a European country obtains in an Eastern state is not an end in itself; it is a means to the application of its own law to the relations of its own subjects. It is in this position that Great Britain is placed in so far as she exercises jurisdiction by usage and sufferance, and it is in this that she is also placed by the language or the silence of the greater number of treaties [3]. That with the Congo State alone specifies that 'British law' shall be applied both in civil and criminal cases; the Chinese, Japanese, and Corean treaties provide that British subjects 'shall be tried and punished by the consul or other public functionary authorized thereto according to the laws of

As between Great Britain and Eastern states.

---

[1] Tarring, Brit. Cons. Jurisd. p. 94.
[2] Ib. p. 93.
[3] Those with Morocco, Madagascar, Muscat, Siam, China and Japan, Turkey, and with Persia through the most favoured nation clause.

Great Britain;' in no instance is any reserve made in favour of the local law, except in the Congo State, where it is stipulated that British subjects shall not be relieved by the exclusiveness of the jurisdiction 'from the obligation to observe the laws of the said Free State applicable to foreigners, but any infraction thereof by a British subject shall be justiciable only by a British Consular Court[1].'

In like manner English law, either in its purity or with such modifications as may have been introduced by the means provided to that end, becomes applicable whenever British courts exercise jurisdiction or quasi jurisdiction over subjects of an Eastern state or other foreigners in Oriental countries. Whether the individual either as plaintiff or defendant appears independently before the courts, or whether the express consent of his government is given to jurisdiction being assumed by them, he presents himself on the one hand, and cognizance is taken of his case on the other, upon the implied understanding that submission is made to the law which is well known to be habitually administered. The exclusive application of the substance of English law by the courts within the sphere of their ordinary jurisdiction carries with it of necessity its application to whatever matter is voluntarily brought before them.

The same exclusive application of English law which follows from the relation of Great Britain to other states,

With reference to British subjects.

---

[1] It is not easy to reconcile the above stipulation with the provision that jurisdiction shall be exercised in accordance with 'British law,' if the words 'laws applicable to foreigners' are taken in an extended sense. Probably they are only intended to refer to special laws necessitated by the peculiar conditions of the Congo State.

The tacit distinction made between the criminal and civil law in Corea is deprived of significance not merely by the largeness of the terms in which jurisdiction is granted in the first instance, but by the fact that civil justice is, and has been continuously, administered by the Consular Courts according to English law without protest on the part of the Corean authorities.

PART III.
CHAP. 2.

is provided for as between Great Britain and her subjects by the Foreign Jurisdiction Act of 1890, and by the various Orders in Council. The first section of the Act declares that 'it is and shall be lawful for Her Majesty the Queen to hold, exercise, and enjoy any jurisdiction which her Majesty now has or may at any time hereafter have within a foreign country in the same and as ample a manner as if Her Majesty had acquired that jurisdiction by the cession or conquest of territory;' it thus legalises and sanctions legislation by way of Order in Council, and legislation so effected is restricted only by the qualification that if it be repugnant to the provisions of any Act of Parliament extending to Her Majesty's subjects in a foreign country, or repugnant to any order or regulation made under the authority of any such Act of Parliament, it shall be void to the extent of its repugnancy. In general, however, the Orders in Council which, whether made before or after the passing of the Act, are sanctioned by it, effect little substantive legislation, and except in certain necessary matters, simply direct that the civil and criminal jurisdiction in any way vested in the British crown 'shall, subject to the other provisions of the Order, as far as circumstances admit, be exercised on the principles of and in conformity with the common law, the doctrines of equity, the statute law, and other law for the time being in force in and for England [1];' a further important direction being specifically added, that except as to offences made by the order or by a rule or regulation under it, no

---

[1] See the Ottoman, Persian, Chinese and Japanese, Siamese and Morocco Orders. The Africa Order slightly differs in directing that the jurisdiction shall be exercised in conformity with the 'substance' of the law, &c.

The Persian Coasts and Islands are by exception placed in immediate connexion with India; jurisdiction is to be exercised in conformity with Indian enactments, which are enumerated, and in so far as they may be inapplicable, in accordance with justice, equity, and good conscience.

act done by a British subject shall be deemed to be a punishable crime or offence which would not be so deemed by a court having criminal jurisdiction in England.

PART III.
CHAP. 2.

At the same time the qualifying words, 'as far as circumstances admit' which appear universally in the orders, allow of a certain wise elasticity in the application of law, and are paralleled in the Act by the provision that an Order in Council, made in pursuance of it 'shall not be, or be deemed to have been, void on the ground of repugnancy to the law of England unless it is repugnant to the provisions of some such Act of Parliament, order, or regulation,' as before mentioned [1].

It is to be observed, that the law which is to be administered is English law, and that consequently the British courts in Eastern countries can only take notice of Scottish, Colonial, or Indian laws for the purposes and to the extent that those laws are noticed in the English courts [2].

English law the law to be applied.

A further delegation of powers, beyond that which authorizes legislation and application of law by Order in Council, occurs in some instances under provisions in the

Delegation of legislative power to ministers.

---

[1] Sect. xii.

[2] In the treaty with the Congo State it is agreed that British jurisdiction shall be exercised 'in accordance with British law,' and by the treaties with China, Corea, and Japan the law of 'Great Britain' is to be administered. In all these cases, however, the Orders in Council speak of English law, and whatever may have been in the minds of the diplomatists who drafted the treaties, it is unquestionably English law which has to be applied. Possibly 'the law of Great Britain' may have been loosely used as an equivalent for English law ; and not improbably the term 'British law,' which lends itself to a larger interpretation, may be accounted for by the fact that the Congo Treaty was concluded after the decision in re 'Tootal's Trusts,' and before any other decision tending to throw doubt on it had been given. The Order in Council was subsequent to the case of Abd-ul-Messih v. Farra. Comp. § 81.

In view of the variation of laws in different parts of the United Kingdom, and of the inaccuracy with which different terms are sometimes applied, it may be well to point out that the phrase 'law of Great Britain,' excludes the law of Ireland.

PART III. Orders in Council which enable Her Majesty's ministers accredited to Eastern states, and when there are no ministers then the Consuls General, to make 'such regulations as seem fit for the peace, order, and good government of British subjects resident in or resorting to the countries to which they are accredited, and for the observance of the stipulations of treaties,' and of 'local laws and customs.' Sometimes regulations thus made are subject to disallowance by a Secretary of State, sometimes they only come into operation upon his approval. Where approval is needed regulations may be made and enforced in cases of urgency until confirmation or disapproval occurs. In no case can they affect persons with penalties in a consular district until they have been exhibited in the office of the consul for the district during a calendar month, or sometimes unless they have been expressly brought to the notice of a person accused of an offence against them [1].

In what the English law consists which Great Britain, as between herself and Eastern states, has a right to apply.

Reverting at this point to the relation between the British government and an Oriental state, it will be seen that the British law which is inevitably applied within the range of the delegated jurisdiction is not such part of the law governing England or the British dominions as may be found to be capable of application; it is that law, together with whatever special laws or general rules it may seem good to Great Britain to enact or lay down, provided that they do not exceed the powers obtained by treaty, or by usage and sufferance. The grant made by the Oriental state does not imply a simple permission to extend the operation of current law from British to native territory; it implies, in the interest be it said of the Eastern state no less than in that of Great Britain, that

---

[1] The countries in which regulations can be made are China, Japan, Siam, Zanzibar, Muscat, and Brunei; those in which the power is absent are the Ottoman dominions, Persia and Morocco.

permission is given to enact laws at the mere will of the British government which shall be intended to run, and shall run, within that territory. The reason for the permission is simple. The Oriental country does not allow the intrusion of a foreign law into its dominions because it is in its view a good law, but because its own social and legal conditions are incompatible with European ideas; practically it must let people of Western civilization be governed as between themselves in their own way. It is consequently indifferent to permanence or to change in the law which is administered, so long as the boundaries of treaty concession are not overstepped to the detriment of its sovereignty, and so long as the maintenance of good order, the one other point in which the state is interested, remains secure. In this latter respect the possession of legislative authority by the foreign government is of distinct advantage to the territorial state; the foreign country is not hide-bound in laws enacted with a view to other circumstances; it can accommodate itself, as need arises, to the duties which result from its peculiar situation[1].

[1] The terms in which power to make regulations is conferred by the Orders in Council are probably in all cases wide enough to cover every purpose for which regulations can be required. But it is by no means clear that adequate means exist, in the countries where diplomatic or consular officials are not invested with legislative functions, for securing obedience to local laws or administrative measures,—an obedience which it is the more incumbent upon a Western power to enforce upon its subjects that their immunities preclude the territorial state from exercising jurisdiction for itself. In Turkey the Order in Council contemplates that regulations shall be made under the authority of the crown, but no right to issue them is given to any specific person, so that the power must be supposed to reside in the Queen in Council alone until delegation is effected. The courts have jurisdiction in respect of offences against the Capitulations and Treaties irrespectively of the provisions of the Order in Council; but it might be a question whether all offences against the local law can be sufficiently dealt with under their general powers. A Press law is no doubt included amongst laws enacted for the peace and good government of the country, and in the preservation of that peace and good government Great Britain is bound to assist; but if the

PART III.
CHAP. 2.

Organization and powers of the courts. In the Ottoman Empire, China, Japan, and Corea.

§ 77. The courts by which the contentious and criminal jurisdiction of British consuls in the East is administered, are of two types.

In the Ottoman Empire, and in China and Japan, a complete local organization exists with a court of appeal within the respective countries; in other places the organization is more rudimentary, and an appeal lies to the nearest available High or Supreme Court within the British dominions.

At Constantinople is established a supreme court consisting of a judge, who is also consul general, and an assistant judge, who holds a commission of vice-consul. The former must be a barrister of not less than seven years standing at the date of his appointment, or must have held one of certain specified offices which afford a guarantee of legal training and knowledge; the latter must be a barrister of at least seven years standing. A like court is established in Egypt. Below these every commissioned consular officer, with such exceptions as the Secretary of State may think fit to make, and every uncommissioned consular officer, with such exceptions as the supreme court may make, holds a court for his consular district, which is called a provincial court.

An uncommissioned consular officer can take cognizance only of civil suits relating to property of less value than

---

Ottoman government were to call upon the consular officials to enforce an administrative order for the suppression of a newspaper, it is not quite easy to see in what manner a British court, obliged, when not empowered to act otherwise, to follow the analogies of English law, would be able to give effect to its international duty.

Probably if it were wished to aid the local authorities by enforcing any law or regulation made by them, the best form would be an Order in Council identical in terms with the local law or regulation, so that the latter would be absorbed into and become part of the local British law. In cases however where it might be wished to support administrative action caused by circumstances of the moment the want might be felt of powers which could be more rapidly applied.

£10, or instituted for the recovery of damages of a less amount than £10, and of criminal cases for which the punishment is a fine of not more than £5. A commissioned consular officer has jurisdiction in all civil suits which are not reserved to the supreme court or the court for Egypt, and in all criminal cases for which a punishment of not more than twelve months, with or without a fine of not more than £50, or the punishment of a fine alone of not more than £50, shall appear to him to be adequate; he has besides concurrent original jurisdiction with that of the courts in his district held before uncommissioned officers. The court for Egypt, besides having an original jurisdiction concurrent with that of the courts below it, is a court of Vice-Admiralty, and can try all crimes up to and inclusive of murder.

From each of these courts an appeal lies to the supreme court at Constantinople. It lies as of course from any order of a provincial court held before an uncommissioned consular officer in a civil suit; and from the court for Egypt and provincial courts held before a commissioned officer as of right in all suits involving a claim or other matter to the value of £50 and upwards, and by permission of the provincial court or of either superior court in matter of less value. An appeal also lies in criminal cases if the person convicted considers that the conviction is erroneous in law, unless the objection appears to be frivolous; and a case can be stated to the supreme court if the court below thinks fit to reserve for consideration any question of law arising on the trial. Besides its appellate jurisdiction the supreme court has an original jurisdiction in all matters concurrent with that of the court for Egypt and the provincial courts, an exclusive jurisdiction within the district of the consulate general of Constantinople, jurisdiction within the Ottoman dominions in questions of probate identical with that belonging to the Court of

Probate in England, jurisdiction in matrimonial causes, except as regards dissolution, nullity, or jactitation of marriage, and finally, so far as circumstances permit, all such jurisdiction relative to the custody and management of the persons and estates of persons of unsound mind as in England belongs to the Lord Chancellor.

Neither the court for Egypt nor the supreme court can carry out a punishment for crime of more than twenty years imprisonment, with or without hard labour, and with or without a fine of not more than £500, or the punishment of a fine alone of not more than £500. In cases of murder judgement of death can be recorded, with the sole object apparently of striking the imagination of the local populace; for though the case is reported to the Secretary of State for his direction respecting the punishment to be actually imposed he is unable to inflict the penalty of death, and can only vary the sentence by reducing the term of imprisonment or the amount of fine. The courts also have power, if it be expedient that a crime or offence shall be tried and punished within the British dominions, to send native Indian subjects for trial to Bombay, and other subjects to Malta. When this is done, there is nothing to prevent the penalty of death from being actually inflicted, but it is evident that in general it must be impossible to secure the presence of the necessary witnesses at places so distant as are Malta and Bombay from the scene of the crime.

From the supreme court at Constantinople a last appeal lies of right to the Privy Council, when in a civil suit a final order of the court has been made or given in respect of a sum of £500 or upwards, or has determined directly or indirectly any matter to the value of £500 or upwards; in minor cases the supreme court may give leave to appeal, but there is no appeal as of right [1].

---

[1] Ottoman Order in Council, 1873; and Ottoman Order in Council, 1882.

A like organization is provided for China, Japan, and Corea[1].

Persia offers the most developed specimen of the second type. The system of courts is less elaborate, the forms are looser, the consul general is not required to be a barrister. But in their broad lines the organization and the powers which the courts possess are similar to those of the Turkish courts. Provincial courts of first instance are held by such consular officers and in such districts as the Secretary of State may from time to time direct. Above these the consul general has appellate and concurrent jurisdiction of first instance, and an exclusive jurisdiction extending over the same range as that of the supreme court and the court for Egypt in the Ottoman Empire. There is also an appeal in civil cases from him to the Privy Council. In criminal cases the consul general is unable to imprison for more than five years, with or without hard labour, and with or without a fine of not more than £500; but he can record sentence of death in the same manner as the courts in Turkey; and his inadequate power of actual punishment is corrected by his being able to send native Indian subjects for trial to Bombay, other British subjects to Malta, and persons who are natives of, and domiciled in Cyprus, to that island[2].

In other Eastern countries the organization of powers is so far similar to those in Persia that it need only be mentioned, that in Morocco an appeal lies from the Consular Courts to the chargé d'affaires upon a conviction for breach of treaties or of the rules and regulations made for the peace order and good government of British subjects in the territory, and to the supreme court of Gibraltar in civil cases; that in Muscat and Madagascar there is an

---

[1] China and Japan Orders in Council, 1865 and 1878; and China, Japan, and Corea Order, 1884.
[2] Persia Order in Council, 1889.

PART III.
CHAP. 2.

appeal in civil cases, when the matter at issue is of a certain amount or value, to the high court of Bombay and the supreme court of the Mauritius respectively; and that in Siam there is an appeal to the supreme court of the Straits Settlements[1].

In all the Orders in Council more or less provision is made for the compulsory or facultative employment of juries or assessors in aid of the consul or consular judge. The occasions, and the character of the causes and cases, in which they may or must be used vary in different places, but the differences of this kind, which mark the various orders, are purely of local interest and importance.

It is remarkable that the Consular Courts of the further East, and those of the less civilized countries, have larger powers in criminal cases than those of Turkey and Persia. A death sentence can not only be recorded; it can be carried out. Certain precautions are however taken to prevent inconsiderate execution. In China, Japan, and Corea, for example, no capital sentence can take effect without the direction of the Minister Resident, who has power to commute; the Governor of the Straits Settlements in Council has like powers with respect to Siam; and other places are either affected with equivalent regulations, or provision is made for the trial of persons accused of murder before the court to which an appeal is taken in civil disputes.

Extent to which the divergency

§ 78. Enough has been said incidentally in the foregoing section to render it plain that, albeit the civil and criminal

[1] Morocco Order in Council, 1889; Muscat Order, 1867; Africa Order, 1889; and Siam Order, 1889. It will of course be remembered that the coercive powers of the courts which are necessary to the due exercise of jurisdiction are limited in their application to British subjects. No means exist of compelling the attendance of native or foreign witnesses, except through the aid, prompted only by courtesy, of the territorial authorities, or of the consuls of other states. Nor is there any power of punishing such witnesses, should they be guilty of perjury or contempt of court.

jurisdiction entrusted to consuls is to be exercised, so far as circumstances admit, in conformity with the substance of the law in force in England, and according to the procedure and practice there observed before courts of justice, the necessary divergencies which must take place in the course of application, the variations in the organization of the courts, and the variation in the penalties, constitute very real and very considerable differences. Bare differences however which lead to no doubts of construction or difficulties in practice are for the greater part hardly worth consideration. Some display themselves plainly enough upon the surface of the Orders in Council; others are intangible, and show themselves only in the unrecorded proceedings of the courts. Those points therefore will alone be touched upon which are either of considerable importance in themselves, or which open up disputable questions.

between the law administered in Eastern countries and that administered in England calls for remark.

§ 79. There are a certain number of matters affecting the relations of Great Britain with Oriental states which are either not provided for by English law, or are not dealt with adequately to the occasions which may arise in the East. These are covered in a general way by the power frequently given to ministers and consuls, according to the degrees of authority assigned to them, to make local regulations subject to the approval of the Secretary of State, which shall be calculated to secure the observance of treaties or of native laws and customs, and the peace order and good government of British subjects in reference to matters not legislated for by Order in Council. Some are specifically provided for by the Orders in Council themselves. In the Ottoman dominions, Persia, Morocco, Siam, China, Japan, and Corea, it is made an offence punishable by fine, or by fine and imprisonment for maximum terms of from six months to ten years, to insult or bring into contempt the local religion or its ceremonies, or any place of worship,

Special regulations providing for observance of treaties and maintenance of good order, &c.

tomb or sanctuary. In China, Japan, Corea, Siam, and Madagascar, a British subject taking part in any operation of war, or abetting an insurrection, against the territorial sovereign, while he is at peace with Great Britain, or taking service under him without license from the crown against enemies or insurgents, commits a misdemeanour or offence punishable according to the country with one or two years imprisonment and a fine, or alternatively with fine or imprisonment alone. Smuggling is made an offence by the Orders for Morocco, Madagascar, and Muscat, but not elsewhere.

<small>Powers of deportation,</small>

§ 80. Large powers of deporting British subjects from the territory of Oriental states to British possessions are given to the Consular Courts. They may be exercised either by way of an administrative measure over persons whose presence in the country is undesirable, or as part of the criminal jurisdiction, when it is wished that the trial of an accused person shall take place elsewhere, or that a convicted person shall undergo punishment within the British dominions. In the Ottoman dominions and in Persia, Morocco, Madagascar, China, Japan, and Corea administrative deportation may be ordered, under the respective Orders in Council, on its being shown upon oath that there is reasonable ground to apprehend a breach of the public peace by a British subject, or that his acts or conduct are likely to produce such a breach, or after conviction of any crime or offence before the court, or in Turkey before a court in the sentence of which a British consular officer concurs; subject in both cases to the proviso that the offender shall be alternatively permitted to give security to the satisfaction of the court for his future good behaviour. In Muscat and Siam deportation may be ordered after a second conviction of any kind unless security for good behaviour be given, and after a first conviction, over and above the punishment for the offence, when the crime is of a character, such as arson,

<small>as an administrative measure.</small>

housebreaking, and stabbing, which is particularly inimical to the external good order of the community. In Madagascar the court before which a person has been convicted of levying war, or taking part in insurrection, against the Malagasy sovereign, may order him to be deported in addition to the punishment for his offence. As a check upon arbitrary conduct all cases of administrative deportation must be reported to a superior authority, in some cases to the Secretary of State, in others to the court to which appeals are carried from the particular country. Persons under sentence of deportation can only be sent, except with their own consent, to portions of the British dominions which are appropriate to them, and which are specified in the Orders for natives of Great Britain, India, Malta, &c.

When a person is charged with an offence cognizable by a British court in an Eastern country, and it is expedient that he shall be tried elsewhere, the competent authority may send him for trial to any British possession for the time being appointed by Order in Council[1]. The places so appointed are: Bombay for Muscat; Bombay or Malta for the Ottoman dominions; Bombay, Malta, or Cyprus for Persia; Hong Kong for China, Japan, and Corea; the Mauritius for Madagascar; Gibraltar for Morocco; and one of the British African possessions for the Congo Free State. It is to be observed that the Foreign Jurisdiction Act prescribes that 'the court of the British possession shall admit and give effect to the law by which the alleged offender would have been tried by the British court in the foreign country in which his offence is alleged to have been committed, so far as that law relates to the criminality of the act alleged to have been committed, or the nature or degree of the offence, or the punishment thereof, if the law differs in these respects from the law

With a view to trial of an accused person in a British possession.

[1] Foreign Jurisd. Act, 1890, sect. 6.

PART III. in force in that British possession.' Thus Orders in
CHAP. 2. Council and Regulations made under their authority are
in effect extended to British territory for the purposes of
the trial and punishment of persons accused of having
committed offences within the country to which the Order
or Regulations apply.

For the Finally, while the British courts have the powers of
purpose of imprisonment within Oriental countries which are the
punish-
ment in necessary complement of their powers of criminal juris-
British
territory. diction, they are also enabled to deport convicted criminals
for the purpose of receiving their punishment within
British territory; the places to which prisoners may be
thus sent are specified in the various Orders. If a native
or foreigner, accused of a crime or other offence, prefers the
justice of the British courts in those places where they can
try an offender by consent, to falling into the hands of the
authorities of his own country, he as a matter of course
accepts the jurisdiction with all its consequences, and can
be sent for punishment to a British possession.

Deporta- Doubt has been expressed [1] whether deportation either
tion in
relation with a view to trial or punishment is permissible as
to the
treaties. between Great Britain and the Oriental state if, as is
almost universally the case, no mention of a right to
deport is contained in the treaty. It is argued, more from
the point of view of English law than of international
agreement, that a treaty delegating jurisdiction can only
be understood to refer to territory and places within which
delegation can be made, that is to say within the territory
and waters of the delegating power, and that consequently
both trial and punishment should take place within the
state where the offence has been committed. Where the
Oriental state has not wholly abandoned its jurisdiction,
and retains, as in Corea, the right to put a check upon
the proceedings of the British court, it is evident that

[1] Piggott, Exterritoriality, p. 101.

deportation before trial would not be consistent with the obligations of the treaty; and as in the case of Corea the application of the China Order, which permits deportation, is expressly subordinated to the provisions of the treaty, it must be presumed that no attempt would there be made to carry out a power in the Order the use of which is internationally prohibited. Where also it is simply declared that 'the British consul' shall punish offenders according to English law, a practice of deportation before trial must rest upon a usage and sufferance which, sometimes, as in Turkey for example, is unquestionably adequate. But when there are words conveying unqualified jurisdiction to duly appointed British officers, or words of similar import, it is not easy to see in what way deportation, whether before trial, or after conviction, needs other support than the treaties. No doubt, as a general rule, treaties derogating from sovereignty must be construed strictly, with a presumption against the grantee; but the rule must not be applied pedantically. The interests of the grantor, and the consequent object that he may have had in making a particular concession, are weighty elements of interpretation; and it is only reasonable to give value to the fact that the Eastern state has an evident interest in getting rid from its territory of proved or suspected foreign criminals. The wide words may be assumed to have been employed with intention to convey wide powers. So far indeed as deportation for purposes of punishment is concerned, the gloss, which this natural assumption gives to the language of the treaties, is hardly wanted. Punitive jurisdiction is everywhere abandoned entirely to the foreign authorities; in no treaty is there a trace of care for the accused person from the moment he has been shown to be guilty. If the kind and amount of punishment inflicted is a matter of indifference to the territorial state, it is hard to read into the treaties an intention to dictate the place where the punishment shall be undergone. Whether then sufficient warrant exists for the use of deportation, either administratively or for other reasons, is purely a question of municipal law for the foreign state to settle between itself and its subjects; and in the case of Great Britain ample powers are provided by Act of Parliament and Orders in Council [1].

Exclusiveness of the right of deportation for trial or punishment.

Deportation for trial or with a view to punishment is in the nature of things a right which belongs exclusively to the foreign state. It is impossible that the territorial government shall concurrently own it. The accused person or the criminal must be kept in custody, and power of custody on the part of the territorial state ceases the moment that its agents issue from its frontier on land, or that its ships put the prisoner on the shore of another country. It has no place where a person can be tried or punished after deportation; a government is needed which possesses territory elsewhere.

Administrative deportation.

Administrative deportation is of a different character. It is an end in itself. It is sufficient that the person subjected to it shall be placed outside the territory. There is no question of custody, except in places to which the local jurisdiction extends. There is therefore no material reason why the state should not possess a right of expulsion concurrently with the right of deportation conceded to a Western nation. Has it this right; or is the right of denying residence in an Oriental country to a European the exclusive property of the state to which he belongs? The question is best answered by recurring to the object for which any jurisdiction at all has been granted to the states of European civilization. No concession of sovereignty was intended; simply, a *modus vivendi* was arranged between peoples of unlike laws and moral codes; in working out the *modus vivendi* a power of deportation

[1] Foreign Jurisd. Act, 1890, sects. vi, vii, viii, ix, xii.

was found to be convenient; and in the Ottoman Empire, which has furnished the type upon which the practices more lately formed have been traced, administrative deportation had undoubtedly established itself more than a century ago.

But administrative deportation may be of two kinds. It may be directed to preserve good order, in the ordinary police meaning of the term; or it may be used in the political interests of the government employing it. Deportation of the former sort follows naturally upon criminal jurisdiction; under the conditions which prevail in Oriental countries it may almost be said to be inevitably complementary; and if the jurisdiction is exclusive, the right of deportation may reasonably be taken to be exclusive also. It forestalls disorder, and anticipates punishable crime. The right of deportation for political or quasi political reasons touches sovereignty more nearly, and there can never be certainty that it will always be used with a single eye to the good of the territorial sovereign, and in accordance with his will. It would be unreasonable that he should be deprived of a self-defensive weapon which in some circumstances may be of the highest value, and which he may need against the very state which also possesses it. Were the foreign state to hold it to the exclusion of the territorial authorities, the latter might have to stand powerless in the face of intrigues directed against their existence under the sanction of the foreign government itself. It is impossible that such a state of things can have been contemplated on both sides; and it cannot therefore be held that Eastern states have in this respect abdicated their sovereign rights. The European state has unlimited power of deportation over its own subjects; the Oriental state retains concurrent power of expulsion for due cause. It may, however, be added that in the Ottoman Empire it would be in the spirit of the

PART III. Capitulations, and that in other Eastern states it would be
CHAP. 2. in harmony with the relations set up by the treaties and
usages, that before expulsion is effected the reasons for the
measure, and proof of the facts in the case, should be
communicated to the diplomatic agent of the power, whose
subject is accused of ill conduct, so that inquiry may be
made and the circumstances relied upon to justify expulsion
be if possible disproved [1].

Domicil in Oriental countries.
§ 81. The first and by far the most important subject which strikes the eye on looking at the civil jurisdiction exercised by Great Britain in the East, is the law of domicil. It is also that in which there is most of complexity and doubt. Can a British subject acquire a domicil in an Eastern state? Can he have a local domicil out of England in which he is nevertheless governed by the law of England? Or must he retain that of the part of the

---

[1] There can be no doubt that in Turkey deportation for political reasons was never contemplated when the Capitulations, and at least the earlier treaties, were framed; but no objection can be taken to the terms of an Edict, the equivalent of an Order in Council, by which the French government in 1778 directed that 'dans tous les cas qui intéressent la politique ou la sûreté de commerce de nos sujets dans les pays étrangers, pourront nos consuls faire arrêter et renvoyer en France par le premier navire de la nation tout Français qui, par sa mauvaise conduite ou ses intrigues, pourrait être nuisible au bien général.' The edict was obviously directed solely against conduct which might create difficulties between France and Turkey, and it in no way displaces the sovereign power of the Ottoman Empire. No protest seems ever to have been made by the Porte, and such rights as can be founded upon the edict, when read in its true intent, have become established by prescription, and, like all other rights obtained by a Western nation, are shared by Great Britain. France, *more suo*, has converted a tacit permission into an exclusive and over-ruling right; and when a French journalist was expelled from Bulgaria for political intrigue and propagation of noxious falsehoods in the journals with which he was connected, after several applications for his deportation had been vainly made to the French consul, the French ambassador at Constantinople was instructed to complain that the Bulgarian authorities had acted otherwise than through the intervention of the consul. There is a sophistical, but interesting article on 'Les Capitulations et l'incident Franco-Bulgare du 1891,' by M. Merignhac in the Rev. de Droit Int. xxiv. 147.

British Empire where he was domiciled before settling in the East?

It is hardly necessary to clear the ground by reminding the reader that a British subject, on going to an Oriental country, carries his domicil with him, be it English, or Scottish, or Colonial. The question only is, can this domicil be changed?

It has never been decided either expressly or by implication that domicil cannot be acquired in an Eastern state. Nevertheless a certain vague atmosphere of doubt seems to hang about the subject, which is scarcely warranted by the language used by judges who have had occasion to allude to it. Dr. Lushington, in a well-known case[1], said with much truth that 'every presumption is against the intention of British Christian subjects voluntarily becoming domiciled in the dominions of the Porte,' and in another part of his judgment he developed the idea latent in this sentence by arguing that if the treaties between Great Britain and the Porte 'did not apply to domicil, as residence would often become fused into domicil, British merchants, and in case of their deaths, their families, would find themselves suddenly, and contrary to their intention, and to the presumption of intention, subject to a code of laws wholly contrary to their religious persuasions, their feelings, customs, and contemplation in making arrangements for the welfare of themselves and families.' The case, however, was decided purely upon the effect of the treaties, and Dr. Lushington, while stating his desire 'not to be supposed to have given an opinion upon any questions not necessary to be decided in this case,' and while therefore giving 'no opinion whether a British subject can or cannot acquire a Turkish domicil,' incidentally remarked that 'as to British subjects, originally Mussulmans, as in the East Indies, or becoming Mussulmans, the same reasoning does

[1] Maltass v. Maltass, i Robertson, Ecc. Rep. 70.

not apply to them as Lord Stowell has said does apply in cases of a total and entire difference of religion, customs, and habits[1].' Taking the foregoing language as a whole it appears to yield a very reasonable doctrine. There is nothing in the nature of an Eastern state which renders it impossible that a British subject shall wish to take up his permanent abode there, and identifying himself with its religious and social institutions, abandon all intention of ultimate return to his British domicil. Some Englishmen have become Mohammedans. If such a person were to settle in an Eastern state; or if even without making formal profession of Mohammedanism he were to contract polygamous marriages and follow the local customs, satisfying in other respects the conditions needed for the acquisition of domicil, there seems to be no good reason why effect should not be given to his evident intention. The obstacle to imputing an Eastern domicil is the difficulty of supposing that a person of European civilization can intend to place himself under Mohammedan or other Eastern personal laws. In ordinary circumstances the difficulty amounts to an impossibility; as long, therefore, as a person either remains a Christian or lives the usual life of Europeans in an Oriental state, he inevitably keeps

---

[1] The allusion is to the judgement of Lord Stowell in 'The Indian Chief' (iii Rob. Adm. 29). 'In the East,' he said, 'from the oldest times an immiscible character has been kept up; foreigners are not admitted into the general body and mass of the society of the nation; they continue strangers and foreigners as all their fathers were—Doris amara suam non intermiscuit undam; not acquiring any national character under the general sovereignty of the country, and not trading under any recognized authority of their own original country, they have been held to derive their present character from that of the association or factory under whose protection they live and carry on their trade.' Lord Stowell was thinking of the indisposition of Eastern nations to admit Europeans to social communion with themselves, and of the factory system which was its consequence. The difficulties in the way of domicil in the East are now inverted; but the principle of presumptive immiscib'lity remains the same.

his British domicil; no acts of a common sort, however positive they may appear to be, can be strong enough to destroy the presumption against an intention which is incompatible with the whole tenour of the person's conduct. Dr. Lushington, it will have been observed, remarked that the reasoning which excludes, or almost excludes, the possibility that a British subject, while remaining Christian, can acquire an Oriental domicil, does not apply to British subjects whose religion and social customs are identical with, or resemble in essentials, those of an independent Oriental state. There seems at any rate to be no reason why a Sunní Mohammedan of India should not acquire a domicil in Turkey, or a Shiite with equal facility become domiciled in Persia.

The answer to the further question whether a British subject can acquire a local domicil in which he is governed by the law of England, or whether he must retain the British domicil possessed by him before he arrived in the Oriental country which he inhabits, is supplied by the cases of Tootal's Trusts and Abd-ul-Messih v. Farra[1]. In the former, the point at issue was whether a person of the name of Tootal, who died at Shanghai, retained his English domicil of origin, or whether long residence in China in an organized community of British subjects, governed by English law, and exempt from Chinese jurisdiction, when that residence was coupled with expressed intention of never returning to England, had given him a fresh domicil, which might be described as Anglo-Chinese. Mr. Justice Chitty held, in conformity with the usual definitions, that 'residence in a territory is an essential part of the legal idea of domicil,' he also held that there is 'no authority in English law that an individual can become domiciled as a member of a community which is not the community possessing the supreme or sovereign territorial power;'

[1] L. R. Chan. Div. xxiii. 532; and App. Cases, xiii. 431.

PART III.
CHAP. 2.

that the sovereignty in the soil of Shanghai remains vested in the Emperor of China; and that consequently there was a want of the tie between the territory and the community which is needed as a foundation for domicil[1]. Mr. Tootal was relegated to his English domicil of origin. In Abd-ul Messih *v.* Farra the question was whether a person of Turkish origin, under British protection, who had taken up his permanent abode in Cairo, and died there, had acquired an Anglo-Egyptian domicil. The two cases have little, that is apparent, in common; it is not easy to see that 'the domicil in Turkey of a Chaldean Catholic Ottoman subject had any analogy either to an Anglo-Turkish or an Anglo-Indian domicil, by reason of his having British protection[2].' But the judicial committee of the Privy Council expressed their entire concurrence in the reasoning by which Mr. Justice Chitty supported his decision in the case of Tootal's Trusts, and must therefore be understood to hold that an Anglo-Oriental domicil is impossible[3]. Thus the present law is that British subjects in Eastern countries in all cases retain their domicil in that portion of the British Empire where they were domiciled previously to taking up their abode in the Oriental state.

Advisability of creating an Anglo-Oriental domicil.

It is perhaps to be regretted that a change in the law is not made which a short Order in Council could easily effect. Anglo-Oriental domicil has its reasonable, it may almost be said, its natural place. Conflicts between the

[1] The decision was partly based on the impression that Dr. Lushington held Mr. Maltass to have been domiciled in England. In spite of some language to that effect, the distinct statement made by Dr. Lushington that he did not intend to decide the question of domicil, and the general run of the judgement, are fatal to this view. Comp. Westlake, Private International Law, 3rd ed. p. 294.

[2] Westlake, p. 293. On the whole subject, see ib. 289-99.

[3] It may perhaps be as well to mention expressly that the judicial committee of the Privy Council did not, by the above decision, hold that a person of English domicil of origin is incapable in any circumstances of acquiring a purely Oriental domicil of choice.

differing laws of England, of Scotland, of the various self-governing colonies, are inevitable within British jurisdiction in the East; but it is unnecessary to multiply the points of collision. So long as persons have not identified themselves with the life of a new community, they must each keep his own law; but as soon as they have shown their wish and intention to cut themselves adrift from the association of birth, they prove their indifference to the personal law attendant on their domicil of origin; there is, therefore, no reason why simplicity and unity of law should not be gained for British subjects by attributing community in the laws of England to all of European blood. There is also every reason for avoiding very grave difficulties of another kind, which are opened through invariable preservation of the domicil of origin. English families, even in the present day, often remain through more than one generation in Oriental countries as their permanent place of abode; formerly the history of persons whose domicil might become a matter of importance was generally known sufficiently well; many are now of obscure antecedents and of an origin uncertain among the numerous places from which British subjects can derive. As no domicil can be acquired in an Anglo-Oriental community, it becomes every year more probable that cases will occur in which the determination of the domicil of a father, perhaps of a grandfather, may become necessary, and in which it may be equally impracticable to impute an English domicil or to attribute any other with fair probability. It would be a great advantage that in such cases there should be a fixed rule which should correspond with the obvious facts, and that the courts, instead of searching with infinite trouble and expense for an ancestral domicil, should be enabled to find that a domicil had been acquired in the Eastern country which carried with it the application of English law;—that, in other words, residence in China under English law, with the *animus manendi*, should imply domicil in China under the condition of the applicability of the special law of the English community established there, as that law is defined by Order in Council. Theoretically the conception of such a domicil is unobjectionable if once the mind is cleared of the notion, at present dominant, that domicil is the creature of place and intention alone. In Europe it is so, because residence in a place implies subjection to the common territorial law, and to no other; in the East it is not necessarily so, because residence there implies subjection to the law of one or other of several different communities the personal laws of which receive equal recognition from the territorial sovereign power. Association with place is necessary to domicil; but it is not always the sole determinant factor. In any case, even if the conception of domicil here suggested be anomalous, the convenience of giving effect to it is large enough to excuse a certain sacrifice of logical principle.

Bankruptcy.

§ 82. The Orders in Council, after giving general powers to the Consular Courts in civil matters, and declaring that they shall be courts of law and equity, by language which, though somewhat varied, is always identical in effect, go on to confer certain special powers of which the first is jurisdiction in bankruptcy. It is provided that the supreme or appellate and every other court shall, as far as circumstances admit, with respect to British subjects and to their debtors and creditors, being either British subjects or foreigners submitting to the jurisdiction of the court, have all such jurisdiction as belongs to Bankruptcy and County Courts in England.

The extremely mixed national character of the foreign population in most Oriental countries, and the number of different laws which are consequently administered in most Eastern mercantile communities, probably introduce an unusual amount of complication into bankruptcy proceedings. There must generally be assets within more than one foreign jurisdiction. The effect of such circumstances, however, and all questions that spring from the differences between English and foreign bankruptcy laws may be dismissed from consideration here. No practical difficulties, to which they may give rise, are caused by the fact of bankruptcy jurisdiction being exercised by Great Britain under the special local conditions, or by any peculiarity in the jurisdiction itself. Foreign debtors and creditors are in the same position with regard to proceedings in the Consular Courts as foreign debtors and creditors in Europe are with reference to proceedings in a Bankruptcy Court in England. It is only to be noticed that foreign creditors, and debtors if they choose to submit themselves to the jurisdiction, are subjected to the same requirements in respect of consents, security, and so forth, as are exacted in ordinary suits.

The only real difficulty which presents itself is consequent upon the state of the law of domicil. An Anglo-Oriental domicil being impossible, a bankruptcy petition in an Eastern state can only be presented against a debtor if he shall have ordinarily resided or had a dwelling-house or place of business in the country within a year before the presentation of the petition. Were such a domicil possible, a petition could be presented against him, in the event of his being domiciled there, irrespectively of residence [1]. The instances may not be very numerous in which a debtor would be found to have a domicil in the East, without having also such business connexion with the seat of jurisdiction as to enable a petition to be presented on other grounds. But the circumstance may occur. The difficulty can only be touched and left; its solution is dependent on the external fact of the opinion

[1] Bankruptcy Act, 1883, 46 and 47 Vict. c. 52, sect. 6.

PART III. which may ultimately prevail, as to the advisability or
CHAP. 2. inadvisability of allowing an Anglo-Oriental domicil to
be obtained.

Matrimonial causes.

§ 83. The Orders in Council which govern the more numerous and important of the British communities in Eastern states confer upon the superior courts a limited jurisdiction in matrimonial causes. The jurisdiction, so far as it goes, is not exclusive; and the Divorce Court in England has concurrent powers in all cases of which the conditions of domicil or residence prescribed by English law allow it to take cognizance.

The Supreme Court of Constantinople has exclusively, 'as far as circumstances admit, for and within the Ottoman dominions, with respect to resident subjects and protected persons, all such jurisdiction, except the jurisdiction relative to dissolution or nullity or jactitation of marriage, as for the time being belongs to the court for divorce and matrimonial causes in England.' The Supreme Court of Shanghai has like jurisdiction for China, Japan, and Corea over 'British subjects,' the term being only explained as meaning 'all subjects of Her Majesty, whether by birth or naturalization.' In Persia the consul general has the same jurisdiction with respect to 'resident British subjects,' among whom are subjects of the Indian protected states resident in the country. From Morocco all matrimonial causes in which British subjects and British protected persons, inclusive of natives of the protected states of India, are concerned go before the Supreme Court of Gibraltar, which exercises such, 'if any, jurisdiction' in respect of them as it has in Gibraltar[1].

It will be observed that in the Ottoman Empire and Persia jurisdiction is exercised only in respect of persons

[1] No matrimonial powers are given to the Consular Courts in the Congo State, Madagascar, Muscat, the Persian Coasts and Islands, and Siam.

who are resident; the Court at Shanghai can take cognizance of all causes between 'British subjects.' The Turkish and Persian Orders are thus founded on the assumption that no domicil within the Ottoman and Persian Empires is possible to a British subject, and where jurisdiction is dependent on domicil the parties are relegated to the English court or to whatever other court is competent in the matter. The China Order is more elastic; if domicil were possible in China and Japan, cases based upon it could be taken, as well as those which are based upon residence; so long as it is not possible, such cases must be dealt with elsewhere. The number which could ever be affected by the difference of powers is probably not very great. In Turkey and Persia grave inconvenience would apparently be felt only on the supposition that a person domiciled there marries, resides, and gives occasion for the exercise of jurisdiction, in a country where no power of giving relief exists.

The inclusion of native Indian subjects of the Empire, of protected persons in the Ottoman dominions, and of subjects of the Indian protected states in Persia and Morocco, amongst persons over whom matrimonial jurisdiction can be exercised, raises a question which at first sight may seem to be of some difficulty. Many of these persons are polygamous in fact, or potentially polygamous by their personal law. To what extent is the jurisdiction which is exercised over them to be in accordance with English law? English law only recognizes monogamous marriage; is this principle to be carried into the East and is cognizance only to be taken of matrimonial causes between the very small proportion of the above classes who are monogamous? Or is the proviso that English law is to be administered 'as far as circumstances admit' sufficiently large to allow of jurisdiction being exercised over causes arising out of marriages contracted under a polygamous law?

PART III.
CHAP. 2.

In choosing between two senses of words in an Order in Council, as in an Act of Parliament, that must be taken which will allow the words to have operative effect; and it can hardly be said that operative effect is given to language which covers many millions of people, when it is permitted only to touch an infinitesimal portion of them. A jurisdiction over Indian subjects of the Crown and Indian protected persons must be illusory which ignores alike the marriage laws of Mohammedans and Hindoos. It seems reasonable then to suppose that the personal law of the original domicil was intended so far as possible to accompany such persons into foreign countries where they live under the protection of Great Britain, and have recourse to the justice of her courts. In order that this shall be effected it is only necessary to apply the construction of the Order in Council, regulating the jurisdiction of the Consular Courts in Turkey, which was adopted by the judicial committee of the Privy Council in the case of Abd-ul-Messih v. Farra[1]. It was stated in the judgement in that case that 'according to section six' the Consular Courts 'are to administer the law for the time being in force "in and for England," an expression which simply denotes the law for the time being administered in the courts of England,' and includes the law which is administered in Indian appeal cases; in other words, with relation to the matter in hand, the law applicable in India to matrimonial causes between native Indian subjects of Great Britain, is applicable under the Orders in Council to the extent that jurisdiction is given by them.

Probate jurisdiction.

§ 84. The Consular Courts are courts of probate, and can grant probate of wills or administration with the will annexed, or can grant letters of administration, with respect to the property of British subjects, who are resident in Turkey and Persia, who are even momentarily in the

[1] App. Cases xiii. p. 442.

country in Muscat, and who in China, Japan, Siam, the Congo State, and Madagascar, have had their fixed places of abode in the country. The last expression introduces an element of uncertainty, and its meaning is not easy to seize. It must be supposed, since it is used instead of the obvious word residence, to be intended to signify something more permanent than that term is usually employed to indicate; it has, however, no definite legal force, and seems to leave the occasions upon which the courts can exercise their probate jurisdiction very largely within their own discretion. It is not evident in any interpretation of the expression why it is used to define the jurisdiction of the Court of Shanghai without being also applied to that of Constantinople. The latter place being much nearer to England than the former it would seem natural, if a difference in the extent of probate jurisdiction were to be made, that it should be the seat of narrower rather than of larger powers.

PART III.
CHAP. 2.

More important is it to remark that the Consular Court has no probate jurisdiction in cases where the deceased British subject dies outside the country where the court is established. The powers of the court seem in that case to be limited to taking possession of the personal property of the deceased, so that it may be kept until it can be dealt with according to law, or to granting, if necessary, a protective administration to an officer of the court.

§ 85. A few final words may be devoted to the powers of the Consular Courts in relation to British officials and to the government of the country in which the courts are established.

Jurisdiction of Consular Courts

Although all powers which they hold spring remotely from a delegation made by the sovereign of the territorial state, their authority is immediately derived from the British government, which has instituted them, not in the capacity of an agent, but independently, in

in respect to British officials;

virtue of rights acquired by treaty. They are British courts. They have therefore like jurisdiction in respect of diplomatic and consular agents as is possessed over persons in the service of the state by the courts in England, except in so far as their powers are limited in the Orders in Council either expressly or by implication. The jurisdiction is no doubt in practice not always available. In Turkey, Egypt, China, Japan, and Morocco, jurisdiction is possessed by the Court of Appeal concurrently with the Consular Courts both in civil and criminal matters [1]; and the High Court of Bombay has concurrent civil powers with the consul at Muscat. But with regard to Siam jurisdiction can only be exercised by the court at Singapore with the consent of the consul general at Bangkok; and in Persia and the countries covered by the Africa Order there is no provision of means by which the superior consular officer in a given state or region can be made either civilly or criminally amenable to the law. The powers of the court in the latter class of places are obviously illusory as against the superior consular official; they are equally futile in some instances for his protection. Where he is alone, where the civil jurisdiction of a district court is insufficient, or where it possesses no criminal jurisdiction, he may be without any available remedy against a wrong, and without any means of punishing a crime of which he was himself the object, since it would be impossible for him to act as judge in his own cause. The difficulty in either direction can only be got over where, as is the case in Madagascar, Great Britain is empowered to delegate authority to any 'officer duly appointed' as well as to the consul.

[1] It will be remembered that in Shanghai there is a Supreme Court; that the Consular Court at Alexandria has concurrent jurisdiction with the Provincial Consular Courts within its district; and that the Supreme Court of Constantinople has concurrent jurisdiction with it; finally, that the Supreme Court of Gibraltar is the Court of Appeal for Morocco.

For the same reason that the Consular Court is a British court the territorial sovereign, if he chooses to bring an action in it, submits himself, by doing so, as absolutely to the jurisdiction as any other litigant, and must take the consequences of his submission as fully as it has long been settled law that he must take them in England[1].

PART III. CHAP. 2.

in respect to a foreign sovereign suing in the court.

If a question arises between a Consular Court and the government of the country in which it is established as to whether a particular case falls within the jurisdiction of the former, it is for the court to decide in the first instance upon its own competence, and it is not until after appeal to the judicial committee of the Privy Council that the dispute can enter the diplomatic phase. Great Britain, in respect to her own courts, can only act upon the theory of their complete independence, except to the extent that it has been restricted by express legislation[2]. It is for them to declare the law which it is their duty to administer; if it be found that the law conflicts with treaties or with other international obligations, the state must make what satisfaction may be possible at the moment and must provide for the future by effecting the necessary alterations; but it cannot move until the law has been ascertained. It can neither supersede nor interfere with the action of its courts.

Questions of competence.

§ 86. The Foreign Marriage Act, 1892, applies to Oriental as well as to Western countries; diplomatic and consular agents therefore, if duly authorized to be marriage officers, have the same powers as like agents in the territory of European or American states, and exercise them in the same manner, and subject to the same conditions[3]; except that, owing to the diversity of marriage institutions, con-

Marriages in Oriental countries.

---

[1] A sovereign 'brings with him no privileges that can displace the practice as applying to other suitors.' The King of Spain *v.* Hullet and Widder, 1 Clark and Finnelly, H. of L. 333.

[2] Comp. § 71.

[3] See Part II. chap. iii.

PART III. siderations of comity are absent; and that the question
CHAP. 2. whether a particular marriage, valid by reason of its having been performed according to the local law, is valid also by English law need not be entered into, there not being in the vast majority of instances sufficient facilities, within the reasonable meaning of the Order in Council [1], for the solemnization of the marriage in accordance with the law of the country.

Generally marriages, contracted in Oriental countries, to which British subjects are parties, will be celebrated under the provisions of the Foreign Marriage Act; but it will be remembered that its enactments are permissive, and not directory to the exclusion of all other forms than those prescribed. It is necessary therefore to inquire whether there are any different forms of marriage which can be used under the sanction of English law, and whether there are any forms of marriage good under territorial laws which are capable of effecting marriages good according to English law.

Marriages *per verba de praesenti* before a person in episcopal orders.

§ 87. It has been seen that by the law of England as it stood antecedently to Lord Hardwicke's Act marriages were valid, if contracted *per verba de praesenti* before a clergyman in episcopal orders, and that the Act in question confined the changes which it introduced to the United Kingdom. It follows that British subjects still carry with them the ancient law into foreign places where British jurisdiction exists, and into heathen or Mohammedan countries where there is no local law which is applicable to the marriage of Europeans [2]. There can therefore be no doubt that marriages performed by a clergyman of the Church of England or of the United States, or by a priest of the Church of Rome [3], in places

---

[1] Foreign Marriages Order in Council, 1892.

[2] 26 Geo. II, c. 33 (1753); Lautour *v.* Teesdale, viii Taunt. 830 (1816).

[3] In the Lautour case the marriage was performed by a Portuguese Roman Catholic priest at Madras. There seems to be no reason for making

and countries of the above kinds, are perfectly good, and even if there be local forms, or forms recognized by the local law, which are available, the existence of the jurisdiction conceded by the local sovereign to Great Britain secures the validity of the contract. Marriages thus celebrated under the ancient law of England can be performed in any place, and without any obligation of residence or of notice. The jurisdiction possessed by the British crown is co-extensive with the territory of the sovereign authority from which it is derived, if concession be taken as its basis; and as between the Crown and its subjects, whether opportunities of marriage are afforded on the ground of derivative powers or of powers assumed because of the absence of a local law which can be applied, the enabling jurisdiction is in either case, not locally circumscribed, but general and personal. The absence of any need for residence or notice is consequent upon the fact that no requirement in these respects was made by the law which was formerly general, and which still regulates marriages of the sort under consideration.

While the law is clear, it has to be kept in mind that certain practical difficulties attach no less to those marriages in Eastern countries which are unquestionably valid, than to those of a validity more hard to establish, which may perhaps be contracted in some circumstances in European or American states. There may be great difficulty in proving the celebration of a marriage *per verba de praesenti*, before a person in episcopal orders, if the necessity for doing so should arise; and unless it could be shown that recourse to a consul had been impossible, and that con-

any distinction between the episcopal orders of different churches. There is indeed at least one case in which clergymen not in English episcopal orders have received appointments with a view to the marriage of British subjects. In the end of last century the Hudson's Bay Company, finding it difficult to procure a sufficient number of English chaplains for their territories, appointed persons in orders of the Swedish church.

sequently no choice offered itself as to the means by which the marriage should be performed, the conduct of the parties in entering upon wedlock through a side door would expose them, where proof was not of the clearest nature, to suspicions and inferences which might bring the regularity of their marital connexion into the utmost peril. The local consequences also may not be less inconvenient in Oriental than in European countries. In Turkey, for example, and no doubt in all other Mohammedan countries, a marriage good by the law of any religious community is good for all purposes in the territorial dominions. A marriage *per verba de praesenti* before a priest in episcopal orders is therefore one which Turkish courts, and Turkish administrative authorities, would be fully prepared to recognize, and in most cases do recognize [1]. But a British ambassador or consul has at present no authority to declare the law; he cannot give any assurance that a marriage of the sort is valid by the law of the Church of England. The Turkish courts therefore might not recognize it; and as they take cognizance of all cases in which real property is directly or indirectly involved, the consequence of non-recognition might be serious, notwithstanding its social unimportance. An Order in Council could clear away the difficulty in principle; but in practice, unless a certificate from a clergyman or other person in orders were admitted as evidence of the marriage for all purposes, there would still be difficulty arising from the want of formal proof. The Turkish courts would either demand a certificate of marriage from the consul, or would have to be permitted to go into the question of validity after their own fashion, and in effect to adjudicate upon

---

[1] It seems to have always been, and still to be, the general custom among Europeans in the Ottoman dominions to be married at their church, Catholic, Protestant, or Greek, as the case may be. See Salem (Advocate at Salonica), in Rev. de Droit Int. Privé, xvi. 28-9. There are now certain compulsory exceptions.

questions of English marriage law. Like embarrassments might be caused, especially in cases of mixed marriages, if the nationality of the children were at issue[1].

§ 88. Beyond marriages *per verba de praesenti* effected before a person in episcopal orders, there lies another class of contracts purporting to be marriages, which are made by a simple exchange of declarations in the presence of witnesses. Whether these are ever valid at all, and if so in what circumstances, and under what conditions, is a question of no small difficulty and delicacy. At the first blush the matter looks simple enough. In the very carefully weighed case of the Queen *v.* Millis[2] the House of Lords decided, in perfectly general language, that by the common law of England a marriage *per verba de praesenti* must be entered into before a person in orders, and that therefore a marriage of that kind, not so made in a place where the common law reigns, is invalid. The law is thus fixed for all cases which are necessarily governed by the decision; but there is still much uncertainty as to the extent of ground which it will be permitted to cover.

The case was one in which the validity of a marriage contracted before a Protestant dissenting minister in Ireland was at issue; it was a marriage in a country of European civilization, where other means of effecting marriage were provided. Notwithstanding therefore that the language of the decision in the House of Lords was without reserve or limitation, it may be argued that there is no such parity of circumstance between a marriage in Ireland and marriages in Eastern countries under the pressure of extreme difficulty or necessity, that it is needful or even justifiable to test both by the same principles, and to apply the common law in all its integrity to the latter.

---

[1] On the attitude taken up by the Ottoman government with respect to religious marriages of foreigners, see Salem, loc. cit.
[2] x Clark and Finnelly, 534.

PART III.
CHAP. 2.

This at any rate is the view which seems to have been taken by judges of great authority. Lord Cranworth in delivering judgement in the later case of Beamish v. Beamish[1] went out of his way to say, 'I wish to guard myself against its being supposed to be clear that the decision in the Queen v. Millis applies to the case of marriage of necessity entered into where the presence of a minister in holy orders may have been impossible. That question must be considered in this House as still open to be determined whenever it may arise'; and Mr. Justice Willes in giving to the House of Lords the opinions of himself and of Justices Byles and Hill upon the same case, expressed a doubt whether the Queen v. Millis could be 'ever rightly held to apply to British subjects in the colonies and foreign countries, where no priest could be procured[2].'

That a distinction will be made between marriages entered into in Oriental and barbarous countries and marriages of the sort contemplated by the decision in the Queen v. Millis, is rendered the more probable that the correctness of the law there laid down, even with regard to the marriages undoubtedly covered by it, is very far from being unimpeached. The House of Lords were equally divided in opinion; and if the judgement given can rest upon the great legal authority of Lord Lyndhurst, it failed to commend itself to Lord Campbell and Lord Brougham, who delivered judgements in favour of the legality of a simple contract before witnesses. The judges, who were consulted on the law, reported in favour of the view that prevailed, but it appears from observations which dropped from Lord Cranworth and Lord Wensleydale in the case of Beamish v. Beamish that they had wished to consider the point more maturely, and that it was only with great doubt that they adopted the conclusion which was reached; Lord Wensleydale confessed that with the

[1] ix Clark, House of Lords Cases, 274.   [2] Ib. 332.

Queen v. Millis before him at that moment as an undecided case he would concur in the opinion which Lord Campbell had supported[1].

If the decision in the Queen v. Millis represented the common law of England rightly, it is nevertheless certain that in the American Colonies and in India 'only such portions of the common law' can have been understood to be 'introduced as were suitable to the condition of the country[2].' In New York, Pennsylvania, South Carolina, Kentucky and Georgia 'the consent of the parties is all that is required;' and as this doctrine has always been supposed to be that 'of the common law, and also of the canon law, which governed marriages in England prior to the Marriage Act of 26 Geo. II,' it is unquestionably that of the common law, as understood to be applicable in America, upon which practice was modelled, and the courts decided, before the separation of the United States from Great Britain, in the states mentioned, and in others where the law is now altered[3]. In India it was the policy of the East India

---

[1] Dr. Lushington, whose authority was great in cases of marriage law, practically ignored the decision in the Queen v. Millis. In his judgement in Catterall v. Catterall (1 Robertson, 582) he says, 'In the Queen v. Millis nothing fell from any of the Law Lords in the House of Lords which in any way intimated that such a marriage,' viz. a marriage *per verba de praesenti* without the presence of a person in orders, 'would not be sufficient to enable this Court to proceed to a separation *a mensâ et thoro*. I am not disposed to carry the decision in that case one iota further than it went, . . . until I am controlled by a superior authority—for no further examination of the question will induce me to change my opinion—most unquestionably I shall hold in this and all similar cases that where there has been a fact of consent between two parties to become man and wife, such is a sufficient marriage to enable me to pronounce when necessary a decree of separation.' He seems to leave open the question of the right of the wife to dower, and of the legitimacy of the children.

[2] Sir Erskine Perry in Maclean v. Crystall. Supreme Court of Bombay, 1849, Perry, Oriental Cases, 75.

[3] Kent, Comment. on Amer. Law, Ed. 1873, *85, *87, *88. Hautz v. Sealy, vi Binney, 408; Jewell's lessee v. Jewell, i Howard (Supreme Court of the United States), 233; Patterson v. Gaines, vi Howard, 587.

Company to encourage marriages at their factories, and it appears that 'ship loads of young ladies' were sent out by the corporation in the end of the seventeenth century; it was not till the beginning of the eighteenth century that chaplains were provided, and then so sparingly that within the memory of persons living in 1849 there were only three chaplains assigned to the whole Bombay Presidency, and the native states in connexion with it. Great numbers of marriages must have been contracted by mere consent before witnesses both within and without the territories under British jurisdiction; indeed 'the practice which has existed so far back as any trace can be discovered' appears to have been 'to celebrate marriages in the absence of a clergyman in as solemn a manner as the nature of the case permitted. Any European who has been any time in the country is able to enumerate many of his friends amongst whom or amongst whose connexions such marriages have taken place.' In the case of a marriage performed at Surat by a missionary not in episcopal orders, there not being a Protestant clergyman nearer than Ahmedabad, about a hundred and forty miles distant, the marriage was held by the Supreme Court of Bombay to be good, although there was a Roman Catholic priest in the town. The court considered that so much only of the common law having been imported into India as was suitable to the condition of the country, the requirement of the presence of a minister in holy orders at the celebration of a marriage was not included in the portion introduced[1]. The Surat marriage was

[1] Maclean v. Crystall, loc. cit. In deciding the case of Catterall v. Catterall (loc. cit.), Dr. Lushington said : 'Were I to hold the presence of a priest in the orders of the Church of England to be necessary, I should be going the length of depriving thousands of couples married in the colonies and the East Indies (where till of late there were no chaplains) of the right to resort to this court for such redress as it can give in cases of cruelty and adultery.'

It is to be noted that in Catherwood v. Caslon (xiii Meeson and

found to be good, and the wife having committed adultery, a bill for its dissolution was brought into Parliament and passed. In discussing the bill the House of Lords was of course acting in its legislative and not in its judicial capacity; but it is inconceivable that the House would have passed an Act considered by the Law Lords to be in contravention of the law of England; the decision of the Supreme Court of Bombay, therefore, must be taken to have received an important, though informal, confirmation.

PART III. CHAP. 2.

It is not for a mere writer to anticipate the ultimate decision of the courts, and to formulate a judgement of his own. It is enough to say that though facilities for concluding marriages in a regular manner are commonly provided far more fully than in the earlier days of the American colonies, or than in India during a great part of the present century, there are places in no inconsiderable number where the requirement of a person in episcopal orders would be found to constitute a prohibition of marriage as absolute as would be an imperative legal obligation to have recourse to a consul.

§ 89. Subject to such qualifications as may be imported by the existence of local laws recognizing Christian marriages, it is generally impossible for a marriage, which shall be valid within the British dominions, to be contracted by British subjects in a polygamous country in accordance with the local law, except when the parties to it are themselves members of a polygamous religious community belonging to territories where such marriages

Lex loci marriages in polygamous countries.

Welsby, 261; 1844), it was decided that a marriage was invalid which had been performed at Beyrut in 1834, between two British subjects, by an American missionary not in episcopal orders. The judgement was no doubt inspired by that given in the Queen *v.* Millis; but as at that time consuls were not empowered to marry, and there was probably no person in orders within many hundreds of miles, the case would evidently fall within the exceptions to the Queen *v.* Millis, if exceptions there be, and the decision will either be overruled or confirmed according to the view which is ultimately adopted by the House of Lords.

are good by the local British Law. Between British subjects of European blood, as between subjects of every other country of European civilization, marriage and its effects are founded upon the assumption of monogamy; and the status which is created by it, the relations of married persons to each other, the consequences in respect of legitimacy and property, the whole social and legal incidents of marriage, are so different under monogamous and polygamous systems that it is impossible to work the two together. Polygamous marriage is wholly rejected by English law [1].

In monogamous Eastern countries.

§ 90. In a monogamous Oriental country, such as Japan, on the other hand, a marriage valid by the local law is valid also in the British dominions. The form of celebration is immaterial: so soon as an English Court is convinced that no second wife can be taken during the lifetime of the first, unless the latter be divorced, it recognizes that the essential element of a European marriage is present, and it gives effect to the relation [2].

Registration of marriages.

§ 91. It is probably superfluous to note that as the eighteenth section of the Foreign Marriage Act and the

[1] Comp. on the essential difference from the legal point of view of Christian and polygamous marriages, Lord Brougham in Warrender *v.* Warrender, ii Clark and Finnelly, 529 ; Lord Penzance in Hyde *v.* Hyde, Law Rep. i Prob. and Div., 130; and Sir J. Hannen in Brinkley *v.* the Attorney-General, Law Rep. xv Prob. and Div. 76 (1890).

[2] 'The principle,' said Sir J. Hannen, 'which has been laid down' by the Hyde and Bethell cases 'is that a marriage which is not that of one man and one woman to the exclusion of all others, though it may pass by the name of a marriage, is not the status which English law contemplates when dealing with the subject of marriage. . . . Though throughout the judgements that have been given on this subject, the phrase "Christian marriage," "marriage in Christendom," or some equivalent phrase, has been used, that has only been for convenience to express the idea. But the idea which was to be expressed was this, that the only marriage recognized in Christian countries and in Christendom is the marriage of the exclusive kind I have mentioned, and here it was proved that in Japan marriage is of that character.' Brinkley *v.* the Attorney-General, loc. cit.

eighth article of the Foreign Marriage Order in Council, 1892, extend to marriages contracted in Oriental states, it is the duty of the consular officer, subject to the reserve made in the latter article, to register marriages solemnized in accordance with the local law, in the manner prescribed for the registration of like contracts in European or American countries, provided the marriages are of such sort that they are, or may conceivably be, valid in the British dominions. Where the local law contemplates polygamous marriages only, or in any case in which a marriage has been so concluded as to leave open the right of taking further wives, it is considered not merely that no duty of registering the marriage arises, but that the consular officer ought to refuse to register it, even with an appended remark indicating the character of the union. He is called upon at most to secure the perpetuation of evidence that a ceremony has been gone through purporting to set up a good marriage according to the law of some country which holds fundamentals of law in common with England, and possibly having for its effect the conclusion of a marriage that may be recognized in the British dominions. It is wholly outside his functions to perpetuate evidence with regard to a ceremony which, whatever effect it may have, is destitute at least of the power of setting up that relation which is called marriage in Christendom.

CHAPTER III.

PROTECTORATES, SPHERES OF INFLUENCE, AND BARBAROUS COUNTRIES.

PART III.
CHAP. 3.

Essential characteristic of a protectorate.

§ 92. The term 'protectorate' is one of which the meaning is somewhat indefinite; or rather perhaps it may be said with more correctness to have different meanings in different circumstances and in the mouths of different persons. A protectorate of the kind which used to be exercised by a European power over a smaller civilized state is far from being identical with the relation which links an Eastern protected state or community with a European country; and a protectorate as understood by the German government signifies the assumption of much fuller control than has seemed to Great Britain to be legitimate. So different indeed are the meanings of the word, that they can in truth be only said to have one element in common. In all cases a state or community under the protection of a European state has parted with freedom of action in foreign affairs.

Difference between protectorates of

It was usual for the older writers on international law to describe protected states as retaining their independence[1]. Of insufficient power to guard it themselves,

---

[1] Vattel, for example, says: 'Un état faible, qui, pour sa sûreté se met sous la protection d'un plus puissant, et s'engage, en reconnaissance, à plusieurs devoirs équivalents à cette protection, sans toutefois se dépouiller de son gouvernement et de sa souveraineté, cet état, dis-je, ne cesse point pour cela de figurer parmi les souverains qui ne reconnaissent d'autre loi que le droit de gens.' Le Droit de Gens, Liv. I. cap. i. § 6; and comp. cap. xvi. § 192.

they placed their foreign relations under the tutelage of a country strong enough to provide for their security; but they retained, or at least were in law supposed to retain, their complete rights of internal sovereignty.

PART III. CHAP. 3. the European and the Eastern types.

Typical examples half a century ago were Monaco and the Ionian Islands. However doubtful may be the propriety of ascribing independence in any serious sense to these states, they had at least a core of independent administration, the limits of which coincided with the range of those matters with which, apart from politics, other countries or their subjects were concerned. They had an internal government, a police, laws, and courts, of the ordinary European type. Whether the justice provided were good or bad, it was offered in such form and under such external guarantees that the country responsible to foreign states could not reasonably be called upon to displace any of the internal powers of the local government; there was no more probable risk of scandalous deficiency in public order or of gross injury to foreign subjects than exists in many independent states of the European type of civilization. In these respects there is a wide, and as will presently be seen a cardinal, distinction between protectorates of the kind which was formerly familiar, and those which have sprung into existence of late years in the East and in Africa. For practical purposes in fact there is no analogy between the two sorts in the essential particular of the authority to which a foreign state must in reason look for due provision of administrative and judicial safeguards of the interests of its subjects.

§ 93. It is not likely that the ancient doctrine, or the precedents supplied by protectorates in Europe, weighed much with English statesmen and lawyers when they found it necessary to define the relation of Great Britain towards Eastern states[1] and barbarous communities over

Views formerly entertained by Great Britain as to the relation

---

[1] Among Eastern protected states I do not include the native states

PART III.
CHAP. 3.

between protecting and protected states.

which protectorates had been established. It is more probable that the Austinian theory of the indivisibility of sovereignty furnished the influence under which they long persisted in regarding protected states or communities as independent, and which induced them, arguing logically from their premises, to repudiate all possession of power within the territory, whether by way of privilege or obligation, except over British subjects. The territory was foreign, its inhabitants were foreign; over neither therefore could jurisdiction be exercised, still less could it be assumed over subjects of other European states. So recently as 1888 an Agreement was concluded with the Sultan of Brunei under which 'the state is to continue to be governed and administered by the Sultan and his successors as an independent state, under the protection of Great Britain'; jurisdiction is reserved to British consular officers over British subjects and 'protected subjects,'—that is to say protected persons,—but the British courts are not invested with civil or criminal jurisdiction over the subjects

within the Empire of India. They form a class apart. With many of them treaties were entered into long ago which, if no subsequent change in the relations so established had taken place, would warrant their being looked upon as independent, save in the one point of incapacity to maintain diplomatic intercourse with any European or Eastern power, or any fellow Indian protected state. Since then, however, sometimes by fresh compact, universally by usage, internal independence has been invaded to an extent which is no doubt very different in the case of the Nizam from that of the petty chiefs of Káthiáwad or the Rajpút princelings of the Himalayas; but which everywhere involves the exercise to a greater or less degree of territorial jurisdiction by the paramount power, and implies the reserve on its part of a certain dominant 'residuary jurisdiction,' and even of the right to disregard the plain terms of the treaties themselves when the supreme interests of the empire are touched, or when the interests of the subjects of the native princes are gravely affected. Were the sovereignty of Great Britain less marked in fact, it would still be impossible to hold that the native states of India preserve so much independence as remains in the hands of an ordinary protected state. From the moment that the Queen was proclaimed Empress of India the sovereign powers which native princes enjoyed, and enjoy, ceased to be relics of their independence; they were kept by sufferance or delegation.

of foreign states[1]. There is thus no means of protecting British subjects against the misdeeds of foreigners whose government may not choose to cede jurisdiction, nor of securing civilized justice to foreigners in either civil or criminal matters where natives or subjects of third powers are concerned.

§ 94. The views which commend themselves to foreign countries, as to the powers and duties attendant on a protectorate, are of a very different complexion to those which have been entertained in England. It is believed that all the states represented at the Berlin Conference of 1884-5, with the exception of Great Britain, maintained that a protectorate includes the right of administering justice over the subjects of other civilized states; and by the first article of the General Act of the Brussels Conference of July, 1890, the powers, in this instance inclusive of Great Britain, declared 'that the most effective means for counteracting the slave trade in the interior of Africa are the following:—(1) Progressive organization of the administrative, judicial, religious, and military services in the African territories placed under the sovereignty or protectorate of civilized nations'; in the second to the seventh paragraphs are prescribed the establishment of occupied stations, roads, railways, inland steam navigation, telegraph lines, and the maintenance of restrictions on the importation of fire arms and ammunition[2]. Evidently on the one hand acts of the nature contemplated and prescribed compel extensive interference with the internal sovereignty of a community and involve a commensurate assumption of

Views entertained by foreign powers.

---

[1] Hertslet, Commercial Treaties, xviii. 228. Sarawak is governed still more completely as an independent state, the control of foreign relations being alone reserved to Her Majesty's government. The arrangement in this case is natural; but it is curious that the 'independent' sovereignty of a company created by charter should be recognized, and that the authority of the British Crown within the 'State of North Borneo' should be 'extraterritorial.'

[2] Parl. Papers, Africa, No. 7, 1890.

PART III. sovereignty by the protecting state; on the other the
CHAP. 3. objects aimed at can hardly, if at all, be attained compatibly with the exemption of European traders and adventurers from the local civilized jurisdiction.

It is in this sense that the general rights accruing from the possession of a protectorate are interpreted by Germany and France, and that the conventional rights given by the General Acts of the conferences of Berlin and Brussels are unquestionably understood by the former power; it is equally certain that France will not adopt a reading in any
Germany. particular more unfavourable to herself. The law regulating jurisdiction in the German protectorates, as modified by alterations introduced by Imperial Decree of March 15, 1888, expressly declares that it is competent to the Imperial authority to extend jurisdiction over all persons irrespectively of their nationality, and to place natives of the territory on the same footing as German subjects with regard to the right of flying the Imperial flag. Further, it is evident that the protected territories are put at least under the suzerainty of the German Empire, and that the protectorate has consequently a distinct territorial character; so much is this so that foreigners settling within the jurisdiction
France. may be naturalized and become German subjects. France on her part, wherever she has found it possible, has assumed powers not inferior to those taken by Germany. When the protectorate of Madagascar was acquired, treaties had already been concluded by its sovereign with Great Britain and the United States which barred France from obtaining jurisdiction over all foreigners, and the Malagasy government has since shown no disposition to abandon control of its internal affairs; French jurisdiction therefore is no greater than that which it had by treaty before the existence of a protectorate, or than that which is enjoyed by Great Britain; the powers of the protecting state are in fact extremely shadowy and its whole position far from

assured. Tunis may almost be said to have been absorbed; it is a protectorate only in name, and lies too far away on the opposite extreme from Madagascar to be of much use in illustrating the necessary authority of a protecting state. Apart from some minor protectorates, and from districts in the interior of Africa, which are claimed, but which no attempt has as yet been made to organize, there remain Annam and Cambodia. There the domestic administration is nominally left in the hands of the native government, and the resident only utters his commands in the form of advice. The protectorate is thus of the most normal type. Foreigners of every nationality are however placed under French jurisdiction, both in criminal and civil matters, and in contentions between themselves as well as in mixed causes[1]. That jurisdiction will be exercised as a matter of course over foreigners in all French protectorates may be inferred from a recent decision of the Cour de Cassation, reversing a judgement of the Appeal Court of Réunion, which had declared itself incompetent to try a British subject for murder committed in the protected island of Anjouan (Johanna)[2].

[1] Rev. de Droit Int. Privé, xvii. 205; Reichs-Gesetzblatt of March 15, 1888; Treaty of Houdong of April 14, 1863, State Papers, lvii. 739; Treaty of Hué, of June 6, 1884, State Papers, lxxv. 100.

Foreigners in Annam are expressly subjected to French jurisdiction by the Treaty of Hué. The treaty of Houdong between France and Cambodia only states that 'différends' between French citizens and other Europeans are to be adjudicated upon by the Resident; and no change is in terms made in this respect by the Treaty of Pnom-Penh of June 17, 1884 (State Papers, lxxv. 992); but the First and Fourth Articles open a door to the exercise of complete jurisdiction by providing that France may assume any power which she may think fit to take.

[2] Affaire Magny et autres; Cour de Cassation, Oct. 27, 1893. A portion of this judgement is worth quoting. 'Attendu,' it says, 'que si ce traité' of 1892 'à l'exemple des deux précédents, ne contient aucune disposition qui attribue expressément tout ou partie de la justice criminelle aux tribunaux français, cette attribution résulte implicitement de son article 3, ainsi conçu: "le Résident de France aura sous ses ordres le personnel de la police. Aucune force publique ne pourra se recruter, s'organiser, ni se

PART III.
CHAP. 3.

Powers exercised by Great Britain in her protectorates.

Malay Peninsula.

Zanzibar and Brunei.

§ 95. The powers exercised by Great Britain in protectorates are singularly various both in form and extent. In the Malay Peninsula no definite jurisdiction is appropriated; authority is vested in a Council of State, on which both the native chief and the British resident have a seat, and which is so invariably guided by the advice of the latter in all matters relating to the interests of foreigners, that it has been found practicable to dispense with the establishment of special British courts. The continuance of so simple an organization has no doubt been facilitated by the almost total absence of European subjects of Western states. In Zanzibar and Brunei, where well developed Oriental governments existed previously to the establishment of a protectorate, the powers acquired or asserted are strictly based on treaty, and do not exceed those possessed by Great Britain in several independent Eastern states, except in the one particular of the transference of foreign relations into the hands of the British government. Such is the self-restraint of Great Britain, that in the very agreement with the Sultan of Brunei, by which he accepted protection, it is provided that in mixed civil cases arising between British and British protected subjects and the subjects of the Sultan, the trial shall take place in the courts of the defendant's nationality, an officer appointed by the government of the plaintiff's nationality being entitled to be present at, and to take part in, the proceedings, without

mouvòir que par les ordres du Résident." Attendu en effet, qu'il eût été contradictoire de donner à la France pour la repression des crimes les mesures préparatoires de police et celles d'exécution et de laisser à la juridiction locale l'appréciation des actes criminels, autres du moins que ceux concernant exclusivement les indigènes, et cela sans aucune des garanties qui sont assurées aux accusés devant les juridictions françaises.. la cour cesse et annule' &c. The court is troubled with no doubts as to the power of the Sultan of Johanna to cede jurisdiction over foreigners, and has no hesitation in going beyond the words of the treaty in order to give effect to what it conceives to be their logical consequences.

however having a voice in the decision[1]. In Zanzibar, by a recent arrangement, in all cases in which a British subject is concerned, 'and the defendant or accused is a subject of His Highness the Sultan, or of other non-Christian power not represented by consuls, the Sultan hereby delegates all his judicial powers, as defined in' Article XVI of the Treaty of April 30, 1886, 'to Her Britannic Majesty's agent and consul general or to any person or persons appointed by the Secretary of State for that purpose. His Highness however retains the right to appoint a kathi to be present at the hearing of such cases and to act as assessor[2].'

In neither case is any jurisdiction, taken by the Order in Council applicable to the respective states, exercisable over foreigners in either civil or criminal matters; it is even provided in the Brunei Order, issued subsequently to the assumption of the protectorate, that if a foreigner institutes civil proceedings against a British subject, or is willing to appear as a defendant, in a British court, he must first file his consent to the jurisdiction, and if required must produce the consent of a competent authority of his own government; in Zanzibar, by a provision which has not been rescinded since the establishment of the protectorate, the latter condition is imperative. The Somali Coast is placed under an Order in Council, which simply applies the Persia Coasts and Islands Order, and which therefore recognizes that causes in which a foreign European subject is concerned can only be entertained in a British court by consent[3]. The orders in the above

Somali Coast.

---

[1] Hertslet, Com. Treaties, xviii. 228.
[2] Declaration between Great Britain and Zanzibar of Dec. 16, 1892.
[3] Brunei Order in Council, 1890; Zanzibar Order in Council, 1884; Somali Order in Council, 1889.

The requirement that a foreigner shall obtain the consent of his government before submitting as a defendant to the jurisdiction of the British court, is necessary in Zanzibar with reference to subjects of all powers possessing extraterritorial jurisdiction under a treaty concluded before the assumption of the protectorate by Great Britain. Besides all Oriental

PART III.
CHAP. 3.

cases are evidently inspired by the somewhat pedantic, and certainly erroneous, notion that sovereignty is indivisible, and that as Zanzibar, Brunei, and the Somali Coast are not completely under British sovereignty, they cannot be so for any purpose; it is supposed that Great Britain as a protecting state can only exercise delegated powers, and that an Eastern state cannot grant jurisdiction over persons who are neither its own subjects, nor subjects of the country to which the powers are delegated[1].

countries, however, there must be many Western states that have no such treaties.

A provision identical with that still existing in Zanzibar was even contained in the Western Pacific Order of 1877, which applied to New Guinea, the Solomon Islands, and other such places; the Order has now been superseded by that of 1893 which is different in this respect.

Larger powers can now be taken on the Somali Coast by the simple process of the issue by a Secretary of State of Consular Instructions, or of a notification under the Africa Order. Africa Order, 1889, Arts. 4, 5, and 7. The inclusion of this protectorate within the limits affected by the Africa Order need not involve the substitution of English law for the law of British India, which is at present administered. Africa Order of June 28, 1892.

[1] The terms of Dr. Lushington's judgement in the case of Papayanni v. the Russian Steam Navigation and Trading Company (2 Moore, P. C. 183) suggest at first sight that in the opinion of the Judicial Committee of the Privy Council an Eastern state can in no circumstances grant jurisdiction over persons who are neither its own subjects nor subjects of the power to which jurisdiction is delegated. 'Though,' he said, 'the Ottoman Porte could give, and has given, to the Christian powers of Europe authority to administer justice to their own subjects according to their own laws, it has neither professed to give, nor could give, to one such power any jurisdiction over the subjects of another power. But it has left those powers at liberty to deal with each other as they thought fit, and if the subjects of one country desire to resort to the tribunals of another, there can be no objection to their doing so with the consent of their own sovereign and that of the sovereign to whose tribunals they resort. There is no compulsory power in Turkey in an English court over any but English subjects.' In weighing the meaning of this language, however, it must be borne in mind that Dr. Lushington had certain facts only before his eyes, and that he neither had, nor could have had, in his mind the facts which are characteristic of a modern protectorate. He had before him in the Ottoman Empire a state which retained its full sovereignty and independence, and which had no intention of ceding any portion of either; and he had to ask himself whether, consistently with this attitude, a jurisdiction could be conferred on Great Britain, acceptance

The Africa, South Africa, and Pacific Orders in Council are of a different character[1]. Under the first, which by consular instructions or notification on the part of a Secretary of State can be applied to any existing or future African protectorate inclusively of the Niger protectorate, providing that no other Order in Council is already in force, jurisdiction extends to all persons 'with respect to whom any state, king, chief, or government, whose subjects, or under whose protection they are, has by any treaty or otherwise agreed with Her Majesty for, or consented to, the exercise of power or authority by Her Majesty.' This provision amounts to the assumption of jurisdiction over the natives of the country, and over the subjects of every European state, which needs for the present purpose to be considered, in all protectorates where the Order in Council is applied. The General Act of the conference of Berlin contemplated the assumption of protectorates by various powers on the coasts of Africa, and indirectly acknowledged a British protectorate

PART III.
CHAP. 3.

Africa, South Africa, and Pacific.

of which involved the assumption, and delegation of which involved the abandonment, of a portion of the international responsibilities of the Turkish sovereign. To the question put in this form there can be but one answer. It does not follow that Dr. Lushington would have expressed himself with regard to protectorates in the same manner, still less that an English court, in dealing with them, would now feel bound by the terms of a judgement prompted by circumstances to which those of a protectorate offer no analogy.

[1] Africa Order in Council, 1889; South Africa Order in Council, 1891; Pacific Order in Council, 1893. The only jurisdiction established in an ostensible protectorate by the Africa Order is that of the Niger Coast Protectorate, formerly called the Oil Rivers Protectorate. The territory of the British East Africa Company also forms a jurisdiction, which for practical purposes may be ranked with protectorates. 'The Nyassa districts' constitute a third jurisdiction. So far as I am aware there is nothing to show whether these last are to be considered a protectorate or a possession, or simply a barbarous country over which a jurisdiction of an unclassed description has been assumed. In none of these cases are definite territorial boundaries set to the jurisdiction. Presumably it extends over the territories named so far as they have known boundaries and elsewhere will follow delimitation as it occurs, in the meantime reaching wherever the actual presence of authorized British officers or agents enables it to be exercised.

as already existing on the Niger; an obligation was taken to insure the establishment of authority in occupied regions 'sufficient to protect existing rights, and, as the case may be, freedom of trade and of transit under the conditions agreed upon'; Great Britain specifically undertook 'to protect foreign merchants and all the trading nationalities in all those portions of the Niger which are or may be under her sovereignty or protection as if they were her own subjects.' The evident meaning of the Berlin Act is emphasized by the declaration, already quoted, of the Brussels Act which enjoins a progressive administration and judicial organization of territories taken under the protectorate of civilized nations[1]. It would be impossible for the signatories of agreements pointing so clearly to the establishment of whatever jurisdiction may be found necessary or advisable by a protecting state for the attainment of prescribed objects, and pointing moreover to a development of organization as an end in itself, to deny the grant of implied consent to the exercise by Great Britain of civil and criminal jurisdiction over their subjects in British protectorates duly set up upon the coasts of Africa; and as the conditions under which protectorates can exist upon the coast and in the interior parts of the continent, to which the agreements do not extend, differ only in the greater difficulty of maintaining effective jurisdiction in inland places, the signatory governments are morally precluded from objecting to the assumption of equal powers in the one case to those which they have given in the

---

[1] Arts. 30, 34, 35 of the General Act of the Conference of Berlin, Parl. Papers, Africa, No. 3, 1886; Art. 1 of the General Act of the Brussels Conference, Parl. Papers, Africa, No. 7, 1890. In view of the heading of the sixth chapter of the Berlin Act, the phrase 'occupied regions' in the 35th article, though suggestive of occupation in full sovereignty, must obviously be read so as to include the protectorates mentioned in the 34th Article.

The Brussels Act was signed by all the signatories of the Berlin Act, and in addition by the United States, and some other countries of less importance.

others. It is to be observed however that no power is taken by the Africa Order over subjects of powers which have not consented expressly or by implication to the exercise of jurisdiction.

In an indirect and confused, but sufficient, manner the Pacific Order asserts jurisdiction over natives and the subjects of foreign states irrespectively of consent. The jurisdiction taken in the first instance is indefinite; subsequently it is stated to extend 'only over Her Majesty's subjects' in places which are 'not British settlements or under the protection of Her Majesty,' and to the usual requirement of consent in civil actions the qualification is added that 'the foregoing provisions of this article shall take effect only in places within the limits of the Order which are not British settlements or under the protection of Her Majesty.' In this case authority over foreign subjects is appropriated independently of consent on the part of other European states. It rests upon the implied assertion that exercise of jurisdiction on all persons within a protected territory is so necessary, or at least so natural, a consequence of the protectorate, where native administration and judicial organization is inadequate, that foreign powers may be expected to acquiesce in its enforcement in the same manner as they acquiesce in the effects of complete sovereignty [1].

The same powers can now apparently be called into existence without having recourse to an Order in Council in protected territory adjacent to the Gold Coast Colony, to which neither the Berlin Act nor the Africa Order in Council of 1889 apply. By an Order in Council of December 29, 1887, it was provided that it should be 'lawful for the Legislative Council for the time being of the Gold Coast Colony, by Ordinance, or Ordinances, to

[1] The groups of islands in the Pacific which are now under British protection are the Union, the Phoenix, the Cook, the Gilbert, and the southern Solomons.

PART III.
CHAP. 3.
exercise and provide for giving effect to all such powers and jurisdiction as Her Majesty may, at any time before or after the passing of this Order in Council, have acquired in the said territories adjacent to the Gold Coast Colony.' Subject to such instructions as may at present be in force, it would seem to be competent to the Legislature to apply the principle embodied in the Pacific Order to the territories in question.

South Africa.

The South Africa Order establishes a protectorate over 'the parts of South Africa bounded by British Bechuanaland, the German protectorate, the rivers Chobe and Zambesi, the Portuguese possessions, and the South African Republic.' Within this region the High Commissioner for South Africa may 'by Proclamation provide for the administration of justice, the raising of revenue, and generally for the peace, order, and good government of all persons within the limits' of the Order, 'including the prohibition and punishment of acts tending to disturb the public peace.' Until the issue of such proclamation any jurisdiction exercisable under a charter granted by the Crown remains in full force. The South African Company consequently, by virtue of its Charter [1], for the present holds complete power of government and jurisdiction, and is under an obligation 'to the best of its ability to preserve peace and order in such ways and manner as it shall consider necessary' within a 'field of operations' which, on its vague description may be larger, or smaller than, or identical with the area comprised in the protectorate. The charter appears to grant jurisdiction over all inhabitants, whether native or European, and the Order in Council unquestionably subjects to the jurisdiction 'all persons' within the limits defined to the authority of the High Commissioner.

Niger Territories.

In the Niger territories a protectorate is exercised through the agency of the Royal Niger Company, which

[1] London Gazette of Dec. 20, 1889.

by its Charter[1] is 'authorized and empowered to hold and retain the full benefit of' certain specified cessions of territory made by native chiefs, 'and all rights, interests, authorities, and powers for the purposes of government, preservation of public order, protection of the said territories, or otherwise of what nature or kind soever, under or by virtue thereof, or resulting therefrom.' Under this charter, which, as it was granted subsequently to the Conference of Berlin, must be understood as being intended to give effect to the obligations contracted there by Great Britain, the company maintains order and a civil administration, and has established Courts of Justice with civil and criminal jurisdiction over foreigners. None of the signatories of the general Act have disputed the validity of the jurisdiction. In one instance it has been distinctly admitted by implication, the German government having appealed to that of Great Britain on behalf of a German subject against a decision given by the local courts, on the alleged grounds that a certain district was outside the British protectorate, and that the particular regulations which had been infringed were in contravention of the provisions of the Niger Navigation Act [2].

[1] London Gazette of July 13, 1886.
[2] A portion of the territorial history of the protectorate seems to be curious. It would appear that in 1884 thirty-seven treaties were concluded by Consul Hewitt with various tribes on or near the rivers Niger and Benue, by which 'the Queen of Great Britain and Ireland' undertook to extend to the chiefs 'and to the territory under their authority and jurisdiction her gracious favour and protection,' the chiefs on their part promising 'to refrain from entering into any correspondence, agreement, or treaty with any foreign nation or power, except with the knowledge and sanction of Her Britannic Majesty's Government.' In most cases jurisdiction over British subjects and property was ceded to Great Britain, and an engagement was entered into to act in all other matters upon the advice of British Consular or other officers. A like number of treaties of cession, concluded in the same year by the Company, which was not yet chartered, appears to have vested in it the territories of the tribes in question. These latter treaties are taken in the charter as the foundation of the territorial rights of the

PART III.
CHAP. 3.

The true character of the relations between a protecting and protected state or territory.

§ 96. From the foregoing sketch it will be seen that the views held by Great Britain as to the powers and obligations attached to a protectorate over semi-civilized or barbarous countries have tended to assimilate themselves to the conceptions which had been formed in other countries at a somewhat earlier date, but that there are still considerable differences both between some of the British protectorates and those of other nations, and between British protectorates themselves. It will not therefore be superfluous to recur for a moment to the essential fact which distinguishes a protected from a fully independent state, and to see what consequences flow from it under the conditions prevailing in uncivilized territories. The mark of a protected state or people, whether civilized or uncivilized, is that it cannot maintain political intercourse with foreign powers except through or by permission of the protecting state. Whatever results from this fact is necessary to the relation created by a protectorate; whatever is independent of it descends from some other source. Starting from this point, it becomes at once evident that the interposition of the protecting state between the protected country and foreign powers deprives the latter of the means of exacting redress for themselves for wrongs which their subjects may suffer

Company, and it is empowered to enjoy the benefit of them. The two sets of treaties would have been to a great extent mutually exclusive, since both jurisdiction and all lesser powers necessarily follow cession, were it not that every cession received by a British subject enures to the benefit of the British crown; as things are the charter must be regarded as a grant of all powers acquired by the British Crown that are inconsistent with it, as recognizing the full property and sovereignty obtained by the above and other subsequent cessions received before the Charter was granted, and as extinguishing in consequence a protective jurisdiction which was to be exercised over and in favour of the previous territorial owners. As a protectorate is nevertheless considered to exist, it must now be founded upon, and must consist in, the reserved power of control contained in the charter itself. The protectorate is over the Chartered Company, and not directly over the native tribes. On the other hand, where the treaties concluded by the Company have fallen short of cession in their effect, the protectorate is doubtless over the native tribes themselves.

at the hands of the native rulers or people; and that, as the protecting state interposes voluntarily and for its own selfish objects, it is not morally in a position to demand that foreign governments shall patiently submit to wrongdoing from persons whose natural responsibility it covers with the shield of its own sovereign independence. A state must be bound to see that a reasonable measure of security is afforded to foreign subjects and property within the protected territory, and to prevent acts of depredation or hostility being done by its inhabitants. It must consequently exercise whatever amount of control may be found necessary for the purpose. Naturally this must vary greatly with the degree to which a people is advanced towards civilization, with the readiness with which it lends itself to guidance, with the number and character of the Europeans who visit or reside in the country. There are cases in which social order may be amply preserved by the means which suffice in the Malay Peninsula; there are instances in which the more difficult and complex conditions of the problem justify, or require, a complete organization of legal machinery and the maintenance of a force of police. With such exercise of jurisdiction however, and such means of giving effect to it as may be reasonable in the circumstances, the strict consequences of the establishment of a protectorate cease; a foreigner cannot demand an amount of protection in the upper waters of the Benue which he might properly expect at Zanzibar; and beyond protection he can ask for nothing. Correlatively also to the protection, which can be claimed for him, his government must consent to the exercise of jurisdiction over him. Others must be protected against him as fully as he is against others; if he must be given the opportunity of suing, he must submit to be sued; if a person is punished for committing a crime against him, he must be liable to punishment on committing a crime himself.

From the substitution then, in relation to foreign governments, of the protecting state for the protected country or people are inevitably derived the right and the obligation to assume so much jurisdiction as is at once needed and possible in the circumstances. If the protecting state goes further, and takes into its hand any portion of the administration which is not directed to this end, it travels beyond the true limits of the protective function, and unnecessarily usurps the internal sovereignty of the community.

If the foregoing remarks are well founded, it is clear that Great Britain is justified in varying the forms of her protective jurisdiction. It is also clear that in the less developed instances she has assumed smaller powers than might reasonably have been taken, and that in some cases, as for example on the Somali coast, enough power has certainly not been appropriated to meet the demands which may rightly be made by foreign states, or to prevent the continuance or establishment of foreign extraterritorial jurisdictions, the existence of which may be productive of grave embarrassment in the future. On the other hand, in the protectorates where she has invested herself with fuller powers, while refraining from any undue invasion of internal sovereignty, she has secured to herself sufficient authority to meet all contingencies.

§ 97. The extent of the powers which may be assumed by Great Britain in its protectorates being well ascertained in principle, and for practical purposes being sufficiently ascertained with reference to other European and American states, it remains to inquire whether an identical amount of jurisdiction has been conferred by those statutes which, so far as they reach, have defined the prerogative rights of the Crown; for although foreign governments may internationally admit the rights of Great Britain in ample degree, it must always be open to an individual foreigner to test the municipal legality of a jurisdiction, to which he may have been subjected, by appealing to the British courts.

It must be confessed that if the courts are bound to guide themselves solely by reference to the Foreign Jurisdiction Act, the right of exercising jurisdiction over subjects of foreign powers hardly seems to rest upon so solid a foundation as might be wished.

The Foreign Jurisdiction Act of 1890, after reciting that 'by treaty, capitulation, grant, usage, sufferance and other lawful means, Her Majesty the Queen has jurisdiction within divers foreign countries,' declares that 'it is and shall be lawful for Her Majesty the Queen to hold, exercise, and enjoy any jurisdiction which Her Majesty now has or may at any time hereafter have within a foreign country.' The recital and the operative language are both nearly identical with the corresponding portion of the Act of 1843; they differ only in being somewhat narrower, the earlier Act speaking of a 'country or place' where the later makes mention of a 'country' alone. That the Act of 1843 referred only to certain wholly independent states, in which a limited jurisdiction over British subjects had been obtained in the various ways specified in the recital, is unquestionable. It is equally unquestionable that neither then, nor during the long subsequent period when successive Acts were passed [1], was Great Britain supposed to have asserted by statute any other than a strictly extra-territorial jurisdiction, limited to her own subjects. It may be doubted whether the provision that it shall be lawful for the Crown to exercise such power or jurisdiction as it may 'at any time hereafter have within any country out of Her Majesty's dominions' can be stretched so far

---

[1] Foreign Jurisdiction Amendment Acts of 1865 (28 & 29 Vict. c. 116), of 1866 (29 & 30 Vict. c. 87), of 1875 (38 & 39 Vict. c. 85), and 1878 (41 & 42 Vict. c. 67); now repealed by and consolidated in the Foreign Jurisdiction Act, 1890.

beyond the analogy of the species of jurisdiction contemplated through a series of years, as to include powers that have at least a strong flavour of sovereignty, which are not specifically given by treaty or acquired by prescription, and to cover persons so broadly different from those at which the Act originally aimed as are the subjects of foreign European and American states. It is to be remembered that the Act of 1890 is a consolidating Act, and that therefore new meanings cannot arbitrarily be read into language which reproduces the terms of preceding statutes.

Whatever be the value of these doubts, it is to be feared that something more than uncertainty must in any case remain as to the operation of the Act with regard to foreign subjects in precisely those regions where it is most necessary that large jurisdiction shall be taken. By the second section it is provided that 'where a foreign country is not subject to any government from whom Her Majesty the Queen might obtain jurisdiction in the manner recited by this Act, Her Majesty shall by virtue of this Act have jurisdiction over Her Majesty's subjects for the time being resident in or resorting to that country, and that jurisdiction shall be jurisdiction of Her Majesty in a foreign country within the meaning of the other provisions of this Act.' The jurisdiction contemplated is jurisdiction over British subjects alone; foreign subjects are by implication excluded. In barbarous countries therefore, where no local administration exists, the British government appears upon the bare terms of the Act to be precluded on the one hand from safeguarding foreigners, on the other from protecting natives or subjects of its own.

The prerogative in its relation to protectorates.

§ 98. Unless, as hardly seems likely, there are reasons of policy which render it inadvisable to draw the attention of governments, who were not signatories of the Berlin or Brussels Acts, to the assumption by Great Britain of jurisdiction over foreigners in protectorates, it would be well to affirm that jurisdiction by legislation. In the meanwhile it is at least possible that jurisdiction may be maintainable independently of statute.

It can scarcely any longer be seriously argued that the sovereign powers of a state are incapable of being divided between different persons or bodies of persons, or that the persons sharing them must be identified solely with the state itself. Evidence to the contrary was always plentiful, though the eyes of English lawyers declined to rest upon it. In the older European cases the respective powers of a protected or semi-sovereign country and of the protecting or paramount state were frequently, and indeed generally, sharply defined; the latter could only exceed the powers assigned to it by an act of force, or in other words by action which was practically war, while the limits of the inferior sovereignty were marked with equal distinctness. It is possible that the sharpness of the division tended to distract attention from the fact that there was a sovereignty in common. Whether this be so or not, it is unnecessary to enumerate or discuss either these or the more modern instances in which sovereignty is divided in varying proportions between two governments, neither of which sometimes is local. It is enough to point to a single case, in which Great Britain has placed itself by treaty in the position of being a joint sovereign with another country. In Cyprus the powers that, taken together, make up the plenitude of sovereignty, are shared between it and the Ottoman Empire. Internationally the island remains a Turkish possession; to Turkey belongs the external sovereignty; Great Britain enjoys no right of alienation. On the other hand, all legislative and administrative powers have been ceded unreservedly to Great Britain, and in no circumstances has the Turkish government a right of control or interference; to Great Britain belongs the internal sovereignty. Bosnia and Herzegovina are in similar case. To pretend that the Porte has kept full sovereignty in its hands, and that Great Britain and Austria make laws, administer civil and criminal justice, and levy taxes and dues in the capacity of subordinates to whom delegated functions are entrusted, is to be satisfied with barren phrases; to deny that some sovereignty rests with the Porte is to ignore the patent fact that the bare territorial sovereignty has never been transferred [1].

If once it be granted that sovereign powers are divisible, there can be no reason why the British Crown, in the exercise of its prerogative rights, should not acquire a portion of the territorial sovereignty of a state or tribal community for the purpose of establishing a protectorate, in the same way as it can undoubtedly acquire the whole of such sovereignty by cession or conquest for the purpose of annexing territory to the Empire. The name is different; the powers which are taken are smaller; but in essence nothing would be done, in doing this, that has not already been done in Cyprus. There the power of governing and organizing was desired; internal sovereignty was consequently obtained. In protectorates the exclusion of foreign European states is the primary object; external sovereignty is therefore appropriated together with so much of the internal sovereignty as is needed to be its complement.

It cannot be validly objected to this view that though the powers, which are obtained by cession or seizure, may have been obtained, as any powers may be, through the same right by which the Crown concludes treaties or makes war, yet that the effects following upon cession or conquest cannot attach to them, because of their being dissociated from territory. The powers exercised in a protectorate are in fact territorial. Each and every sovereign power is terri-

---

[1] Comp. on the divisibility of sovereignty, Maine, International Law, p. 58.

torial in that it obliges every person within the territory of the state or community to the extent of its applicability; and inversely, every power which extends over the whole territory is a part of or an emanation from the state sovereignty.

If the foregoing statement of the position held by Great Britain within a protected territory is accurate, it may be expected that the English courts will consider that, in assuming a protectorate, the crown takes to itself powers which, so far as they go, are identical with those that it would have in a conquered country. It can prescribe laws until parliament chooses to legislate; and it can subject to its administration all persons upon the protected soil. This is done in those protectorates where general jurisdiction is claimed. The Crown, in the exercise of its prerogative rights, legislates by applying English law, so far as it is suitable to a rough state of society; and it applies the law indifferently to all persons whom it finds within the territory over which, by agreement or assumption, it has obtained a limited territorial jurisdiction.

§ 99. Some mention has already been made of the exceptional international situation in which Cyprus is placed. Its internal organization is equally distinct. Under an Order in Council of September 14, 1878, it is ruled by a high commissioner, who administers the government 'in the name and on behalf of Her Majesty,' with the assistance of a legislative and of an executive council. With the advice of the former he makes such laws and ordinances as may be necessary from time to time, subject to such instructions as may be issued under the Queen's sign-manual, and subject to a power reserved to the Crown to confirm or disallow such laws and ordinances either wholly or in part, and to make laws or ordinances by Order in Council. The high commissioner has power in cases of emergency to make ordinances for

PART III
CHAP. 3.

the peace, order, and good government of the island independently of the legislative council; and together with the necessary general executive powers, may grant lands, appoint judges and all necessary officers, and has power of suspending any such persons from the exercise of their functions until the Queen's pleasure be known; finally he enjoys the prerogative of pardon, and of remitting fines, penalties, or forfeitures. Thus the entire internal sovereignty is assumed and its exercise is provided for; so fully indeed is the sovereignty assumed that the island has been taken over released from the Capitulations; the privileges of the subjects of European states have disappeared[1].

In this instance the powers granted led so immediately to administrative and legislative action that the case at once declares itself to be one of limited cession of territorial sovereignty. That it has hitherto been possible to avoid seeing that a similar cession takes place also in protectorates is merely due to the circumstance that the portion of sovereignty ceded directly or · by implication does not necessarily require to be applied so instantaneously or so systematically.

Natives of protectorates in places under foreign jurisdiction.

§ 100. The law which is administered, and the machinery for administering the law, being identical in protectorates and in independent states where extraterritorial jurisdiction is organized under Orders in Council, there is one consequence only of the position occupied by protected territories which calls for remark, outside those political relations

[1] As the Capitulations are treaties of which the Porte cannot rid itself within its territory, the acquiescence of European powers in their supersession by British law constitutes a proof that, in the opinion at least of foreign states, the internal sovereignty of Cyprus has been completely ceded. As a matter of practice natives of the island of Cyprus are not considered to be protected subjects of the Queen in countries foreign to the Ottoman Empire, or even in Egypt, still less therefore in other parts of the Ottoman dominions. On the other hand extradition of criminals and accused persons is provided for by an Order in Council of July 15, 1881. It is needless to say that extradition is essentially an act of territorial sovereignty.

which have already been dealt with. Are the natives of a protectorate to be regarded as simple foreigners when in countries other than their own, or can they demand to be placed in the same situation as is accorded to persons whom, for one reason or another, Great Britain has been in the habit of protecting? Up to the present time they seem to have been relegated to the former category, consistently no doubt with the opinion which has usually been held in England as to the powers acquired by establishing a protectorate. If however the views expressed in the foregoing sections are well founded, it becomes logically necessary that the amount of protection shall be afforded to the members of a protected community, when within the territory of a foreign state, which is implied in the political connexion between Great Britain and their country, and which is correlative to the security offered by Great Britain to persons who enter its protectorates under the wing of a foreign power. In other words they share the right of subjects to enjoy the advantages of such good order as, in different degrees, is maintained within the civilized possessions of a European state and in its protected territories, and they share also the right to diplomatic protection when occasion for it arises.

If this view be not adopted, the practical inconvenience will make itself felt that natives of foreign protectorates will have to receive more favourable treatment in British protected territories than can be conversely demanded. That foreign European states will regard natives of their protectorates as being in the same position as subjects when in places under the political control of Great Britain there can be no doubt; German law goes even so far as to allow them to be put by Imperial Ordinances on the same footing as German subjects with regard to the right of flying the Imperial flag [1].

[1] Gesetz betreffend die Rechtsverhältnisse der Deutschen Schutz-

PART III.
CHAP. 3.

Spheres of influence.

§ 101. The term 'sphere of influence' is one to which no very definite meaning is as yet attached. Perhaps in its indefiniteness consists its international value. It indicates the regions which geographically are adjacent to or politically group themselves naturally with, possessions or protectorates, but which have not actually been so reduced into control that the minimum of the powers which are implied in a protectorate can be exercised with tolerable regularity. It represents an understanding which enables a state to reserve to itself a right of excluding other European powers from territories that are of importance to it politically as affording means of future expansion to its existing dominions or protectorates, or strategically as preventing civilized neighbours from occupying a dominant military position.

The business of a European power within its sphere of influence is to act as a restraining and directing force. It endeavours to foster commerce, to secure the safety of traders and travellers, and without interfering with the native government, or with native habits or customs, to prepare the way for acceptance of more organized guidance. No jurisdiction is assumed, no internal or external sovereign power is taken out of the hands of the tribal chiefs; no definite responsibility consequently is incurred. Foreigners enter the country with knowledge of these circumstances,

gebiete, vom 15. März 1888, Art. 2, § 7, in the Reichsgesetzblatt of that date.

So far has Great Britain been from adopting this attitude that doubts have arisen in very recent years as to the precise status and privileges which should be accorded to ships from Cutch, trading to the Persian Gulf, and belonging to subjects of Indian protected states. As they are not owned by British subjects they cannot be registered as British ships, nor can they hoist the British merchant flag; if therefore the Persian Gulf and its shores were not so completely as they are under the influence of this country, disagreeable consequences might easily occur. The reluctance shown fully to protect natives of Cutch is the more remarkabel that they are of course in a widely different legal position from the inhabitants of an ordinary protectorate. Comp. p. 128.

and therefore to a great extent at their peril. While then the European state is morally bound to exercise in their favour such influence as it has, there is no specific amount of good order, however small, which it can be expected to secure.

The position of a European power within its sphere of influence being so vague, the questions suggest themselves, whether any exclusive rights can be acquired as against other civilized countries through the establishment of a sphere, and in what way its geographical extent is to be ascertained.

The answer to both these questions lies in the fact that the phrase 'sphere of influence,' taken by itself, rather implies a moral claim than a true right. If international agreements are made with other European powers, such as those between Great Britain and Germany and Italy, the states entering into them are of course bound to common respect of the limits to which they have consented; and if treaties are entered into with native chiefs which, without conveying any of the rights of sovereignty involved in a protectorate, confer exclusive privileges or give advantages of a commercial nature, evidence is at least afforded that influence is existent, and it would be an obviously unfriendly act within a region where any influence is exercised to try to supplant the country which had succeeded in establishing its influence. But agreements only bind the parties to them; and no such legal results are produced by the unilateral assertion of a sphere of influence as those which flow from conquest or cession, or even from the erection of a protectorate. The understanding that a territory is within a sphere of influence warns off friendly powers; it constitutes no barrier to covert hostility. The limit of effective political influence is practically the limit of the sphere, if another European state is in waiting to seize what is not firmly held; and an aggressive state is not likely to consider itself excluded, until the state exercising influence is ready, if her legal situation be challenged, to take upon herself the responsibility of a protectorate. Even as between an influencing state and powers which are friendly in the full sense of the words, it has to be remembered that the exercise of influence is not in its nature a permanent relation between the European country and the native tribes; it is assented to as a temporary phase in the belief, and on the understanding, that within a reasonable time a more solid form will be imparted to the civilized authority. It is not likely therefore that an influencing government will find itself able for any length of time to avoid the adoption of means for securing the safety of foreigners, and consequently of subjecting the native chiefs to steady interference and pressure. Duty towards friendly countries, and self-protection against rival powers, will alike compel a rapid hardening of control; and probably before long spheres of influence are destined to be merged into some unorganized form of protectorate analogous to that which exists in the Malay Peninsula.

Powers which can be exercised in barbarous countries not under the protection of a civilized power. With respect to British subjects.

§ 102. In barbarous countries which are neither in the possession nor under the protection of any civilized power a like jurisdiction can be exercised by the British Crown over its subjects to that which it exercises over them in independent Eastern states and protectorates. By the Pacific Islanders Protection Act of 1875, it was enacted that it should be 'lawful for Her Majesty to exercise power and jurisdiction over her subjects within any islands and places in the Pacific Ocean not being within Her Majesty's dominions, nor within the jurisdiction of any civilized power in the same and as ample a manner as if such power or jurisdiction had been acquired by the cession or conquest of territory;' and by the Foreign Jurisdiction Act of 1890 it was more largely provided that 'where a foreign country is not subject to any government from which Her Majesty the Queen might obtain jurisdiction in the manner recited by this Act, Her Majesty shall by virtue of this Act have jurisdiction over Her Majesty's subjects for the time being resident in or resorting to that country, and that jurisdiction shall be jurisdiction of Her Majesty in a foreign country within the meaning of the other provisions of this Act,' that is to say, the same jurisdiction as that given in the above quoted section of the Pacific Islanders Protection Act [1]. Powers have been taken under these Acts by the Pacific Order in Council, 1873, over the Navigators, Friendly, Ellice, and Santa Cruz Islands, and other minor islands scattered within specified limits of latitude and longitude. The operation of the Acts may be extended, as occasion may require, to such rare islands as are not yet appropriated by civilized or semi-civilized powers, or to regions in the interior of Africa which are in a similar position.

Within places of the kind at present under consideration it would evidently be improper to assert jurisdiction over persons other than British subjects. Great Britain neither pretends to complete sovereignty nor to the rights which accompany a protectorate [2]. It can merely, with some exceptions to be mentioned below, compel the observance of law among persons who are within her grasp in virtue of the authority which she possesses over her own subjects, wherever it is not displaced by the territorial sovereignty of another organized community. Accordingly in the Pacific Order in Council it is declared that 'in islands and places which are not British Settlements, or under the protection

[1] 38 & 39 Vict. cap. 51, sect. 6; 53 & 54 Vict. cap. 37, sect. 2.
[2] The 7th section of the Pacific Islanders Protection Act declares that 'nothing herein or in any such Order in Council contained shall extend or be construed to extend to invest Her Majesty, her heirs or successors, with any claim or title whatsoever to dominion or sovereignty over any such islands or places as aforesaid, or to derogate from the rights of the tribes or people inhabiting such islands or places, or of chiefs or rulers thereof, to such sovereignty or dominion.'

PART III. of Her Majesty, jurisdiction under this order shall be exer-
CHAP. 3. cised (except only as in this order expressly provided)'
that is to say in certain cases of consent, 'only over Her
Majesty's subjects, and any foreigners or natives, in so far
as by reason of being, or having been[1], on board a British
ship or otherwise, they have come under a duty of
allegiance to Her Majesty, and their property, and pro-
prietary rights and obligations.'

With respect to foreigners.

Foreigners can thus only be made amenable to British
courts in independent barbarous countries by the express
or implied consent of the state to which they belong, or by
the consent of the individual. Express consent to a general
exercise of jurisdiction has in no instance been given; and
the conditions under which jurisdiction would be exercised
being wholly unlike those which are found in a protectorate, implied consent cannot in present circumstances be
supposed. Jurisdiction can therefore only be based upon
a particular consent on the part of foreign authorities, for
giving effect to which no provision is made; or on the
consent of the individual, which the courts can take as
founding jurisdiction in civil suits, provided that the
foreign plaintiff or defendant, if required, 'obtains and
files a certificate in writing from a competent authority
of his own government, to the effect that no objection
is made by that government to the foreigner submitting in
the particular cause or matter to the jurisdiction of the
court[2].'

Organization of British jurisdiction in barbarous territories in the Pacific.

§ 103. The organization, by means of which the jurisdiction taken in the independent Pacific Islands is exercised,
necessarily differs considerably from that established in
more civilized independent countries and in protected

---

[1] Great Britain takes jurisdiction over crimes committed by any
British subject who has within the previous three months belonged to
any British ship, irrespectively of the place where the crime is committed.
17 & 18 Vict. cap. 104, sect. 267.

[2] Pacific Order in Council, 1893, Art. 109.

territories. The whole of the islands of the Western Pacific, which are not under the control or in the possession of other powers of European civilization, whether they are a colony or settlement[1], a protected territory, or independent, are placed to the extent of the jurisdiction belonging in them to Great Britain, under a high commissioner, whose court, sitting in Fiji, has both appellate and original jurisdiction. Subordinate to him are judicial and deputy commissioners; and in addition naval officers employed upon the station are invested with extensive powers. 'Any officer holding Her Majesty's Commission and being in command of any of Her Majesty's ships, or acting for the purposes of this article with the written consent of the officer in command of any such ship,' may apprehend a person alleged to have committed an offence, he may make a preliminary examination and commit for trial, he may with the consent in writing of the accused person in any case which is triable without assessors exercise summary jurisdiction, and he may with like consent of the parties in a civil dispute exercise any of the powers which can be exercised by a deputy commissioner, either by way of conciliation or arbitration or by way of judicial determination[2]. Through this very valuable provision control can to a great extent be maintained in wild outlying islands over the scattered traders, who would otherwise in practice completely escape from the restraint of British authority[3].

---

[1] Amongst the Pacific Islands are some which have been occupied by British subjects, under licence from the Crown, for the purpose of collecting guano, planting cocoa nuts, and other like industries. They were not inhabited before they were so occupied, and they are now inhabited only by the licencees and their servants; they are consequently regarded as territory acquired by settlement, and as forming part of the British dominions. They are only mentioned here in order that they may not be confused with the various other categories of islands over which the Pacific Order extends.   [2] Art. 18.

[3] Among the extremely miscellaneous European population of the

PART III.
CHAP. 3.

Independent natives of barbarous places.

§ 104. The natives of the barbarous islands of the Pacific, which are not under the protection or entire sovereignty of a European power, being foreigners, and their territory being foreign territory, jurisdiction in the proper sense of the word cannot be exercised over them; it is therefore considered that all acts done in repression of lawlessness on their part are acts of war, and must both be of the usual nature of such acts, and followed by the consequences thought to be appropriate in Europe. The detention of culprits in British territory by way of punishment is illegitimate, still more so would be their execution. It is believed that officers on the spot have occasionally somewhat overstepped the bounds of strict legality with very wholesome effect; but in general the punitive measures adopted after cases of murder or plunder have consisted in shelling villages, or in landing and burning them. Unless life happens to be taken, the penalty is not

Pacific Islands occurrences not infrequently take place, which sometimes suggest that improvement in the international police of these regions would be desirable, and sometimes point to weaknesses in English law which it would be well, though no doubt it might be difficult, to cure. The following case to a certain extent illustrates both points. A person of English name, but claiming to be a French citizen, acquired naturalization in Australia, and in virtue of his naturalization obtained a British colonial register for a vessel with which he traded to the Pacific Islands. The person in question committed an act of violence against a native, in retaliation for which a murder was committed. The very delicate question was opened up of the national character of the former delinquent. As master and owner of a British vessel he was no doubt amenable to British jurisdiction for acts done on board his ship. But the act of violence was done on shore in an island within no civilized jurisdiction. Persons naturalized in the Australian colonies are not in strictness British subjects for any purpose outside the limits of the colony in which they are naturalized; and although it is the practice to grant them passports, entitling them to protection elsewhere than in their country of origin, it can neither be expected that the authorities of their own nation will regard them as English, nor can their British character be insisted upon adversely to them by British authorities. In this particular case the difficulty of bringing the culprit under British jurisdiction was the more unfortunate that France has no legal means of dealing with her citizens in the independent islands.

greatly deterrent in itself, when the houses are mere sheds made of branches, which can be rebuilt in a few hours from the neighbouring forest; and whatever be the punishment inflicted, it is at least better that it should strike the actual perpetrators of a crime than that it should involve a whole community which, sometimes at any rate, is innocent of complicity. It is little short of ridiculous to apply the principles of European international law with prudish exactness to the savages of the Santa Cruz Islands; and it is unfortunate that naval officers are not enabled to use towards independent natives the powers entrusted to them as deputy commissioners in protectorates. Even if it were necessary to authorize them to inflict capital punishment in clear and flagrant cases, it would be better to do so than that the whole population of a village should be exposed to indiscriminate bombardment. No doubt there are cases in which punishment of the village is needed, there are others in which it is the only practicable measure; but if only for the sake of the Europeans who live isolated among the natives, it is assuredly wiser to enlist as a general rule the interests of a tribe in surrendering a criminal than to make it a matter of indifference whether or not he is concealed or his escape connived at.

§ 105. The conditions of marriage in protectorates and barbarous countries differ in no essential point from those which have been already considered in treating of marriage in civilized foreign states.

Marriage in protectorates and barbarous countries.

The Foreign Marriages Act of 1892 provides that besides consuls, high commissioners, residents, and any persons appointed in pursuance of the marriage regulations to act in place of a high commissioner or resident, may receive warrants enabling them to act as marriage officers. There are thus no protectorates or spheres of influence, where the British officials are appointed by the Crown, to which the machinery established by the Act is inapplicable.

In most places it has not been found necessary to vary the usual arrangements, but by the Pacific Order in Council of 1893 a special class of officers has been created. It is provided that the high commissioner for the Western Pacific 'upon receiving a requisition from any minister of religion ordinarily officiating as such, or from the head of the denomination to which such minister belongs, stating that he is a British subject, specifying the religious denomination of such minister and his designation and usual place of residence, together with the place where he officiates, and desiring that he may be registered as a minister for celebrating marriages in the Western Pacific, shall forthwith without fee register the name of such minister with the foregoing particulars in a register book to be kept for that purpose.' It is further provided that within the limits of the Order 'marriages between persons who would if in England be legally competent to contract marriages, and of whom one at least is a British subject, may be celebrated by a minister of religion ordinarily officiating as such if he is a British subject, and if his name, designation and ordinary place of residence, together with the place where he officiates is at the time of the marriage registered in the office of the high commissioner.' There is provision for the registration of marriages, but it is not required that the registers or copies of them shall be sent to a Secretary of State. No power is taken in the Order to enable marriages to be performed by any other persons than ministers of religion, and though the Order cannot of course displace the Foreign Marriage Act, so that under it marriage officers of the usual kind can be appointed, the class of persons mentioned are evidently alone intended to be entrusted with the celebration of marriages. This in the circumstances is very likely a matter of necessity; in any case missionaries are often the only fit persons, and must everywhere be the fittest and most responsible persons in the outlying protectorates and the independent islands of the Pacific. It is a matter for some surprise that like arrangements have not been made for supplying the marriage wants of the remoter parts of protectorates elsewhere, since there must always be a possibility that a minister of religion not in episcopal orders may be found in places far away from the station of a clergyman of the Church of England or of a priest of the Church of Rome.

Upon the language of the Act it would not seem that administrators and other officials appointed by chartered companies are capable of being authorized to act as marriage officers. In territories therefore which are administered through such companies, and in barbarous places which do not fall within the scope of the Pacific Order, British subjects are thrown back exclusively upon such other forms of marriage as may be open to them in the local circumstances. In places also, it is to be remembered, where consular marriages or marriages under the Pacific Order can take place, a valid contract can always be effected under a sufficient local law, if such a law exists, or under the common law of England.

Marriages per verba de praesenti and by local forms.

As the form of a marriage contract is unessential the possibility of marriages being entered into by performance of a local rite must unquestionably be admitted; but that the voluntary union for life of one man and one woman to the exclusion of all others, would be so accomplished by any such rite as to satisfy the requirements of English law is in the highest degree unlikely. If, as would usually at least be the case, the local customs were polygamous, a marriage celebrated in native form would be inevitably void. It has already been seen that polygamous marriage is wholly rejected by English law[1]. Even if the local

---

[1] § 89. What is above said does not apply to members of polygamous communities belonging to British territories where polygamous marriages are good by the local British law. Any difficulties in contracting a legal marriage which they might meet with would be of a different kind.

customs were professedly monogamous the effect of concubinage would probably have to be considered. Where one wife only is permitted, but concubines can be taken, who enter the man's house with recognized ceremonies, and who, as well as their children, have ascertained rights, the system under which the wife is married is in effect polygamous. It must again be doubtful how far a union would be regarded as permanent in the sense needed in English law which could, for example, be dissolved at the will of the husband on paying a given amount to the wife or her relations.

That marriages entered into *per verba de praesenti* before a clergyman in episcopal orders in any territories of the kinds under consideration would be good in the British dominions, it is hardly necessary to repeat[1]; and except perhaps in organized Mohammedan states of the type of Zanzibar and Brunei there can be no doubt of their local validity, if local validity be a matter of any importance whatever. Whether marriages *per verba de praesenti* made through the performance of a ceremony by a minister not in episcopal orders, or through a simple exchange of declarations in the presence of witnesses, are valid or invalid must necessarily depend, as previously stated, upon the views which ultimately prevail upon the question in the English courts[2].

[1] § 87. [2] See § 88.

CHAPTER IV.

JURISDICTION ON THE HIGH SEAS AND IN RESPECT OF ACTS DONE THERE.

§ 106. THE high seas are the last region in which it is open to Great Britain to exercise more or less of jurisdiction. That which she has upon them, or in respect of acts done upon them, is based upon somewhat varied grounds, and falls under different heads. No principles however are involved differing from those to which reference has already been made. The case is simply one of application to the particular circumstances [1].

PART III. CHAP. 4.

Jurisdiction on the high seas over

British jurisdiction is naturally felt in its largest extension by British subjects sailing in British vessels. On board such vessels no competing law is possible. Whether they are commissioned vessels of the state, or whether they are in the less intimate relation to it of merchant ships, they are entirely covered by the national sovereignty in places where no equal or superior sovereignty exists. British subjects therefore are solely governed on board British ships by whatever law is able to accompany them

British subjects in British vessels.

---

[1] A great portion of the subjects which might naturally be discussed at large in the following chapter is sufficiently treated in works so universally known as Russell on Crimes and Stephen's History of the Criminal Law of England. I feel therefore that it is only necessary to offer a very general view both of the facts and of their relation to the principles which have already been stated, or which at least have underlain much that has been said in the earlier parts of the present work.

on leaving the shores of the British dominions. With regard to the nature and extent of this law, it is enough to repeat that the common law of England reigns in so far as the ordinary statute law does not operate outside the United Kingdom, or in so far as special laws such as the Merchant Shipping Acts or the Slave Trade Acts fail to reach; and to point out that since the laws enacted by the governments of India and the Colonies take effect only within the territories which they are expressly made to touch, an Indian or Colonial subject of the Crown on embarking in a British ship, leaves behind him all laws under which he was locally placed that are not identical with the law of England.

The fact that a person remains subject to English law is of course wholly independent of the question whether a particular court is competent to deal with his acts. Apart from special legislation or from authorization given under the general powers of the Foreign Jurisdiction Acts, a British Court established in an Eastern state or in a foreign state of European civilization can only take cognizance of acts done within the territory or territorial waters of the state in question. Acts done upon the High Seas must be brought before a court sitting within the British dominions. The Merchant Shipping Acts confer jurisdiction upon the naval courts in respect of certain minor offences, and in China and Japan special authority is given by the Order in Council to the local British courts to take cognizance of crimes or offences committed by a British subject within a British vessel at a distance of not more than a hundred miles from the shores of those countries[1]. As a general rule, however, persons accused of offences of a grave nature must be sent for trial to the United Kingdom or to a British possession.

[1] Arts. 101–5. Power is also given to take cognizance of crimes or offences so committed by a British subject within a Chinese or Japanese vessel, or a vessel not lawfully entitled to claim the protection of the flag of any state.

IN RESPECT OF ACTS DONE THERE.   241

Foreigners in a British ship when on the high seas find themselves in the same legal position as they occupy within British territory. Children born to them are British subjects; if they wish to perform a civil act which shall be valid in the British dominions, and in some cases if they desire that it shall be valid in their own country, they must comply with the forms of English law; and if they commit crimes or misdemeanours they are justiciable by the English Courts[1].

PART III.
CHAP. 4.

Foreigners in British vessels.

In the case of British subjects on board foreign ships jurisdiction primarily belongs to the country of which the vessel carries the flag; and as a general rule Great Britain makes no attempt to exercise jurisdiction concurrently. By exception however a British subject who commits an offence on board a foreign ship of the crew of which he does not form a part can be tried in any British court which would have cognizance of the offence if it were committed on board a British ship within the jurisdiction of the court[2],

British subjects in respect of acts done on foreign vessels.

[1] Merchant Shipping Act, 18 & 19 Vict. cap. 91, sect. 21 (1855).
The term 'British seaman' in the Merchant Shipping Act of 1854 (Sect. 267) 'may mean one who, whatever his nationality, is serving on board a British ship.' Mr. Justice Blackburn in R. v. Anderson, L. R. 1 C. C. R. 162.
For jurisdictional purposes it is immaterial whether a foreigner is on board a British vessel voluntarily or without his own consent. He is in either case equally amenable to the British Courts if he commits a crime, except perhaps if, not being in lawful custody, he does an act which would otherwise be criminal with the object of effecting his escape. Reg. v. Lopez, Dearsley and Bell, 525.
It is to be remembered that, except to the extent of the competence of Naval Courts, misdemeanour and crimes committed by foreigners on board British ships can only be tried by those British Courts which sit in British territory, or in protectorates where jurisdiction over foreigners has been assumed. In Oriental states where Great Britain has extra-territorial jurisdiction, and in protectorates of the earlier type, no power of trying foreign subjects exists.
On concurrent jurisdiction of the Courts of the state to which the criminal belongs, see p. 81, note 2.
[2] Merchant Shipping Acts, 18 & 19 Vict. cap. 91, sect. 21 (1855); and 30 & 31 Vict. cap. 124, sect. 11 (1867).
There are weighty practical objections which militate against the

R

PART III. and even if he be a member of the crew of the foreign vessel
CHAP. 4. he can be tried for treason or misprision of treason.

Regulation of fisheries.
§ 107. A certain amount of regulatory jurisdiction affecting waters outside territorial limits is exercised by Great Britain through Imperial or Colonial legislation with the object of controlling industries connected with the products of the sea. Of this kind are the Sea Fisheries Act of 1868, the Herring Fishery (Scotland) Act of 1889, and the Canadian Fisheries Statute, of the Dominion Parliament, of 1886. The last of these asserts jurisdiction on the high seas over Canadian subjects alone; the two former contemplate the possibility of bye laws being enforced upon foreigners as well

assumption of jurisdiction over British sailors serving on board foreign ships, and it is very certain that it would be unwise to take power to try them for offences committed on the high seas except under reciprocal agreements with foreign powers, the scope of which should be confined within jealously guarded limits. At the same time occurrences sometimes happen which cause legitimate regret that it is not possible to keep a jurisdiction in reserve by which flagrant crime could be prevented from going wholly unpunished. A few years ago a couple of Englishmen, part of the crew of a German ship, committed murder on the high seas. The vessel put into Table Bay, where for some reason which is not apparent the men were landed or allowed to go on shore. When application for them was made to the Colonial authorities, the latter were unable either to try the men or to detain them for extradition. Again, in the course of a mutiny on board an Uruguayan vessel, some Englishmen murdered a Russian. The ship was ultimately brought into a French port. The French courts had no jurisdiction, because the crime was committed by foreigners on board a foreign ship; the English courts had no jurisdiction, because the British criminals belonged to the ship's crew; the Uruguayan government took no steps; and the men escaped all punishment. In principle Great Britain is not opposed to the exercise of jurisdiction (comp. p. 81. note 2). It is to be wished that arrangements could at least be made under which the courts should be allowed to take cognizance of grave offences upon request to that effect being made by the consul of the state on a vessel belonging to which the offence had been committed; and it would be of great advantage that the case of a British subject, member of the crew of a foreign ship, who commits a crime on board that ship, and afterwards escapes into British territory, should be excepted from the operation of the provisions for the non-surrender of nationals which occur in nearly all the extradition treaties concluded between Great Britain and other powers.

as upon British subjects in non-territorial waters, but the powers taken with this object were intended only to meet the case of a fishery treaty by which the subjects both of Great Britain and of the other contracting state would be placed under regulations in common, and as a matter of fact no bye laws affecting foreigners have been made. Save in so very exceptional a case as that mentioned below, Great Britain neither has the right, nor does she attempt, to exercise jurisdiction over foreigners on the high seas in respect of fisheries, apart from international agreement. To support jurisdiction there must be sovereignty over place or person, or there must be consent, or finally the urgency of necessity [1].

PART III.
CHAP. 4.

§ 108. To another form of jurisdiction, resting on a totally different basis, foreigners by the terms of the law are equally subordinated on the high seas with subjects of Great Britain. It is provided by statute that 'the master of every ship required to have a manifest on board shall produce such manifest to any officer of the customs who shall come on board his ship after her arrival within four leagues of the coast of the United Kingdom or of the coast of the Isle of Man, and who shall demand the same for his inspection.' A copy of the manifest is to be given if demanded; and a penalty of £100 is imposed for non-production of the

Protective Jurisdiction for revenue purposes.

[1] 31 & 32 Vict. c. 45 ; 52 & 53 Vict. c. 23 ; Revised Statutes of Canada, c. 95, sects. 6 & 7.
There is one exceptional instance in which it would seem that jurisdiction over fisheries outside territorial limits is enforced upon foreigners. The pearl fisheries of Ceylon, which extend to a distance of twenty miles from land, have been the subject of a series of ordinances and regulations affecting all persons whether British subjects or not. The circumstances however are peculiar. 'The claim of Ceylon is not to an exceptional extent of water forming part of the high seas as incidental to the territorial sovereignty of the island, but is a claim to the products of certain submerged portions of land which have been treated from time immemorial by the successive rulers of the island as subjects of property and jurisdiction.' Behring Sea Arbitration ; Counter Case of Her Majesty's Government ; Parl. Papers, United States, No. 3, 1893, p. 93.

original or for non-delivery of the copy. Foreign vessels not being square rigged, on board of which there are subjects of the Queen, may be forfeited if found with spirits on board within four leagues of the shores of the United Kingdom; and within a hundred leagues the act of shooting maliciously at a vessel or boat belonging to the British navy or in the revenue service is punishable by penal servitude for life[1]. The jurisdiction thus taken is however uncontentious. Whether the law represents a custom or a pretention, foreign nations, in so far as they are practically affected by it, have conceded to it their acquiescence. The powers taken are not put forward as a right; they merely formulate consent. Against a state which resisted their exercise they would not be maintained. But in their present shape, used with moderation, they repose on an agreement which though tacit is universal. No civilized country encourages offences against the laws of a foreign state when it sees that the laws are just and necessary; and the justice and necessity of taking precautionary measures outside territorial waters, in order that infractions of revenue laws shall not occur upon the territory itself, is in principle uncontested. Under the Acts in question therefore no right to action is taken by Great Britain in the high seas, and no right to jurisdiction is assumed over subjects of foreign powers, apart from the acquiescence of the foreign state to which they belong[2].

[1] 8 & 9 Vict. c. 86. 9 Geo. II. c. 35, was to similar effect. The provision of the Act with reference to malicious shooting &c. would no doubt not apply to a foreigner on board a foreign vessel. Comp. § 109.

[2] Comp. Wheaton, Elements of International Law, ed. by Dana, § 179, note 108.

In Le Louis (ii Dodson 245) Lord Stowell said, 'maritime states have claimed a right of visitation and enquiry within those parts of the ocean adjoining to their shores which the common courtesy of nations has for their common convenience allowed to be considered as parts of their dominions for various domestic purposes, and particularly for fiscal or defensive regulations more immediately affecting their safety and welfare.

In a more limited degree the Quarantine Act[1] sanctions the exercise of like powers. It does not confer jurisdiction over persons or vessels upon the high seas, but it asserts jurisdiction in respect of acts done on the high seas. Certain 'formalities are enjoined on vessels liable to quarantine so soon as they pass within two leagues of the British coasts; but the Act provides no machinery for enforcing these regulations on vessels that do not come within the ordinary limits, or communicate with the shore, and the Privy Council are aware of no instance of any attempt to interfere with any vessel simply passing outside the three mile limit, and in fact such interference would have been, as far as they understand, both unnecessary and illegal[2].' Quarantine laws are possessed by all countries; to such as are of a reasonable nature universal consent is, and always would be, given; and behind universal consent it is unnecessary for practical purposes to go. Were there any reason for doing so, enforcement of the British statute upon foreigners might be amply justified upon two grounds, either of which is independently sufficient. It is admitted as a principle of international law that motives of self-preservation, sufficiently grave and urgent, warrant a nation in overstepping the usual limits of its rights, and in taking exceptional measures for its security. Though the legislation effected by the Quarantine Act is continuing, the occasions on which it is put in force are occasions of emergency when the attack of pestilence is to be fended off, and when in the view of the framers of the statute no measures less general than those prescribed would be adequate for the purposes of defence. If therefore jurisdiction

Such are our hovering laws, which within certain limited distances, more or less moderately assigned, subject foreign vessels to such examination.'
[1] 6 Geo. IV. c. 78 (1825).
[2] Argument of Sir C. Russell before the Tribunal of Arbitration in the matter of the Behring's Sea. Report of the Proceedings, Part v. p. 1106.

were exercised in respect of acts completed on the high seas, but calculated to produce effects upon the territory, its imposition would conflict with no principle governing the relations of states. But the acts which are pointed at by the statute are either not completed upon the high seas or are such as to give rise to an absolute presumption that they are not intended to be completed there. Communication with the territory is of the former kind; of the latter is approach to a port without showing the signals which indicate that the vessel approaching is infected.

Classification of the foregoing instances of jurisdiction.

§ 109. If the foregoing cases in which Great Britain actually exercises, or claims the right to exercise, jurisdiction on the high seas, or with reference to acts done there, be regarded from the point of view of the ground upon which they can be severally supported, they will be found for practical purposes to divide themselves into three classes:—

1. Instances in which jurisdiction is exercised over persons in virtue of their being British subjects.
2. Instances in which jurisdiction is exercised over foreigners in virtue of their association with a British vessel.
3. Instances in which jurisdiction is exercised, or the right to exercise it with or without the consent of foreign states, is claimed over foreigners irrespectively of the national character of the vessel in which they are, on the ground of protective necessity.

The first class calls for no further remark than has already been made. Upon the second it is almost as unnecessary to comment. Although the sovereignty of a state is imperfectly embodied in its merchant ships, there is enough of it to exclude the possibility that any other sovereignty shall make itself felt; and no principle of international law is more universally recognized than that merchant vessels on the high seas are under the administrative, the civil, the criminal, and the protective jurisdiction of the state to which they belong. With regard to the third class, it has been seen that the range is extremely small within which the right to exercise jurisdiction over foreigners is asserted; and that a right of jurisdiction is only asserted at all when reasons of a wholly exceptional character can be assigned in justification. Limited as the range obviously is, there is a rule of English law which reduces its extent within a narrower space than on a cursory reading of the Acts it might seem to cover. It is a presumption of the courts that Parliament is unlikely to intend to legislate for the rights or liabilities of foreigners who are in no way within the jurisdiction of Great Britain, and that to overcome the presumption the words of an Act must be express, or the context exceedingly clear. When therefore 'the language of a statute is general and may include foreigners' so circumstanced 'or not, the true canon of construction is to assume that the legislature has not so enacted as to violate the rights of other nations[1].' Applying this principle to the Act of 8 & 9 Victoria, it becomes evident that the provision, which renders malicious shooting at a vessel belonging to the British navy punishable by penal servitude for life, is not applicable to foreigners on board a foreign ship; and that a foreigner so acting can neither be seized at the moment nor be apprehended and tried under the Act if subsequently found upon British soil or in a British vessel. Every enactment, consequently, or provision in an enactment, which affects persons upon the high seas with liabilities must be carefully scanned before it is applied to foreign subjects who are not already within the jurisdiction of Great Britain.

---

[1] Chief Justice Cockburn in R. v. Keyn, ii. L. R. Ex. Div. 63.

APPENDIX I

THE NATURALIZATION ACT, 1870.

33 Vict. c. 14.

Whereas it is expedient to amend the law relating to the legal condition of aliens and British subjects:

Be it enacted by the Queen's most Excellent Majesty, by and with the advice and consent of the Lords Spiritual and Temporal, and Commons, in this present Parliament assembled, and by the authority of the same, as follows:

1. This Act may be cited for all purposes as 'The Naturalization Act, 1870.' {Short title.}

Status of Aliens in the United Kingdom.

2. Real and personal property of every description may be taken, acquired, held, and disposed of by an alien in the same manner in all respects as by a natural-born British subject; and a title to real and personal property of every description may be derived through, from, or in succession to an alien, in the same manner in all respects as through, from, or in succession to a natural-born British subject: Provided,— {Capacity of an alien as to property.}

> (1) That this section shall not confer any right on an alien to hold real property situate out of the United Kingdom, and shall not qualify an alien for any office or for any municipal, parliamentary, or other franchise:

(2) That this section shall not entitle an alien to any right or privilege as a British subject, except such rights and privileges in respect of property as are hereby expressly given to him:

(3) That this section shall not affect any estate or interest in real or personal property to which any person has or may become entitled, either mediately or immediately, in possession or expectancy, in pursuance of any disposition made before the passing of this Act, or in pursuance of any devolution by law on the death of any person dying before the passing of this Act.

Power of naturalized aliens to divest themselves of their status in certain cases.

3. Where Her Majesty has entered into a convention with any foreign state to the effect that the subjects or citizens of that state who have been naturalized as British subjects may divest themselves of their status as such subjects, it shall be lawful for Her Majesty, by Order in Council, to declare that such convention has been entered into by Her Majesty; and from and after the date of such Order in Council, any person being originally a subject or citizen of the state referred to in such Order, who has been naturalized as a British subject, may, within such limit of time as may be provided in the convention, make a declaration of alienage, and from and after the date of his so making such declaration such person shall be regarded as an alien, and as a subject of the state to which he originally belonged as aforesaid.

A declaration of alienage may be made as follows; that is to say,—If the declarant be in the United Kingdom in the presence of any justice of the peace, if elsewhere in Her Majesty's dominions in the presence of any judge of any court of civil or criminal jurisdiction, of any justice of the peace, or of any other officer for the time being authorized by law in the place in which the declarant is to administer an oath for any judicial or other legal purpose. If out of Her Majesty's dominions in the presence of any officer in the diplomatic or consular service of Her Majesty.

4. Any person who by reason of his having been born within the dominions of Her Majesty is a natural-born subject, but who also at the time of his birth became under the law of any foreign state a subject of such state, and is still such subject, may, if of full age and not under any disability, make a declaration of alienage in manner aforesaid, and from and after the making of such declaration of alienage such person shall cease to be a British subject. Any person who is born out of Her Majesty's dominions of a father being a British subject may, if of full age, and not under any disability, make a declaration of alienage in manner aforesaid, and from and after the making of such declaration shall cease to be a British subject. How British-born subjects may cease to be such.

5. From and after the passing of this Act, an alien shall not be entitled to be tried by a jury *de medietate linguæ*, but shall be triable in the same manner as if he were a natural-born subject. Alien not entitled to jury *de medietate linguæ*.

Expatriation.

6. Any British subject who has at any time before, or may at any time after the passing of this Act, when in any foreign state and not under any disability voluntarily become naturalized in such state, shall, from and after the time of his so having become naturalized in such foreign state, be deemed to have ceased to be a British subject and be regarded as an alien: Provided,— Capacity of British subject to renounce allegiance to Her Majesty.

> (1) That where any British subject has before the passing of this Act voluntarily become naturalized in a foreign state and yet is desirous of remaining a British subject, he may, at any time within two years after the passing of this Act, make a declaration that he is desirous of remaining a British subject, and upon such declaration herein-after referred to as a declaration of British nationality being made, and upon his taking the oath of allegiance, the declarant shall be deemed to be and to have been continually

a British subject; with this qualification, that he shall not, when within the limits of the foreign state in which he has been naturalized, be deemed to be a British subject unless he has ceased to be a subject of that state in pursuance of the laws thereof, or in pursuance of a treaty to that effect:

(2) A declaration of British nationality may be made, and the oath of allegiance be taken as follows; that is to say,—if the declarant be in the United Kingdom in the presence of a justice of the peace; if elsewhere in Her Majesty's dominions in the presence of any judge of any court of civil or criminal jurisdiction, of any justice of the peace, or of any other officer for the time being authorized by law in the place in which the declarant is to administer an oath for any judicial or other legal purpose. If out of Her Majesty's dominions in the presence of any officer in the diplomatic or consular service of Her Majesty.

Naturalization and resumption of British Nationality.

Certificate of naturalization.

7. An alien who within such limited time before making the application herein-after mentioned as may be allowed by one of Her Majesty's Principal Secretaries of State, either by general order or on any special occasion, has resided in the United Kingdom for a term of not less than five years, or has been in the service of the Crown for a term of not less than five years, and intends, when naturalized, either to reside in the United Kingdom, or to serve under the Crown, may apply to one of Her Majesty's Principal Secretaries of State for a certificate of naturalization.

The applicant shall adduce in support of his application such evidence of his residence or service, and intention to reside or serve, as such Secretary of State may require. The said Secretary of State, if satisfied with the evidence adduced, shall take the case of the applicant into consideration, and may, with or without assigning any reason, give or withhold a certificate as he thinks most conducive to the public good, and no appeal shall lie from his decision, but such certificate shall not take effect until the applicant has taken the oath of allegiance.

<small>APPENDIX I.</small>

An alien to whom a certificate of naturalization is granted shall in the United Kingdom be entitled to all political and other rights, powers, and privileges, and be subject to all obligations, to which a natural-born British subject is entitled or subject in the United Kingdom, with this qualification, that he shall not, when within the limits of the foreign state of which he was a subject previously to obtaining his certificate of naturalization, be deemed to be a British subject unless he has ceased to be a subject of that state in pursuance of the laws thereof, or in pursuance of a treaty to that effect.

The said Secretary of State may in manner aforesaid grant a special certificate of naturalization to any person with respect to whose nationality as a British subject a doubt exists, and he may specify in such certificate that the grant thereof is made for the purpose of quieting doubts as to the right of such person to be a British subject, and the grant of such special certificate shall not be deemed to be any admission that the person to whom it was granted was not previously a British subject.

An alien who has been naturalized previously to the passing of this Act may apply to the Secretary of State for a certificate of naturalization under this Act, and it shall be lawful for the said Secretary of State to grant such certificate to such naturalized alien upon the same terms and subject to the same conditions in and upon which such certificate might have been granted if such alien had not been previously naturalized in the United Kingdom.

8. A natural-born British subject who has become an alien in pursuance of this Act, and is in this Act referred to as a statutory alien, may, on performing the same conditions and adducing the same evidence as is required in the case of an alien applying for a certificate of nationality, apply to one

<small>Certificate of re-admission to British nationality.</small>

APPENDIX I.

of Her Majesty's Principal Secretaries of State for a certificate, herein-after referred to as a certificate of re-admission to British nationality, re-admitting him to the status of a British subject. The said Secretary of State shall have the same discretion as to the giving or withholding of the certificate as in the case of a certificate of naturalization, and an oath of allegiance shall in like manner be required previously to the issuing of the certificate.

A statutory alien to whom a certificate of re-admission to British nationality has been granted shall, from the date of the certificate of re-admission, but not in respect of any previous transaction, resume his position as a British subject; with this qualification, that within the limits of the foreign state of which he became a subject he shall not be deemed to be a British subject unless he has ceased to be a subject of that foreign state according to the laws thereof, or in pursuance of a treaty to that effect.

The jurisdiction by this Act conferred on the Secretary of State in the United Kingdom in respect of the grant of a certificate of re-admission to British nationality, in the case of any statutory alien being in any British possession, may be exercised by the governor of such possession; and residence in such possession shall, in the case of such person, be deemed equivalent to residence in the United Kingdom.

Form of oath of allegiance.

9. The oath in this Act referred to as the oath of allegiance shall be in the form following; that is to say,

'I   do swear that I will be faithful and bear true allegiance to Her Majesty Queen Victoria, her heirs and successors, according to Law. So help me GOD.'

National status of married women and infant children.

National status of married women and infant children.

10. The following enactments shall be made with respect to the national status of women and children:

(1) A married woman shall be deemed to be a subject of the state of which her husband is for the time being a subject:

(2) A widow being a natural-born British subject, who has become an alien by or in consequence of her marriage, shall be deemed to be a statutory alien, and may as such at any time during widowhood obtain a certificate of re-admission to British nationality in manner provided by this Act:

(3) Where the father being a British subject, or the mother being a British subject and a widow, becomes an alien in pursuance of this Act, every child of such father or mother who during infancy has become resident in the country where the father or mother is naturalized, and has, according to the laws of such country, become naturalized therein, shall be deemed to be a subject of the state of which the father or mother has become a subject, and not a British subject:

(4) Where the father, or the mother being a widow, has obtained a certificate of re-admission to British nationality, every child of such father or mother who during infancy has become resident in the British dominions with such father or mother, shall be deemed to have resumed the position of a British subject to all intents:

(5) Where the father, or the mother being a widow, has obtained a certificate of naturalization in the United Kingdom, every child of such father or mother who during infancy has become resident with such father or mother in any part of the United Kingdom, shall be deemed to be a naturalized British subject.

Supplemental Provisions.

11. One of Her Majesty's Principal Secretaries of State may by regulation provide for the following matters:— *Regulations as to registration.*

(1) The form and registration of declarations of British nationality:

APPENDIX I.

(2) The form and registration of certificates of naturalization in the United Kingdom:

(3) The form and registration of certificates of re-admission to British nationality:

(4) The form and registration of declarations of alienage:

(5) The registration by officers in the diplomatic or consular service of Her Majesty of the births and deaths of British subjects who may be born or die out of Her Majesty's dominions, and of the marriages of persons married at any of Her Majesty's embassies or legations:

(6) The transmission to the United Kingdom for the purpose of registration or safe keeping, or of being produced as evidence, of any declarations or certificates made in pursuance of this Act out of the United Kingdom, or of any copies of such declarations or certificates, also of copies of entries contained in any register kept out of the United Kingdom in pursuance of or for the purpose of carrying into effect the provisions of this Act.

(7) With the consent of the Treasury the imposition and application of fees in respect of any registration authorized to be made by this Act, and in respect of the making any declaration or the grant of any certificate authorized to be made or granted by this Act.

The said Secretary of State, by a further regulation, may repeal, alter, or add to any regulation previously made by him in pursuance of this section.

Any regulation made by the said Secretary of State in pursuance of this section shall be deemed to be within the powers conferred by this Act, and shall be of the same force as if it had been enacted in this Act, but shall not so far as respects the imposition of fees be in force in any British possession, and shall not, so far as respects any other matter, be in force in any British possession in which any Act or ordinance to the contrary of or inconsistent with any such direction may for the time being be in force.

Appendix I.

12. The following regulations shall be made with respect to evidence under this Act:—

Regulations as to evidence.

(1) Any declaration authorized to be made under this Act may be proved in any legal proceeding by the production of the original declaration, or of any copy thereof certified to be a true copy by one of Her Majesty's Principal Secretaries of State, or by any person authorized by regulations of one of Her Majesty's Principal Secretaries of State to give certified copies of such declaration, and the production of such declaration or copy shall be evidence of the person therein named as declarant having made the same at the date in the said declaration mentioned:

(2) A certificate of naturalization may be proved in any legal proceeding by the production of the original certificate, or of any copy thereof certified to be a true copy by one of Her Majesty's Principal Secretaries of State, or by any person authorized by regulations of one of Her Majesty's Principal Secretaries of State to give certified copies of such certificate:

(3) A certificate of re-admission to British nationality may be proved in any legal proceeding by the production of the original certificate, or of any copy thereof certified to be a true copy by one of Her Majesty's Principal Secretaries of State, or by any person authorized by regulations of one of Her Majesty's Principal Secretaries of State to give certified copies of such certificate.

(4) Entries in any register authorized to be made in pursuance of this Act shall be proved by such copies and certified in such manner as may be directed by one of Her Majesty's Principal Secretaries of State, and the copies of such entries shall be evidence of

any matters by this Act or by any regulation of the said Secretary of State authorized to be inserted in the register:

(5) The Documentary Evidence Act, 1868, shall apply to any regulation made by a Secretary of State, in pursuance of or for the purpose of carrying into effect any of the provisions of this Act.

Miscellaneous.

Saving of letters of denization.

13. Nothing in this Act contained shall affect the grant of letters of denization by Her Majesty.

Saving as to British ships.

14. Nothing in this Act contained shall qualify an alien to be the owner of a British ship.

Saving of allegiance prior to expiration.

15. Where any British subject has in pursuance of this Act become an alien, he shall not thereby be discharged from any liability in respect of any acts done before the date of his so becoming an alien.

Power of colonies to legislate with respect to naturalization.

16. All laws, statutes, and ordinances which may be duly made by the legislature of any British possession for imparting to any person the privileges, or any of the privileges, of naturalization, to be enjoyed by such person within the limits of such possession, shall within such limits have the authority of law, but shall be subject to be confirmed or disallowed by Her Majesty in the same manner, and subject to the same rules in and subject to which Her Majesty has power to confirm or disallow any other laws, statutes, or ordinances in that possession.

Definition of terms.

17. In this Act, if not inconsistent with the context or subject-matter thereof,—

'Disability' shall mean the status of being an infant, lunatic, idiot, or married woman:

'British possession' shall mean any colony, plantation, island, territory, or settlement within Her Majesty's dominions, and not within the United Kingdom, and all territories and places under one legislature are deemed to be one British possession for the purposes of this Act:

'The Governor of any British possession' shall include any person exercising the chief authority in such possession:

'Officer in the Diplomatic Service of Her Majesty' shall mean any Ambassador, Minister or Chargé d'Affaires, or Secretary of Legation, or any person appointed by such Ambassador, Minister, Chargé d'Affaires, or Secretary of Legation to execute any duties imposed by this Act on an officer in the Diplomatic Service of Her Majesty:

'Officer in the Consular Service of Her Majesty' shall mean and include Consul-General, Consul, Vice-Consul, and Consular Agent, and any person for the time being discharging the duties of Consul-General, Consul, Vice-Consul, and Consular Agent.

Repeal of Acts mentioned in Schedule.

18. The several Acts set forth in the first and second parts of the schedule annexed hereto shall be wholly repealed, and the Acts set forth in the third part of the said schedule shall be repealed to the extent therein mentioned; provided that the repeal enacted in this Act shall not affect—

(1) Any right acquired or thing done before the passing of this Act:

(2) Any liability accruing before the passing of this Act:

(3) Any penalty, forfeiture, or other punishment incurred or to be incurred in respect of any offence committed before the passing of this Act:

(4) The institution of any investigation or legal proceeding or any other remedy for ascertaining or enforcing any such liability, penalty, forfeiture, or punishment as aforesaid.

SCHEDULE.

APPENDIX I.

NOTE.—Reference is made to the repeal of the 'whole Act' where portions have been repealed before, in order to preclude henceforth the necessity of looking back to previous Acts.

This Schedule, so far as respects Acts prior to the reign of George the Second, other than Acts of the Irish Parliament, refers to the edition prepared under the direction of the Record Commission, intituled 'The Statutes of the Realm; printed by Command of His Majesty King George the Third, in pursuance of an Address of the House of Commons of Great Britain, from original Records and authentic Manuscripts.'

PART I.

ACTS WHOLLY REPEALED, OTHER THAN ACTS OF THE IRISH PARLIAMENT.

Date.	Title.
7 Jas. 1. c. 2.	An Act that all such as are to be naturalized or restored in blood shall first receive the sacrament of the Lord's Supper, and the oath of allegiance, and the oath of supremacy.
11 Will. 3. c. 6 [1].	An Act to enable His Majesty's natural-born subjects to inherit the estate of their ancestors, either lineal or collateral, notwithstanding their father or mother were aliens.
13 Geo. 2. c. 7.	An Act for naturalizing such foreign Protestants and others therein mentioned, as are settled or shall settle in any of His Majesty's colonies in America.

---

[1] 11 & 12 Wm. 3. (Ruff.)

Date.	Title.
20 Geo. 2. c. 44.	An Act to extend the provisions of an Act made in the thirteenth year of His present Majesty's reign, intituled 'An Act for naturalizing foreign Protestants and others therein mentioned, as are settled or shall settle in any of His Majesty's colonies in America,' to other foreign Protestants who conscientiously scruple the taking of an oath.
13 Geo. 3. c. 25.	An Act to explain two Acts of Parliament, one of the thirteenth year of the reign of His late Majesty, 'for naturalizing such foreign Protestants and others, as are settled or shall settle in any of His Majesty's colonies in America,' and the other of the second year of the reign of His present Majesty, 'for naturalizing such foreign Protestants as have served or shall serve as officers or soldiers in His Majesty's Royal American regiment, or as engineers in America.'
14 Geo. 3. c. 84.	An Act to prevent certain inconveniences that may happen by bills of naturalization.
16 Geo. 3. c. 52.	An Act to declare His Majesty's natural-born subjects inheritable to the estates of their ancestors, whether lineal or collateral, in that part of Great Britain called Scotland, notwithstanding their father or mother were aliens.
6 Geo. 4. c. 67.	An Act to alter and amend an Act passed in the seventh year of the reign of His Majesty King James the First, intituled 'An Act that all such as are to be naturalized or restored in blood shall first receive the sacrament of the Lord's Supper and the oath of allegiance and the oath of supremacy.'
7 & 8 Vict. c. 66.	An Act to amend the laws relating to aliens.
10 & 11 Vict. c. 83.	An Act for the naturalization of aliens.

PART II.

ACTS OF THE IRISH PARLIAMENT WHOLLY REPEALED.

Date.	Title.
14 & 15 Chas. 2. c. 13.	An Act for encouraging Protestant strangers and others to inhabit and plant in the kingdom of Ireland.
2 Anne, c. 14.	An Act for naturalizing of all Protestant strangers in this kingdom.
19 & 20 Geo. 3. c. 29.	An Act for naturalizing such foreign merchants, traders, artificers, artizans, manufacturers, workmen, seamen, farmers, and others as shall settle in this kingdom.
23 & 24 Geo. 3. c. 38.	An Act for extending the provisions of an Act passed in this kingdom in the nineteenth and twentieth years of His Majesty's reign, intituled 'An Act for naturalizing such foreign merchants, traders, artificers, artizans, manufacturers, workmen, seamen, farmers, and others as shall settle in this kingdom.'
36 Geo. 3. c. 48.	An Act to explain and amend an Act, intituled, 'An Act for naturalizing such foreign merchants, traders, artificers, artizans, manufacturers, workmen, seamen, farmers, and others who shall settle in this kingdom.'

PART III.

ACTS PARTIALLY REPEALED.

		Extent of Repeal.
4 Geo. 1. c. 9. (Act of Irish Parliament.)	An Act for reviving, continuing, and amending several statutes made in this kingdom heretofore temporary.	So far as it makes perpetual the Act of 2 Anne, c. 14.
6 Geo. 4. c. 50.	An Act for consolidating and amending the laws relative to Jurors and Juries.	The whole of sect. 47.
3 & 4 Will. 4. c. 91.	An Act consolidating and amending the laws relating to Jurors and Juries in Ireland.	The whole of sect. 37.

APPENDIX II.

THE FOREIGN MARRIAGE ACT, 1892.
55 & 56 VICT. C. 23.

BE it enacted by the Queen's most Excellent Majesty, by and with the advice and consent of the Lords Spiritual and Temporal, and Commons, in this present Parliament assembled, and by the authority of the same, as follows: *[Appendix II.]*

1. All marriages between parties of whom one at least is a British subject solemnized in the manner in this Act provided in any foreign country or place by or before a marriage officer within the meaning of this Act shall be as valid in law as if the same had been solemnized in the United Kingdom with a due observance of all forms required by law. *[Validity of marriages solemnized abroad in manner provided by Act.]*

2. In every case of a marriage intended to be solemnized under this Act, one of the parties intending marriage shall sign a notice, stating the name, surname, profession, condition, and residence of each of the parties, and whether each of the parties is or is not a minor, and give the notice to the marriage officer within whose district both of the parties have had their residence not less than one week then next preceding, and the notice shall state that they have so resided. *[Notice to marriage officer of intended marriage.]*

3.—(1) The marrriage officer shall file every such notice, and keep it with the archives of his office, and shall also, on payment of the proper fee, forthwith enter in a book of notices to be kept by him for the purpose, and post up in some conspicuous place in his office, a true copy of every such notice, and shall keep the same so posted up during fourteen consecutive days before the marriage is solemnized under the notice. *[Filling in registry and posting up of notice.]*

<small>APPENDIX II.</small>

(2) The said book and copy posted up shall be open at all reasonable times, without fee, to the inspection of any person.

<small>Requirement of like consent to marriage as in England, and power to forbid marriage.</small>

4.—(1) The like consent shall be required to a marriage under this Act as is required by law to marriages solemnized in England.

(2) Every person whose consent to a marriage is so required may, at any time before the solemnization thereof under this Act, forbid it by writing the word 'forbidden' opposite to the entry of the intended marriage in the book of notices, and by subscribing thereto his name and residence, and the character by reason of which he is authorized to forbid the marriage; and if a marriage is so forbidden the notice shall be void, and the intended marriage shall not be solemnized under that notice.

<small>Caveat against marriages may be lodged with marriage officer.</small>

5.—(1) Any person may on payment of the proper fee enter with the marriage officer a caveat, signed by him or on his behalf, and stating his residence and the ground of his objection against the solemnization of the marriage of any person named therein, and thereupon the marriage of that person shall not be solemnized until either the marriage officer has examined into the matter of the caveat and is satisfied that it ought not to obstruct the solemnization of the marriage, or the caveat is withdrawn by the person entering it.

(2) In a case of doubt the marriage officer may transmit a copy of the caveat, with such statement respecting it as he thinks fit, to a Secretary of State, who shall refer the same to the Registrar-General, and the Registrar-General shall give his decision thereon in writing to the Secretary of State, who shall communicate it to the marriage officer.

(3) If the marriage officer refuses to solemnize or to allow to be solemnized in his presence the marriage of any person requiring it to be solemnized, that person may appeal to a Secretary of State, who shall give the marriage officer his decision thereon.

(4) The marriage officer shall forthwith inform the parties of, and shall conform to, any decision given by the Registrar-General or Secretary of State.

6. Where a marriage is not solemnized within three months next after the latest of the following dates:—

(a) the date on which the notice for it has been given to and entered by the marriage officer under this Act, or,

(b) if on a caveat being entered a statement has been transmitted to a Secretary of State, or if an appeal has been made to a Secretary of State, then the date of the receipt from the Secretary of State of a decision directing the marriage to be solemnized,

the notice shall be void, and the intended marriage shall not be solemnized under that notice.

7. Before a marriage is solemnized under this Act, each of the parties intending marriage shall appear before the marriage officer, and make, and subscribe in a book kept by the officer for the purpose, an oath—

(a) that he or she believes that there is not any impediment to the marriage by reason of kindred or alliance, or otherwise; and

(b) that both of the parties have for three weeks immediately preceding had their usual residence within the district of the marriage officer; and

(c) where either of the parties, not being a widower or widow, is under the age of twenty-one years, that the consent of the persons whose consent to the marriage is required by law has been obtained thereto, or, as the case may be, that there is no person having authority to give such consent.

8.—(1) After the expiration of fourteen days after the notice of an intended marriage has been entered under this Act, then, if no lawful impediment to the marriage is shown to the satisfaction of the marriage officer, and the marriage has not been forbidden in manner provided by this Act, the marriage may be solemnized under this Act.

officer and two witnesses.

(2) Every such marriage shall be solemnized at the *official house* of the marriage officer, with open doors, between the hours of eight in the forenoon and three in the afternoon, in the presence of two or more witnesses, and may be solemnized by another person in the presence of the marriage officer, according to the rites of the Church of England, or such other form and ceremony as the parties thereto see fit to adopt, or may, where the parties so desire, be solemnized by the marriage officer.

(3) Where such marriage is not solemnized according to the rites of the Church of England, then in some part of the ceremony, and in the presence of the marriage officer and witnesses, each of the parties shall declare,

> 'I solemnly declare, that I know not of any lawful impediment why I A. B. [or C. D.] may not be joined in matrimony to C. D. [or A. B.].'

And each of the parties shall say to the other,

> 'I call upon these persons here present to witness, that I A. B. [or C. D.] take thee, C. D. [or A. B.], to be my lawful wedded wife [or husband].'

Marriage fees to marriage officer and registration of marriages.

9.—(1) The marriage officer shall be entitled, for every marriage solemnized under this Act by him or in his presence, to have from the parties married the proper fee.

(2) He shall forthwith register in duplicate every such marriage in two marriage register books, which shall be furnished to him from time to time for that purpose by the Registrar-General (through a Secretary of State), according to the form provided by law for the registration of marriages in England, or as near to that form as the difference of the circumstances admits.

(3) The entry in each book of every such marriage shall be signed by the marriage officer, by the person solemnizing the marriage, if other than the marriage officer, by both the parties married, and by two witnesses of the marriage.

(4) All such entries shall be made in regular order from the beginning to the end of each book, and the number of the entry in each duplicate shall be the same.

(5) The marriage officer by whom or in whose presence a marriage is solemnized under this Act may ask of the parties to be married the several particulars required to be registered touching the marriage.

10.—(1) In January in every year every marriage officer shall make and send to a Secretary of State, to be transmitted by him to the Registrar-General, a copy, certified by him to be a true copy, of all the entries of marriages during the preceding year in the register book kept by him, and if there has been no such entry, a certificate of that fact; and every such copy shall be certified, and certificate given, under his hand and official seal.

(2) The marriage officer shall keep the duplicate marriage register books safely until they are filled, and then send one of them to a Secretary of State, to be transmitted by him to the Registrar-General.

11.—(1) For the purposes of this Act the following officers shall be marriage officers, that is to say :—

- (*a*) Any officer authorized in that behalf by a Secretary of State by authority in writing under his hand (in this Act referred to as a marriage warrant); and
- (*b*) Any officer who, under the marriage regulations hereinafter mentioned is authorized to act as marriage officer without any marriage warrant,

and the district of a marriage officer shall be the area within which the duties of his office are exerciseable, or any such less area as is assigned by the marriage warrant or any other warrant of a Secretary of State, or is fixed by the marriage regulations.

(2) Any marriage warrant of a Secretary of State may authorize to be a marriage officer—

- (*a*) a British ambassador residing in a foreign country to the government of which he is accredited, and also any officer prescribed as an officer for solemnizing marriages in the official house of such ambassador;

(b) the holder of the office of British consul in any foreign country or place specified in the warrant; and

(c) a governor, high commissioner, resident, consular or other officer, or any person appointed in pursuance of the marriage regulations to act in the place of a high commissioner or resident, and this Act shall apply with the prescribed modifications to a marriage by or before a governor, high commissioner, resident, or officer so authorized by the warrant, and in such application shall not be limited to places outside Her Majesty's dominions.

(3) If a marriage warrant refers to the office without designating the name of any particular person holding the office, then, while the warrant is in force, the person for the time being holding or acting in such office shall be a marriage officer.

(4) A Secretary of State may, by warrant under his hand, vary or revoke any marriage warrant previously issued under this Act.

(5) Where a marriage officer has no seal of his office, any reference in this Act to the official seal shall be construed to refer to any seal ordinarily used by him, if authenticated by his signature with his official name and description.

Marriages on board Her Majesty's ships on foreign stations.

12. A marriage under this Act may be solemnized on board one of Her Majesty's ships on a foreign station, and with respect to such marriage—

(a) subject to the marriage regulations a marriage warrant of a Secretary of State may authorize the commanding officer of the ship to be a marriage officer;

(b) the provisions of this Act shall apply with the prescribed modifications.

Avoidance of objections to marriages

13.—(1) After a marriage has been solemnized under this Act it shall not be necessary, in support of the marriage, to give any proof of the residence for the time required by or in pursuance of this Act of either of the parties previous to the marriage, or of the consent of any person whose consent thereto is required by law, nor shall any evidence to prove the contrary be given in any legal proceeding touching the validity of the marriage.

<small>APPENDIX II. on account of want of formalities or authority of officer.</small>

(2) Where a marriage purports to have been solemnized and registered under this Act in the official house of a British ambassador or consul, or on board one of Her Majesty's ships, it shall not be necessary in support of the marriage, to give any proof of the authority of the marriage officer by or before whom the marriage was solemnized and registered, nor shall any evidence to prove his want of authority, whether by reason of his not being a duly authorized marriage officer or of any prohibitions or restrictions under the marriage regulations or otherwise, be given in any legal proceeding touching the validity of the marriage.

14. If a marriage is solemnized under this Act by means of any wilfully false notice signed, or oath made by either party to the marriage, as to any matter for which a notice, or oath, is by this Act required, the Attorney General may sue for the forfeiture of all estate and interest in any property in England accruing to the offending party by the marriage; and the proceedings thereupon, and the consequences thereof, shall be the same as are provided by law in the like case with regard to marriages solemnized in England according to the rites of the Church of England.

<small>Forfeiture of property in case of fraudulent marriage.</small>

15. If a person—
   (a) knowingly and wilfully makes a false oath or signs a false notice, under this Act, for the purpose of procuring a marriage, or
   (b) forbids a marriage under this Act by falsely representing himself to be a person whose consent to the marriage is required by law, knowing such representation to be false,

<small>Punishment of false oath or notice.</small>

such person shall suffer the penalties of perjury, and may be tried in any county in England and dealt with in the same

Appendix II.

manner in all respects as if the offence had been committed in that county.

Evidence.

16.—(1) Any book, notice, or document directed by this Act to be kept by the marriage officer or in the archives of his office, shall be of such a public nature as to be admissible in evidence on its mere production from the custody of the officer.

(2) A certificate of a Secretary of State as to any house, office, chapel, or other place being, or being part of, the official house of a British ambassador or consul shall be conclusive.

Application of Registration Acts to this Act.

17. All the provisions and penalties of the Marriage Registration Acts, relating to any registrar, or register of marriages or certified copies thereof, shall extend to every marriage officer, and to the registers of marriages under this Act, and to the certified copies thereof (so far as the same are applicable thereto), as if herein re-enacted and in terms made applicable to this Act, and as if every marriage officer were a registrar under the said Acts.

Registration of marriages solemnized under local law.

18. Subject to the marriage regulations, a British consul, or person authorized to act as British consul, on being satisfied by personal attendance that a marriage between parties, of whom one at least is a British subject, has been duly solemnized in a foreign country, in accordance with the local law of the country, and on payment of the proper fee, may register the marriage in accordance with the marriage regulations as having been so solemnized, and thereupon this Act shall apply as if the marriage had been registered in pursuance of this Act, except that nothing in this Act shall affect the validity of the marriage so solemnized.

Power to refuse solemnization of marriage where marriage inconsistent with

19. A marriage officer shall not be required to solemnize a marriage, or·to allow a marriage to be solemnized in his presence, if in his opinion the solemnization thereof would be inconsistent with international law or the comity of nations;

Provided that any person requiring his marriage to be solemnized shall, if the officer refuses to solemnize it or allow it to be solemnized in his presence, have the right of appeal to the Secretary of State given by this Act.

20. The proper fee under this Act shall be such fee as may for the time being be fixed under the Consular Salaries and Fees Act, 1891; and the fee so fixed as respects a consul shall be the fee which may be taken by any marriage officer; and the provisions relating to the levying, application, and remission of and accounting for fees under that Act shall apply to the same when taken by any marriage officer who is not a consul.

international law.

Fees 54 & 55 Vict. c. 36.

21.—(1) Her Majesty the Queen in Council may make regulations (in this Act referred to as the marriage regulations)—

Power to make marriage regulations.

(a) Prohibiting or restricting the exercise by marriage officers of their powers under this Act in cases where the exercise of those powers appears to Her Majesty to be inconsistent with international law or the comity of nations, or in places where sufficient facilities appear to Her Majesty to exist without the exercise of those powers, for the solemnization of marriages to which a British subject is a party; and

(b) Determining what offices, chapels, or other places are, for the purposes of marriages under this Act, to be deemed to be part of the official house or the office of a marriage officer; and

(c) Modifying in special cases or classes of cases the requirements of this Act as to residence and notice, so far as such modification appears to Her Majesty to be consistent with the observance of due precautions against clandestine marriages; and

(d) Prescribing the forms to be used under this Act; and

(e) Adapting this Act to marriages on board one of Her Majesty's ships; and to marriages by or before a governor, high commissioner, resident, or other officer, and authorising the appointment of a person

APPENDIX II.

(*f*) Determining who is to be the marriage officer for the purpose of a marriage in the official house of a British ambassador, or on board one of Her Majesty's ships, whether such officer is described in the regulations or named in pursuance thereof, and authorising such officer to act without any marriage warrant; and

(*g*) Determining the conditions under which and the mode in which marriages solemnized in accordance with the local law of a foreign country may be registered under this Act; and

(*h*) Making such provisions as seem necessary or proper for carrying into effect this Act or any marriage regulations; and

(*i*) Varying or revoking any marriage regulations previously made.

(2) All regulations purporting to be made in pursuance of this section may be made either generally or with reference to any particular case or class of cases, and shall be published under the authority of Her Majesty's Stationery Office, and laid before both Houses of Parliament, and deemed to be within the powers of this Act, and shall while in force have effect as if enacted by this Act.

(3) Any marriage regulations which dispense for any reason, whether residence out of the district or otherwise, with the requirements of this Act as to residence and notice, may require as a condition or consequence of the dispensation, the production of such notice certificate, or document, and the taking of such oath, and may authorise the publication or grant of such notice, certificate, or document, and the charge of such fees as may be prescribed by the regulations; and the provisions of this Act, including those enacting punishments with reference to any false notice or oath, shall apply as if the said notice, certificate, or document were a notice, and such oath were an oath, within the meaning of those provisions.

22. It is hereby declared that all marriages solemnized within the British lines by any chaplain or officer or other person officiating under the orders of the commanding officer of a British army serving abroad, shall be as valid in law as if the same had been solemnized within the United Kingdom, with a due observance of all forms required by law.

Validity of marriages solemnized within British lines.

23. Nothing in this Act shall confirm or impair or in anywise affect the validity in law of any marriage solemnized beyond the seas, otherwise than as herein provided, and this Act shall not extend to the marriage of any of the Royal family.

Saving.

24. In this Act, unless the context otherwise requires,—

Definitions.

The expression 'Registrar-General' means the Registrar-General of Births, Deaths, and Marriages in England:

The expression 'Attorney General' means Her Majesty's Attorney General, or if there is no such Attorney-General, or the Attorney General is unable or incompetent to act, Her Majesty's Solicitor General, for England:

The expression 'the Marriage Registration Acts' means the Act of the session of the sixth and seventh years of the reign of King William the Fourth, chapter eighty-six, intituled 'An Act for registering births, deaths, and marriages in England' and the enactments amending the same:

The expression 'official house of a marriage officer' means, subject to the provisions of any marriage regulations, the office at which the business of such officer is transacted, and the official house of residence of such officer, and, in the case of any officer, who is an officer for solemnizing marriages in the official house of an ambassador, means the official house of the ambassador:

The expression 'consul' means a consul-general, consul, vice-consul, pro-consul, or consular agent:

The expression 'ambassador' includes a minister and a chargé d'affaires:

The expression 'prescribed' means prescribed by marriage regulations under this Act.

T

25. This Act shall come into operation on the first day of January next after the passing thereof.

26.—(1) The Acts specified in the schedule to this Act are hereby repealed to the extent in the third column of that Schedule mentioned.

Provided that—

(a) any Order in Council in force under any Act so repealed shall continue in force as if made in pursuance of this Act; and

(b) any proceedings taken with reference to a marriage, any register book kept, and any warrant issued in pursuance of the Acts hereby repealed, shall have effect as if taken, kept, and issued in pursuance of this Act; and

(c) The fees which can be taken in pursuance of the Acts hereby repealed may continue to be taken in like manner as if fixed in pursuance of the Consular Salaries and Fees Act, 1891, and may be altered accordingly; and

(d) The forms prescribed by or in pursuance of the Acts hereby repealed may continue to be used as if prescribed by an Order in Council under this Act.

(2) Every marriage in fact solemnized and registered by or before a British consul or other marriage officer in intended pursuance of any Act hereby repealed shall, notwithstanding such repeal or any defect in the authority of the consul or the solemnization of the marriage elsewhere than at the consulate, be as valid as if the said Act had not been repealed, and the marriage had been solemnized at the consulate by or before a duly authorised consul;

Provided that this enactment shall not render valid any marriage declared invalid before the passing of this Act by any competent court, or render valid any marriage either of the parties to which has, before the passing of this Act, lawfully intermarried with any other person.

27. This Act may be cited as the Foreign Marriage Act, 1892.

SCHEDULE.

ENACTMENTS REPEALED.

Session and Chapter.	Title.	Extent of Repeal.
4 Geo. 4. c. 91.	An Act to relieve His Majesty's subjects from all doubt concerning the validity of certain marriages solemnized abroad.	The whole Act, so far as unrepealed.
12 & 13 Vict. c. 68.	The Consular Marriage Act, 1849.	The whole Act.
31 & 32 Vict. c. 61.	The Consular Marriage Act, 1868.	The whole Act.
33 & 34 Vict. c. 14.	The Naturalization Act, 1870.	In section eleven, the words, 'and of the marriages of persons married at any of Her Majesty's embassies or legations.'
53 & 54 Vict. c. 47.	The Marriage Act, 1890.	The whole Act.
54 & 55 Vict. c. 74.	The Foreign Marriage Act, 1891.	The whole Act.

APPENDIX II. FOREIGN MARRIAGES ORDER IN COUNCIL, 1892.

WHEREAS, by 'The Foreign Marriage Act, 1892' (in this Order referred to as the Foreign Marriage Act), certain enactments relating to the marriage of British subjects outside the United Kingdom are consolidated, and Her Majesty the Queen in Council is authorized to make Regulations for the purposes therein specified:

Now, therefore, Her Majesty, by virtue and in exercise of the powers conferred by the said Act or otherwise enabling Her in this behalf, is pleased, by and with the advice of Her Privy Council, to order, and it is hereby ordered, as follows:—

Embassy Marriages.

1. The person before and by whom a marriage under the Foreign Marriage Act may be solemnized and registered in an Embassy house in a foreign country shall either be the Ambassador, or the officer for the time being performing the duties of the Ambassador, or be any of the Secretaries attached to the Embassy from time to time appointed for the purpose in writing by the Ambassador or by the officer performing his duties; and for the purpose of marriages solemnized in such Embassy house, such Ambassador, officer performing his duties, or Secretary shall, without any marriage warrant, be a Marriage officer.

2. For the purpose of the Foreign Marriage Act and these Regulations, the house in which a British Ambassador resides in the foreign country to the Government of which he is accredited, or which is occupied by him in that country for the purposes of his Embassy, shall be deemed to be the

official house of such Ambassador, and is in this Order referred to as the Embassy house, and every place within the precincts or curtilage of any such house, and any church or chapel annexed to such house, or for the time being used with the consent of the Government to which the Ambassador is accredited as the chapel thereof, shall be deemed to form part of the Embassy house.

For the purpose of marriages in an Embassy house, the expression 'office,' when used with respect to the place where any act or thing shall or may be done, shall be construed to refer to such part of the Embassy house as the Ambassador may from time to time appoint as being sufficiently accessible to the public.

Embassy and Consular Marriages.

3. Where a marriage can be solemnized at a British Consulate in a foreign country, the leave of the Ambassador shall be obtained before the marriage is solemnized in the Embassy house in that country.

4.—(1) Where a marriage according to the local law of a foreign country is valid by English law, then before the marriage is solemnized in that country under the Foreign Marriage Act, whether in an Embassy house or at a Consulate, the Marriage officer must be satisfied either—

(a) That both the parties are British subjects; or

(b) If only one of the parties is a British subject, that the other is not a subject or citizen of the country; or

(c) If one of the parties is a British subject, and the other a subject or citizen of the country, that sufficient facilities do not exist for the solemnization of the marriage in the foreign country in accordance with the law of that country.

(2) If a marriage officer, by reason of anything in this Article, refuses to solemnize or allow to be solemnized in his

presence the marriage of any person requiring such marriage to be solemnized, that person shall have the right of appeal to a Secretary of State given by section 5 of the Foreign Marriage Act.

5. In the case of any marriage under the Foreign Marriage Act, if it appears to the marriage officer that the woman about to be married is a British subject, and that the man is an alien, he must be satisfied that the marriage will be recognized by the law of the foreign country to which the alien belongs.

6. The following modifications of the requirements of the Foreign Marriage Act as to residence and notice which appear to Her Majesty to be consistent with the observance of due precautions against the solemnization of clandestine marriages, shall have effect in cases where one only of the parties has dwelt within the district of the Marriage officer:—

(1) A marriage may be solemnized under the Foreign Marriage Act in the official house of a Marriage officer in whose district one of the parties has dwelt—

    (*a*) If the marriage officer is satisfied that such notice as is mentioned below in Sub-Articles (3) and (4) of this Article, has been given of the intended marriage in the place where the other party has dwelt; or

    (*b*) If a Secretary of State is satisfied that the intended marriage is not clandestine, and that adequate notice has been given, and gives permission for the same to be solemnized.

(2) In either case the oath, affirmation, or declaration under section 7 of the Foreign Marriage Act shall, in addition to the matters specified in sub-sections (*a*) and (*c*) of that section, state that one of the parties has for three weeks immediately preceding had his or her usual place of abode within the district of the marriage officer, and further state the place where the party who has not dwelt within that district has, within three months immediately preceding, had for three

consecutive weeks his or her usual place of abode, and the notice which has been given in that place during those three weeks.

(3) The notice to be given where the marriage is not solemnized with the special permission of a Secretary of State shall, if the party has dwelt in a foreign country, be given, entered, and posted up in the manner and during the period provided by the Foreign Marriage Act, in like manner as if the marriage were to be solemnized by or before a Marriage officer in that country, and the Marriage officer to whom the notice is given in that country shall, on payment of the proper fee, give a certificate that the notice has been so given and posted up, and that he is unaware of any impediment which should obstruct the solemnization of the marriage.

(4) If the party dwells in a place in the United Kingdom, the notice shall be given in the like manner and on payment of the like fee as if that party were about to be married in that place, and in England or Ireland shall be given to the Superintendent Registrar or Registrar, and in Scotland shall be given by proclamation of banns; and the Superintendent Registrar or Registrar shall deal with the notice and give a certificate for marriage in like manner and on payment of the like fee as in the case of a marriage in his district: and the Session Clerk of the parish in which the banns were proclaimed in Scotland shall, in like manner and on payment of the like fee as in the case of a marriage in his district, give a certificate of proclamation of such banns.

Consular Marriages.

7. For the purpose of marriages to be solemnized by or before a marriage officer who is also a Consul as defined by the Foreign Marriage Act, every place within the curtilage or precincts of the house in which the Consul is for the time being resident, or of the building which is for the time being used for the purpose of his office, shall be part of the official house of such marriage officer, and every place to which the

public have ordinary access in such official house shall be deemed to be part of the office of such marriage officer.

Registration of Marriages by Foreign Law.

8.—(1) A Consular officer shall not be required to attend at the solemnization of a marriage solemnized in accordance with the local law unless the marriage is solemnized at the place where he is appointed to reside, nor unless the proper fee has been previously paid to him.

(2) The Consular officer shall forthwith, after the solemnization of the marriage, register the marriage in duplicate in books furnished to him by the Registrar-General through a Secretary of State for the purpose, separate from any register books provided for marriages solemnized by him, and shall register the same in accordance with section 9 of the Foreign Marriage Act, save that if the person by whom the marriage has been solemnized declines to sign the same, the Consular officer shall enter the name of that person, and the fact that he declines to sign the same.

(3) The Consular officer shall transmit copies and the certificate and the book when filled in manner provided by section 10 of the Foreign Marriage Act.

(4) Nothing in this Order shall authorize any officer who is not a Consular officer to register a marriage solemnized in accordance with the local law.

(5) The expression 'Consular officer' includes a Consul-General, Consul, Vice-Consul, Pro-Consul, Consular Agent, and any person for the time being authorized to discharge the duties of Consul-General, Consul, Vice-Consul, or Consular Agent.

High Commissioners, &c.

9.—(1) A Secretary of State, by a written authority under section 11 of the Foreign Marriage Act, may authorize a person to act in the place of a High Commissioner or

Resident mentioned in that section, outside of Her Majesty's dominions.

(2) If a Secretary of State gives such authority, or, in pursuance of the said section, authorizes any High Commissioner, Resident, or other officer outside Her Majesty's dominions, not being an Ambassador or a Consul, to be a marriage officer, then, for the purpose of marriages solemnized and registered by or before any High Commissioner, Resident, or officer, or person so authorized, expressions in the Foreign Marriage Act shall be construed as follows :—

(*a*) Expressions referring to the district of a marriage officer shall be construed to refer to the district for which such High Commissioner, Resident, or officer, or person is authorized to act for the purpose of the Foreign Marriage Act ;

(*b*) The expression 'official house of a marriage officer' shall be construed to refer to the building or part of a building or place specified in the document by which he is authorized to act ;

(*c*) The expression 'office,' when used with respect to the place at which any act or thing shall or may be done, shall be construed to refer to such portion of the building, part, or place so specified as is ordinarily accessible to the public.

Her Majesty's Ships.

10.—(1) Marriages, under the Foreign Marriage Act, on board one of Her Majesty's vessels may be solemnized by or before a commanding officer of such rank and of such vessel as is for the time being authorized for that purpose by or in pursuance of any Admiralty instructions, and for the purpose of any such marriages a commanding officer so authorized shall, without any written warrant, be a Marriage officer, and, for the purpose of such marriages, expressions in the Foreign Marriage Act shall be construed as follows :—

(*a*) Expressions referring to the district of a marriage officer shall be construed to refer to such parts of the foreign station to which the commanding officer is attached as may be specified in that behalf by Admiralty instructions;

(*b*) The expression 'official house of a marriage officer' shall be construed to refer to the vessel of the said commanding officer;

(*c*) The expression 'office,' when used with respect to the place where any act or thing shall or may be done, shall be construed to refer to the part of the ship on which public notices are affixed.

(2) The commanding officer, before he solemnizes a marriage, shall be satisfied that, at the port or place where the marriage is solemnized, sufficient facilities do not exist for the solemnization of the marriage on land, either in accordance with the local law of the country or in accordance with the Foreign Marriage Act.

(3) The requirements of the Foreign Marriage Act as to residence and notice shall be modified as follows, namely, not less than three weeks' notice of the intended marriage must have been given in such public manner, or to such relatives or friends of the parties, as satisfies the commanding officer that as much notice of the intended marriage has been given as would be given if the marriage took place in England, and that the marriage is not clandestine.

11. The forms in the Schedule to this Order, or forms to the like effect, shall be used in all cases to which they are applicable.

Definitions, &c.

12. In this Order the expression 'Ambassador' includes Minister and Chargé d'Affaires, and references to the Embassy or Embassy house shall be construed accordingly.

Other expressions have the same meaning as in the Foreign Marriage Act.

13. This Order shall come into operation on the first day of January, one thousand eight hundred and ninety-three, and from and after that day the Order in Council made on the twenty-fourth November, one thousand eight hundred and ninety-one, with respect to foreign marriages, shall be repealed.

14. This Order may be cited as 'The Foreign Marriages Order in Council, 1892.'

SCHEDULE.

Forms.

No. 1.—*Notice of Marriage.*

To the [British Consul-General *or* Consul] at

I hereby give you notice that a marriage is intended to be had within three calendar months from the date hereof between me and the other party herein named and described (that is to say):—

Name and Surname.	Condition.	Rank or Profession.	Age.	Residence.	Length of Residence.
A. B.	Bachelor		Of full age		
C. D.	Spinster		Minor		

Witness my hand, this   day of

(Signed)   A. B., *or*
                      C. D.

No. 2.—*Form of Oath.*

I, *A. B.*, of   , make oath and say as follows :—

1. A marriage is proposed to be solemnized between me and *C. D.*

2. I believe that there is not any impediment in kindred or alliance, or other lawful hindrance to the above marriage.

3. Both I and *C. D.* have for three weeks immediately preceding this date had our usual place of abode within the district of [*here insert the official title of the marriage officer, and, in the case of a Consul, the place where he is appointed to reside*], that is to say, I at   , and *C. D.*, at

4. Neither I nor *C. D.* is under the age of 21 years; [*or, as the case may be,* I am under the age of 21 years, but I am the widow of   , who died on the   day of   , 18   ], [*or* I am under the age of 21 years, and the consent of *G. H.*, whose consent is required to my marriage, is given as shown by the writing under his hand now shown to me and marked   .]

NOTE.—*Where the requirements of the Foreign Marriage Act as to residence have been dispensed with, the form of paragraph* 3 *of the oath by A. B. will be as follows* :—

I have for three weeks immediately preceding this date had my usual place of abode within the district of [*here insert the official title of the marriage officer, and, in the case of a Consul, the place where he is appointed to reside*], namely, at   , and to the best of my knowledge and belief *C. D.* has, within three months immediately preceding this date, namely, for three consecutive weeks from the   day of   to the   day of   , had his [*or* her] usual place of abode at   , and notice of our intended marriage has been given there during those weeks by   , as appears by the certificate now shown to me and marked   .

And the form of paragraph 3 of the oath by C. D. will be as follows :—

I have within three months immediately preceding this date, namely, for three consecutive weeks from the day of   to the   day of   , had my usual place of abode at   , and notice of our intended marriage was given there during those weeks by   , as appears by the certificate now shown to me and marked   , and to the best of my knowledge and belief *A. B.* has for three weeks immediately preceding this date had her [*or* his] usual place of abode within the district of [*here insert the official title of the marriage officer, and, in the case of a Consul, the place where he is appointed to reside*].

Where a Secretary of State has been satisfied that adequate notice has been given, and gives permission for the solemnization of the marriage, the form of so much of paragraph 3 of the oath as relates to the notice of the intended marriage will be as follows :—

A notice of our intended marriage has been given by [*here state what notice has been given*], as appears by the certificate [*or other evidence of the notice*] now shown to me and marked   , and a Secretary of State has been satisfied that such notice is adequate and has given permission for the marriage to be solemnized.

N.B.—*Any person entitled, under 51 & 25 Vict., cap. 46 (the 'Oaths Act, 1888'), or otherwise, to affirm or declare may make an affirmation or declaration in lieu of an oath.*

No. 3.—*Form of Certificate of Notice.*

I, *A. B.*, British Consul [*or as the case may be*], of   , hereby certify that on the   day of   , 18   , I received the following notice of marriage [*here insert the words of the notice*], and that such notice was entered and was posted up in my Consulate in the manner and during the period provided by the 'Foreign Marriage Act, 1892,' as if the marriage was to be solemnized in my Consulate, and that

APPENDIX II.

I am not aware of any impediment which should obstruct the solemnization of the above marriage.

No. 4.—*Certificate of Copy of Register.*

I,   , [Consul, *or, as the case may be*], residing at   , do hereby certify that this is a true copy of the entries of marriages registered in my office, from the entry of the marriage of *A. B.* and *C. D.*, number *one*, to the entry of the marriage of *R. S.* and *T. V.*, number *fourteen*.

Witness my hand and seal, this   day of   , 18 .

(Signature and official seal of the Marriage Officer.)

APPENDIX III.

FOREIGN JURISDICTION ACT, 1890.

53 & 54 VICT. c. 37.

WHEREAS by treaty, capitulation, grant, usage, sufferance, and other lawful means, Her Majesty the Queen has jurisdiction within divers foreign countries, and it is expedient to consolidate the Acts relating to the exercise of Her Majesty's jurisdiction out of Her dominions: APPENDIX III.

Be it therefore enacted by the Queen's most Excellent Majesty, by and with the advice and consent of the Lords Spiritual and Temporal, and Commons, in this present Parliament assembled, and by the authority of the same, as follows:

1. It is and shall be lawful for Her Majesty the Queen to hold, exercise, and enjoy any jurisdiction which Her Majesty now has or may at any time hereafter have within a foreign country in the same and as ample a manner as if Her Majesty had acquired that jurisdiction by the cession or conquest of territory. Exercise of jurisdiction in foreign country.

2. Where a foreign country is not subject to any government from whom Her Majesty the Queen might obtain jurisdiction in the manner recited by this Act, Her Majesty shall by virtue of this Act have jurisdiction over Her Majesty's subjects for the time being resident in or resorting to that country, and that jurisdiction shall be jurisdiction of Her Majesty in a foreign country within the meaning of the other provisions of this Act. Exercise of jurisdiction over British subjects in countries without regular governments.

3. Every act and thing done in pursuance of any jurisdiction of Her Majesty in a foreign country shall be as valid as if it had been done according to the local law then in force in that country. Validity of acts done in pursuance of jurisdiction.

Evidence as to existence or extent of jurisdiction in foreign country.

4. If in any proceeding, civil or criminal, in a court in Her Majesty's dominions or held under the authority of Her Majesty any question arises as to the existence or extent of any jurisdiction of Her Majesty in a foreign country, a Secretary of State shall, on the application of the court, send to the court within a reasonable time his decision on the question, and his decision shall for the purposes of the proceeding be final.

(2) The court shall send to the Secretary of State, in a document under the seal of the court, or signed by a judge of the court, questions framed so as properly to raise the question, and sufficient answers to those questions shall be returned by the Secretary of State to the court, and those answers shall, on production thereof, be conclusive evidence of the matters therein contained.

Power to extend enactments in First Schedule.

5.—(1) It shall be lawful for Her Majesty the Queen in Council, if She thinks fit, by Order to direct that all or any of the enactments described in the First Schedule to this Act, or any enactments for the time being in force amending or substituted for the same, shall extend, with or without any exceptions, adaptations, or modifications in the Order mentioned, to any foreign country in which for the time being Her Majesty has jurisdiction.

(2) Thereupon those enactments shall, to the extent of that jurisdiction, operate as if that country were a British possession, and as if Her Majesty in Council were the Legislature of that possession.

Power to send persons charged with offences for trial to a British possession.

6.—(1) Where a person is charged with an offence cognizable by a British court in a foreign country, any person having authority derived from Her Majesty in that behalf may, by warrant, cause the person so charged to be sent for trial to any British possession for the time being appointed in that behalf by Order in Council, and upon the arrival of the person so charged in that British possession, such criminal court of that possession as is authorized in that behalf by Order in Council, or if no court is so authorized, the supreme criminal court of that possession, may cause him to be kept in safe and proper custody, and so soon as conveniently may be may inquire of, try, and determine the offence, and on conviction punish the offender according to the laws in force in that behalf within that possession in the same manner as if the offence had been committed within the jurisdiction of that criminal court.

Provided that—

(a) A person so charged may, before being so sent for trial, tender for examination to a British court in the foreign country where the offence is alleged to have been committed any competent witness whose evidence he deems material for his defence and whom he alleges himself unable to produce at the trial in the British possession:

(b) In such case the British court in the foreign country shall proceed in the examination and cross-examination of the witness as though he had been tendered at a trial before that court, and shall cause the evidence so taken to be reduced into writing, and shall transmit to the criminal court of the British possession by which the person charged is to be tried a copy of the evidence, certified as correct under the seal of the court before which the evidence was taken, or the signature of a judge of that court:

(c) Thereupon the court of the British possession before which the trial takes place shall allow so much of the evidence so taken as would have been admissible according to the law and practice of that court, had the witness been produced and examined at the trial, to be read and received as legal evidence at the trial:

(d) The court of the British possession shall admit and give effect to the law by which the alleged offender would have been tried by the British court in the foreign country in which his offence is alleged to have been committed, so far as that law relates to the criminality of the act alleged to have been committed, or the nature or degree of the offence, or the punishment thereof, if the law differs in those respects from the law in force in that British possession.

(2) Nothing in this section shall alter or repeal any law, statute, or usage by virtue of which any offence committed out of Her Majesty's dominions may, irrespectively of this Act, be inquired of, tried, determined, and punished within Her Majesty's dominions, or any part thereof.

Provision as to place of punishment of persons convicted.

7. Where an offender convicted before a British court in a foreign country has been sentenced by that court to suffer death, penal servitude, imprisonment, or any other punishment, the sentence shall be carried into effect in such place as may be directed by Order in Council or be determined in accordance with directions given by Order in Council, and the conviction and sentence shall be of the same force in the place in which the sentence is so carried into effect as if the conviction had been made and the sentence passed by a competent court in that place.

Validity of acts done under Order in Council.

8. Where, by Order in Council made in pursuance of this Act, any British court in a foreign country is authorised to order the removal or deportation of any person from that country, that removal or deportation, and any detention for the purposes thereof, according to the provisions of the Order in Council, shall be as lawful as if the order of the court were to have effect wholly within that country.

Power to assign jurisdiction to British courts in cases within Foreign Jurisdiction Act.

9. It shall be lawful for Her Majesty the Queen in Council, by Order, to assign to or confer on any court in any British possession, or held under the authority of Her Majesty, any jurisdiction, civil or criminal, original or appellate, which may lawfully by Order in Council be assigned to or conferred on any British court in any foreign country, and to make such provisions and regulations as to Her Majesty in Council seem meet respecting the exercise of the jurisdiction so assigned or conferred, and respecting the enforcement and execution of the judgements, decrees, orders, and sentences of any such court, and respecting appeals therefrom.

Power to amend Orders in Council.

10. It shall be lawful for Her Majesty the Queen in Council to revoke or vary any Order in Council made in pursuance of this Act.

11. Every Order in Council made in pursuance of this Act shall be laid before both Houses of Parliament forthwith after it is made, if Parliament be then in session, and if not, forthwith after the commencement of the then next session of Parliament, and shall have effect as if it were enacted in this Act.

<small>Appendix III.

Laying before Parliament, and effect of Orders in Council.</small>

12.—(1) If any Order in Council made in pursuance of this Act as respects any foreign country is in any respect repugnant to the provisions of any Act of Parliament extending to Her Majesty's subjects in that country, or repugnant to any order or regulation made under the authority of any such Act of Parliament, or having in that country the force and effect of any such Act, it shall be read subject to that Act, order, or regulation, and shall, to the extent of such repugnancy, but not otherwise, be void.

<small>In what cases Orders in Council void for repugnancy.</small>

(2) An Order in Council made in pursuance of this Act shall not be, or be deemed to have been, void on the ground of repugnancy to the law of England unless it is repugnant to the provisions of some such Act of Parliament, order, or regulation as aforesaid.

13.—(1) An action, suit, prosecution, or proceeding against any person for any act done in pursuance or execution or intended execution of this Act, or of any enactment repealed by this Act, or of any Order in Council made under this Act, or of any such jurisdiction of Her Majesty as is mentioned in this Act, or in respect of any alleged neglect or default in the execution of this Act, or of any such enactment, Order in Council, or jurisdiction as aforesaid, shall not lie or be instituted—

<small>Provisions for protection of persons acting under Foreign Jurisdiction Acts.</small>

   (a) in any court within Her Majesty's dominions, unless it is commenced within six months next after the act, neglect, or default complained of, or in case of a continuance of injury or damage within six months next after the ceasing thereof, or where the cause of action arose out of Her Majesty's dominions within six months after the parties to the action, suit, prosecution, or proceeding have been within the jurisdiction of the court in which the same is instituted; nor

(*b*) in any of Her Majesty's courts without Her Majesty's dominions, unless the cause of action arose within the jurisdiction of that court, and the action is commenced within six months next after the act, neglect, or default complained of, or, in case of a continuance of injury or damage, within six months next after the ceasing thereof.

(2) In any such action, suit, or proceeding, tender of amends before the same was commenced may be pleaded in lieu of or in addition to any other plea. If the action, suit, or proceeding was commenced after such tender, or is proceeded with after payment into court of any money in satisfaction of the plaintiff's claim, and the plaintiff does not recover more than the sum tendered or paid, he shall not recover any costs incurred after such tender or payment, and the defendant shall be entitled to costs, to be taxed as between solicitor and client, as from the time of such tender or payment; but this provision shall not affect costs on any injunction in the action, suit, or proceeding.

Jurisdiction over ships in certain Eastern seas.

14. It shall be lawful for Her Majesty the Queen in Council to make any law that may seem meet for the government of Her Majesty's subjects being in any vessel at a distance of not more than one hundred miles from the coast of China or of Japan, as fully and effectually as any such law might be made by Her Majesty in Council for the government of Her Majesty's subjects being in China or in Japan.

Provision as to subjects of Indian princes.

15. Where any Order in Council made in pursuance of this Act extends to persons enjoying Her Majesty's protection, that expression shall include all subjects of the several princes and states in India.

Definitions.

16. In this Act,—

The expression 'foreign country' means any country or place out of Her Majesty's dominions:

The expression 'British court in a foreign country' means any British court having jurisdiction out of Her Majesty's dominions in pursuance of an Order in Council whether made under any Act or otherwise:

The expression 'jurisdiction' includes power.

17. The Acts mentioned in the Second Schedule to this Act may be revoked or varied by Her Majesty by Order in Council. *Power to repeal or vary Acts in Second Schedule.*

18. The Acts mentioned in the Third Schedule to this Act are hereby repealed to the extent in the third column of that schedule mentioned: Provided that,— *Repeal.*

(1) Any Order in Council, commission, or instructions made or issued in pursuance of any enactment repealed by this Act, shall, if in force at the passing of this Act, continue in force, until altered or revoked by Her Majesty as if made in pursuance of this Act; and shall, for the purposes of this Act, be deemed to have been made or issued under and in pursuance of this Act; and

(2) Any enactment, Order in Council, or document referring to any enactment repealed by this Act shall be construed to refer to the corresponding enactment of this Act.

19.—(1) This Act may be cited as the Foreign Jurisdiction Act, 1890. *Short title.*

(2) The Acts whereof the short titles are given in the First Schedule to this Act may be cited by the respective short titles given in that schedule.

APPENDIX III.

Sections 5, 19.

SCHEDULES.

FIRST SCHEDULE.

Session and Chapter.	Title.	Enactments which may be extended by Order in Council.	Short Title.
12 & 13 Vict. c. 96.	An Act to provide for the Prosecution and Trial in Her Majesty's Colonies of Offences committed within the jurisdiction of the Admiralty.	The whole Act.	Admiralty Offences (Colonial) Act, 1849.
14 & 15 Vict. c. 99.	An Act to amend the law of evidence.	Sections seven and eleven.	Evidence Act, 1851.
17 & 18 Vict. c. 104.	The Merchant Shipping Act, 1854.	Part X.	
19 & 20 Vict. c. 113.	Act Act to provide for taking evidence in Her Majesty's Dominions in relation to civil and commercial matters pending before Foreign Tribunals.	The whole Act.	Foreign Tribunals Evidence Act, 1859.
22 Vict. c. 20.	An Act to provide for taking evidence in Suits and Proceedings pending before Tribunals in Her Majesty's Dominions, in places out of the jurisdiction of such tribunals.	The whole Act.	Evidence by Commission Act, 1859.
22 & 23 Vict. c. 63.	An Act to afford Facilities for the more certain Ascertainment of the Law administered in one Part of Her Majesty's Dominions, when pleaded in the Courts of another Part thereof.	The whole Act.	British Law Ascertainment Act, 1859.
23 & 24 Vict. c. 122.	An Act to enable the Legislatures of Her Majesty's Possessions Abroad to make Enactments similar to the Enactment of the Act ninth George the Fourth, chapter thirty-one, section eight.	The whole Act.	Admiralty Offences (Colonial) Act, 1860.

APPENDIX III.

Session and Chapter.	Title.	Enactments which may be extended by Order in Council.	Short Title.
24 & 25 Vict. c. 11.	An Act to afford facilities for the better ascertainment of the Law of Foreign Countries when pleaded in Courts within Her Majesty's Dominions.	The whole Act.	Foreign Law Ascertainment Act, 1861.
30 & 31 Vict. c. 124.	The Merchant Shipping Act, 1867.	Section eleven.	
37 & 38 Vict. c. 94.	The Conveyancing (Scotland) Act, 1874.	Section fifty-one	
44 & 45 Vict. c. 69.	The Fugitive Offenders Act, 1881.	The whole Act.	
48 & 49 Vict. c. 74.	The Evidence by Commission Act, 1885.	The whole Act.	

SECOND SCHEDULE.

Acts which may be revoked or varied by Order in Council. Section 17.

Session and Chapter.	Title.	Extent of Repeal.
24 & 25 Vict. c. 31.	An Act for the prevention and punishment of offences committed by Her Majesty's subjects within certain territories adjacent to the colony of Sierra Leone.	The whole Act.
26 & 27 Vict. c. 35.	An Act for the prevention and punishment of offences committed by her Majesty's subjects in South Africa.	The whole Act.

APPENDIX III.

Section 18.

THIRD SCHEDULE.

Enactments repealed.

Session and Chapter.	Title or Short Title.	Extent of Repeal.
6 & 7 Vict. c. 94.	The Foreign Jurisdiction Act, 1843.	The whole Act.
20 & 21 Vict. c. 75.	An Act to confirm an order in Council concerning the exercise of jurisdiction in matters arising within the kingdom of Siam.	The whole Act.
28 & 29 Vict. c. 116.	The Foreign Jurisdiction Act Amendment Act, 1865.	The whole Act.
29 & 30 Vict. c. 87.	The Foreign Jurisdiction Act Amendment Act, 1866.	The whole Act.
33 & 34 Vict. c. 55.	The Siam and Straits Settlements Jurisdiction Act, 1870.	The whole Act.
38 & 39 Vict. c. 85.	The Foreign Jurisdiction Act, 1875.	The whole Act.
39 & 40 Vict. c. 46.	An Act for more effectually punishing offences against the laws relating to the slave trade.	Sections four and six.
41 & 42 Vict. c. 67.	The Foreign Jurisdiction Act, 1878.	The whole Act.

INDEX OF STATUTES

22 Henry VII.	c. 8		31.
33 ,,	c. 23		13.
35 ,,	c. 2		13.
12 & 13 William III.	c. 2		32.
4 George II.	c. 21		19, 21, 28, 125.
9 ,,	c. 35		243 n.
26 ,,	c. 33 (Lord Hardwicke's Act)		110, 119, 194.
13 George III.	c. 21		19, 28, 125.
43 ,,	c. 113		13.
4 George IV.	c. 91		85.
6 ,,	c. 78		244.
5 & 6 William IV.	c. 62		76, 150 n.
6 & 7 Victoria	c. 94 (Foreign Jurisdiction Act, 1843)		9, 150 n, 151 n.
7 & 8 ,,	c. 66		28, 43, 49 n, 75 n.
8 & 9 ,,	c. 86		244, 247.
12 & 13 ,,	c. 68		85.
17 & 18 ,,	c. 104 (Merchant Shipping Act, 1854)		79 n, 232 n, 241 n.
18 & 19 ,,	c. 91		241 n.
24 & 25 ,,	c. 3		13.
28 & 29 ,,	c. 116		31 n, 126, 128.
29 & 30 ,,	c. 87		221 n.
30 & 31 ,,	c. 124		241 n.
31 & 32 ,,	c. 45		242.
33 ,,	c. 14 (Naturalization Act, 1870)		18, 19, 22, 24, 28, 31, 33 n, 41, 45, 49 n, 52, 54, 55, 125, 126, 130, 141.
38 & 39 ,,	c. 51		230.
38 & 39 ,,	c. 85		221 n.
39 & 40 ,,	c. 46		128.
41 & 42 ,,	c. 67		221 n.
42 & 43 ,,	c. 29		118.
44 & 45 ,,	c. 69		155.
52 ,,	c. 10		17, 75.
52 & 53 ,,	c. 23		242.
53 & 54 ,,	c. 37 (Foreign Jurisdiction Act, 1890)		10, 150 n, 151 n, 155, 164, 221, 230.
54 & 55 ,,	c. 50		17.
55 & 56 ,,	c. 23 (Foreign Marriage Act, 1892)		17, 86, 87, 100, 118, 193, 202, 235.

INDEX OF ORDERS IN COUNCIL

	PAGE
Africa	144, 153 n, 156, 159, 164 n. 171-5, 191, 192.
Africa, South	216.
Brunei	166 n, 211.
China	126, 128, 139, 158, 159 n, 164, 166 n, 171-5, 188, 191, 192.
Corea	157, 172-5.
Cyprus	225, 226 n.
Egypt (*see* Ottoman Empire).	
Foreign Marriage (1892)	86, 88, 90, 91, 93, 95, 97, 99, 194, 203.
Gold Coast	215.
Japan (*see* China).	
Morocco	126, 128, 138, 144, 147, 157, 164, 166 n, 171, 173, 188.
Muscat	138, 157, 166 n, 171, 175, 191.
Ottoman Empire	126, 129, 138, 159, 164, 166 n, 167 n, 168, 173-5, 188, 190, 192.
Pacific	215, 231, 232, 236.
Pacific, Western	212 n.
Persia	126, 128, 138, 159, 164, 166 n, 171, 172-5, 188, 190, 192.
Persian Coasts and Islands	161, 164 n.
Siam	126, 138, 144, 155 n, 157, 164, 166 n, 172, 173, 191, 192.
Somali Coast	211, 212 n.
Tripoli (*see* Ottoman Empire).	
Zanzibar	166 n, 211.

INDEX OF CASES

	PAGE
Abbott v. Abbott	147 n.
Abd-ul-Messih v. Farra	136, 165 n, 183, 190.
Atkinson v. The Newcastle Waterworks	84 n.
Beamish v. Beamish	198.
Bourgeoise, Re	35 n.
Brinkley v. The Attorney General	202 n.
Brooke v. Brooke	101 n.
Butler v. Freeman	110 n.
Calvin's Case	19 n.
Catherwood v. Caslon	200 n.
Catterall v. Catterall	199 n.
Dalrymple v. Dalrymple	111 n.
De Geer v. Stone	19 n.
Harvey v. Fitzpatrick	151 n.
Hautz v. Sealy	199 n.
Hyde v. Hyde	202 n.
Indian Chief, The	182 n.
Jewell's lessee v. Jewell	199 n.
Kent v. Burgess	111 n.
King of Spain v. Hullet and Widder	193.
Lacon v. Higgins	111 n.
Lautour v. Teesdale	194 n.
Le Louis	244 n.
Leroux v. Brown	84 n.
Maclean v. Crystall	199, 200 n.
Maltass v. Maltass	181.
Middleton v. Janverin	111 n.
Papayanni v. The Russian Steam Navigation and Trading Company	212 n.
Patterson v. Gaines	199 n.
Pitts v. La-Fontaine	147 n.
Queen v. Millis	197, 201 n.

Reg. *v.* Anderson	14, 241 *n.*
„ Azzopardi	13.
„ Carr	14.
„ Keyn	247.
„ Lopez	241 *n.*
Ruding *v.* Smith	111.
Scrimshire *v.* Scrimshire	110.
Shedden *v.* Patrick	21 *n.*
Tootal's Trusts	165 *n*, 183.
Waldegrave Peerage	120 *n.*
Wall's, Governor, Case	13.
Warrender *v.* Warrender	202 *n.*

INDEX OF TREATIES

	PAGE
Annam	209 n.
Berlin Conference, General Act of	207, 214.
Berlin, Treaty of	138 n.
Brunei	206, 210.
Brussels Conference, General Act of	207, 214.
Cambodia, Treaty of Houdong, 1863	209 n.
,, Pnom-Penh, 1884	209 n.
China	143, 144 n, 149, 158, 162.
Congo Free State	149, 155, 162.
Corea	143, 144 n, 146, 149, 155, 162.
Egypt	152 n, 159 n.
Japan	149, 162.
Madagascar	149, 159, 162.
Morocco, Treaties of 1728 and 1760	140 n.
,, ,, 1856	146, 149, 155.
,, Convention of Madrid	138 n, 147 n.
Muscat	138 n, 155.
Ottoman Empire. Capitulations	133, 226.
,, ,, Treaty of the Dardanelles	133 n, 146, 153 n, 162.
,, ,, ,, Adrianople	134 n, 154 n.
,, ,, Protocol of 1868	143, 147.
Persia, Treaty of Tourkmantchai	143, 154, 160 n.
,, ,, Paris	138 n, 149, 162.
Siam	144 n, 146, 149, 155, 156 n, 162.
Zanzibar	210.

GENERAL INDEX

ABERDEEN, Lord, on persons of British origin born abroad, 66.
Alienage, declaration of, 18, 51.
Annam, 209.
Argentine Confederation, Law of the, 40, 48 n, 49, 62.
Arrest of criminals, 141, 143, 145, 155.
Austria, Law of, 34, 60, 64, 114, 116.

BANKRUPTCY, 186.
Belgium, Law of, 38, 60, 64.
Blackburn, Mr. Justice, quoted, 241 n.
Bolivia, Law of, 47 n, 62, 64.
Bombay, Supreme Court of, 172, 175, 192 n.
Brazil, Law of, 38, 39, 47 n, 62, 64, 65, 113.
British Law, meaning of the term, 165 n, 166.
British seaman, meaning of the term, 241 n.
British subjects, who are, 18-71, 90, 127-31; natural born, 18, 20, 55-65, 139; naturalized, 19, 22, 24, 26, 28, 30, 34-41, 74, 89, 140; Colonial, 28, 74; Indian, 74, 129, 189; registration of, 129; on board foreign vessels, 81 n, 241; in employment in an Eastern state, 151.
Brougham, Lord, quoted, 21.
Brunei, 166 n, 206, 210.
Bulgaria, Law of, 38, 39, 61, 64, 138 n.

CAIRNS, Lord, quoted, 84 n.
Cambodia, 209.
Capitulations, with the Ottoman Porte, 153.
Ceylon, 243 n.
Chapels, ambassadorial and consular, 95, 97, 118 n.
Chile, Law of, 38, 62, 64.
China, 139 n, 153.
Chitty, Mr. Justice, quoted, 183.
Cockburn, Chief Justice, quoted, 32, 67 n, 247.
Colombia, Law of, 38, 48 n.
Comity, 7 n; in relation to consular marriages, 102.

Common Law, its action outside the British dominions, 12, 109-14, 120 n, 194, 197, 237, 240.
Constantinople, Supreme Court of, 147, 168, 188, 191, 192 n.
Consuls, powers and functions of, 15, 73-101, 132-80, 186-93.
Cook Islands, 215 n.
Corea, 155 n.
Costa Rica, Law of, 39, 60, 64, 65.
Courts, Consular, 136, 147, 155 n, 168; jurisdiction in states of European civilization, 78, 81; in eastern states, 129, 142, 147-62, 153, 168-72, 186-93, 212 n; jurisdiction with respect to diplomatic and consular agents, 192; with respect to the territorial sovereign, 193; power of deciding upon their own competence, 151 n, 193.
Cranworth, Lord, quoted, 198.
Cyprus, 223, 225.

DENIZENS 31, 35 n.
Denmark, Law of, 38, 60.
Deportation, administration, 174, 178, 180 n; with a view to trial, 175, 176; for purposes of punishment, 176.
Deserters, Agreements for surrender of, 83.
Diplomatic Agents, powers and functions of, 15, 73, 85.
Divorce, effects of, 41 n, 51, 92.
Domicil, 130 n; as affecting nationality, 57, 59, 61, 64, 65; as affecting marriage, 90; in oriental countries, 180; in relation to bankruptcy, 187; in relation to matrimonial causes, 189.

ECUADOR, Law of, 43, 62, 65.
Egypt, 147 n, 152 n, 159 n; Court for, 169.
Ellice Islands, 231.
Embassies, marriages at, 85, 115-8; the official house, 94.

INDEX. 303

FISHERIES, regulation of, 242.
Foreigners, rights of a state with regard to, 73; under protection of Great Britain, 141, 142 n; on British ships, 240; in independent barbarous countries, 232.
France, Law of, 29 n, 35, 41 n, 42, 56-60, 105 n.
Frelinghuysen, Mr., quoted, 38 n, 64 n.
Friendly Islands, 231.

GERMANY, Law of, 36, 60, 64, 65, 84, 116, 227.
Gibraltar, Supreme Court of, 171, 175, 188, 192 n.
Gilbert Islands, 215 n.
Greece, Law of, 38, 39, 41 n, 60, 64, 65.
Guatemala, Law of, 41 n, 62, 64, 65.

HAITI, Law of, 43.
Hardwicke, Lord, quoted, 110 n.
High Commissioner, 15, 225, 233, 235.
High Seas, British jurisdiction on the, 239-47!; offences committed on board British vessels, 78, 81, 240; offences commited by British subjects on foreign vessels, 81 n, 241.
Hong Kong, Supreme Court of, 175.
Hudson's Bay Company, 195 n.
Hungary, Law of, 35, 60, 64, 65.

ILLEGITIMACY, in relation to nationality, 20, 21, 59, 65.
Indian native states, subjects of, 127, 228 n.
Infants, see Minors.
Ionian Islands, 205.
Italy, Law of, 37, 41 n, 61, 64, 114, 115.

JAPAN, 139 n, 153, 202.

LEVANT COMPANY, 9, 149 n.
Lushington, Dr., quoted, 181, 199 n, 200 n, 212 n.
Luxemburg, Law of, 40.

MADAGASCAR, 153, 208.
Malay Peninsula, 210.
Marriage, effect of, on nationality, 41, 49, 50, 125; nullity of, 44; by British agents in foreign states, 85-118; in eastern countries, 193; in barbarous countries, 235; *per verba de praesenti*, 109, 194, 197, 237; religious, 88, 97, 113, 117; on board vessels of war in foreign ports, 118; within the lines of a British army in foreign territory, 120; recognition of, by territorial state, 97, 106, 109, 114, 120, 196; contracted according to the *lex loci*, 89, 106, 115-7, 196, 201, 202, 237; polygamous, 189, 201, 203; of British women with aliens, 45 n, 49, 90, 103, 108, 109; of foreign women with British subjects, 41, 43, 47 n, 90, 103.
Marriage Officer, 85-90, 99, 106, 193, 235.
Marriage Warrant, 86, 92.
Married women, effect of the Act of 1844 upon the nationality of, 43.
Matrimonial Causes, 188.
Maule, Mr. Justice, quoted, 84 n.
Mauritius, Supreme Court of, 172.
Mexico, Law of, 61, 64, 65.
Minors, 22, 26, 36 n, 52, 91.
Monaco, 205.
Morocco, 140 n, 153, 188.
Muscat, 153.

NATIONALITY, British, 18-70; double, 54, 65, 90, 91, 139; imperfect, 69; persons without any, 30, 49, 51; loss of British, 44; loss of by laws of foreign countries, 34-41; recovery of British, 52, 55; of foreign, 54.
Naturalization in the United Kingdom, its acquisition, 24; its effects, 25, 55; in Colonies, 28, 90, 127, 234 n; in India, 30; in a foreign state, 45; by operation of law, 46; in eastern states, 125; impossibility of in barbarous countries, 130; inchoate or imperfect, 69.
Naturalized aliens, 24, 28, 30, 34, 41, 74, 89.
Naval Courts, 78.
Navigator Islands, 231.
Netherlands, Law of, 38, 61, 64.
New Guinea, 212 n.
Niger Coast Pretectorate, 213 n.
Norway Law of, 38, 39, 60.
Notarial functions of consuls, 17, 75; of diplomatic agents, 75.
Nubar Pasha, quoted, 153 n.
Nyassa districts, 213 n.

OFFICIAL house of diplomatic and consular agents, 93, 95.
Oil Rivers Protectorate, *see* Niger Coast Protectorate.
Orders in Council, provisions respecting in the Foreign Jurisdiction Act, 11.
Ottoman Empire, 147 n, 153; Law of, 124, 125, 138 n, 147 n, 161 n, 196.

PALMERSTON, Lord, quoted, 123.

INDEX.

Paraguay, Law of, 62, 64, 65.
Passports, 74, 128.
Persia, 171, 188.
Peru, Law of, 38, 62, 113.
Phoenix Islands, 215 n.
Police powers, 134 n, 143-5, 154, 173, 179.
Portugal, Law of, 38, 42, 61, 64, 65.
Prerogative, in relation to foreign jurisdiction, 8; to protectorates, 222.
Privy Council, appeals to, 170, 171.
Probate jurisdiction, 190.
Proconsuls, 18, 86.
Protected states in India, 205 n; natives of, 125 n, 127, 128, 189, 228 n.
Protection, right and duty of, in regard to subjects, 4, 72, 134; to whom given, 29, 54, 66, 127 n, 137; of subjects of foreign powers placed under the protection of Great Britain, 142 n; of houses and ships, 143; whether to be given to natives of protectorates, 227.
Protectorates, 204; natives of, 227.
Protectorates, of Brunei, 206, 210; of the Niger, 216, 217 n; of the Niger Coast, 213 n; of North Borneo, 207 n; of Sarawak, 207 n; of the Somali Coast, 211; of South Africa, 216; of Zanzibar, 210; French, 208; German, 208.

QUARANTINE Act, 245.

REGISTRATION, of births and deaths, 77; of marriages, 88, 97, 99, 202; of British subjects in eastern states, 129.
Regulations, power to make for securing conformity to local laws, 165, 167 n, 173.
Residence, in what it consists, 22, 26, 87 n.
Revenue Jurisdiction on the High Seas, 243.
Roumania, Law of, 38, 39, 60, 64, 138 n.
Russell, Lord, quoted, 67 n, 124.

Russell, Sir Charles, quoted, 245.
Russia, Law of, 37, 60, 64, 117.
Russian Jews under British protection, 137 n.

SALVADOR, Law of, 38, 39, 60.
Santa Cruz, 230.
Servia, Law of, 38, 40, 60, 64.
Shanghai, Supreme Court of, 188, 191, 192 n.
Ships, British, in foreign ports, 80, 81 n; in oriental ports, 141, 143; on the high seas, 240.
Ships, foreign, British subjects on board, 81 n, 241.
Ships of war, marriages on, 85, 118.
Spheres of Influence, 228.
Siam, 155 n.
Simpson, Sir E. quoted, 110.
Solomon Islands, 212 n, 215 n.
Somali Coast, 211, 212 n.
Sovereignty, divisibility of, 223.
Spain, 140 n; Law of, 40, 48 n, 60, 65, 103 n.
Stowell, Lord (Sir W. Scott), quoted, 112, 182 n, 244 n.
Straits Settlements, Supreme Court of the, 172, 192.
Strozzi, Letters patent given to Lorenzo, 132.
Sweden, Law of, 38, 39, 60.
Switzerland, Law of, 40, 60, 105 n, 115.

TIDJARET COURT, 161 n.

UNION ISLANDS, 215 n.
United States, Law of, 38, 41, 62, 64, 69, 199.
Uruguay, Law of, 38, 43, 47 n, 62, 64, 65.

VECINDAD, 48 n.

WAR, effect of on persons of double nationality, 68.
Wensleydale, Lord, quoted, 198.
Westlake, Mr., quoted, 184.
Widowhood, effect of, 41 n, 43, 51.
Willes, Mr. Justice, quoted, 198.

ZANZIBAR, 166 n, 210.

THE END.

Clarendon Press, Oxford.

SELECT LIST OF STANDARD WORKS.

DICTIONARIES	Page 1.
LAW	„ 2.
HISTORY, BIOGRAPHY, ETC.	„ 3.
PHILOSOPHY, LOGIC, ETC.	„ 6.
PHYSICAL SCIENCE	„ 7.

1. DICTIONARIES.

A New English Dictionary on Historical Principles, founded mainly on the materials collected by the Philological Society. Edited by James A. H. Murray, LL.D. Imperial 4to.

Vol. I, A and B, and Vol. II, C, half-morocco, 2*l.* 12*s.* 6*d.* each.
Vol. III, D and E.
D. Edited by Dr. Murray. [*In the Press.*]
E. Edited by Henry Bradley, M.A.
E—EVERY, 12*s.* 6*d.* [*Published.*]
EVERYBODY—EZOD. [*Shortly.*] Vol. III. Part II.

An Etymological Dictionary of the English Language, arranged on an Historical Basis. By W. W. Skeat, Litt.D. *Second Edition.* 4to. 2*l.* 4*s.*

A Middle-English Dictionary. By F. H. Stratmann. A new edition, by H. Bradley, M.A. 4to, half-bound, 1*l.* 11*s.* 6*d.*

An Anglo-Saxon Dictionary, based on the MS. collections of the late Joseph Bosworth, D.D. Edited and enlarged by Prof. T. N. Toller, M.A. Parts I–III. A–SÁR. 4to, stiff covers, 15*s.* each. Part IV, § 1, SÁR–SWÍÐRIAN. Stiff covers, 8*s.* 6*d.*

An Icelandic-English Dictionary, based on the MS. collections of the late Richard Cleasby. Enlarged and completed by G. Vigfússon, M.A. 4to. 3*l.* 7*s.*

A Greek-English Lexicon, by H. G. Liddell, D.D., and Robert Scott, D.D. *Seventh Edition, Revised and Augmented.* 4to. 1*l.* 16*s.*

A Latin Dictionary. By Charlton T. Lewis, Ph.D., and Charles Short, LL.D. 4to. 1*l.* 5*s.*

Oxford: Clarendon Press. London: HENRY FROWDE, Amen Corner, E.C.

A Sanskrit-English Dictionary. Etymologically and Philologically arranged. By Sir M. Monier-Williams, D.C.L. 4to. 4*l*. 14*s*. 6*d*.

A Hebrew and English Lexicon of the Old Testament, with an Appendix containing the Biblical Aramaic, based on the Thesaurus and Lexicon of Gesenius, by Francis Brown, D.D., S. R. Driver, D.D., and C. A. Briggs, D.D. Parts I and II. Small 4to, 2*s*. 6*d*. each.

Thesaurus Syriacus: collegerunt Quatremère, Bernstein, Lorsbach, Arnoldi, Agrell, Field, Roediger: edidit R. Payne Smith, S.T.P. Vol. I, containing Fasc. I–V, sm. fol. 5*l*. 5*s*.

Fasc. VI. 1*l*. 1*s*.; VII. 1*l*. 11*s*. 6*d*.; VIII. 1*l*. 16*s*.; IX. 1*l*. 5*s*.

2. LAW.

Anson. *Principles of the English Law of Contract, and of Agency in its Relation to Contract.* By Sir W. R. Anson, D.C.L. Seventh Edition. 8vo. 10*s*. 6*d*.

—— *Law and Custom of the Constitution.* 2 vols. 8vo.

    Part I. Parliament. Second Edition. 12*s*. 6*d*.

    Part II. The Crown. 14*s*.

Baden-Powell. *Land-Systems of British India;* being a Manual of the Land-Tenures, and of the Systems of Land-Revenue Administration prevalent in the several Provinces. By B. H. Baden-Powell, C.I.E. 3 vols. 8vo. 3*l*. 3*s*.

Digby. *An Introduction to the History of the Law of Real Property.* By Kenelm E. Digby, M.A. Fourth Edition. 8vo. 12*s*. 6*d*.

Grueber. *Lex Aquilia.* The Roman Law of Damage to Property: being a Commentary on the Title of the Digest 'Ad Legem Aquiliam' (ix. 2). By Erwin Grueber, Dr. Jur., M.A. 8vo. 10*s*. 6*d*.

Hall. *International Law.* By W. E. Hall, M.A. Third Edition. 8vo. 22*s*. 6*d*.

Holland and Shadwell. *Select Titles from the Digest of Justinian.* By T. E. Holland, D.C.L., and C. L. Shadwell, B.C.L. 8vo. 14*s*.

Also sold in Parts, in paper covers:—
Part I. Introductory Titles. 2*s*. 6*d*.
Part II. Family Law. 1*s*.
Part III. Property Law. 2*s*. 6*d*.
Part IV. Law of Obligations (No. 1). 3*s*. 6*d*. (No. 2). 4*s*. 6*d*.

Holland. *Elements of Jurisprudence.* By T. E. Holland, D.C.L. Sixth Edition. 8vo. 10*s*. 6*d*.

—— *The European Concert in the Eastern Question;* a Collection of Treaties and other Public Acts. Edited, with Introductions and Notes, by T. E. Holland, D.C.L. 8vo. 12*s*. 6*d*.

—— *Gentilis, Alberici, De Iure Belli Libri Tres.* Edidit T. E. Holland, I.C.D. Small 4to, half-morocco, 21*s*.

Oxford: Clarendon Press.

Holland. *The Institutes of Justinian,* edited as a recension of the Institutes of Gaius, by T. E. Holland, D.C.L. *Second Edition.* Extra fcap. 8vo. 5s.

Markby. *Elements of Law considered with reference to Principles of General Jurisprudence.* By Sir William Markby, D.C.L. *Fourth Edition.* 8vo. 12s. 6d.

Moyle. *Imperatoris Iustiniani Institutionum Libri Quattuor;* with Introductions, Commentary, Excursus and Translation. By J. B. Moyle, D.C.L. *Second Edition.* 2 vols. 8vo. Vol. I. 16s. Vol. II. 6s.

—— *Contract of Sale in the Civil Law.* By J. B. Moyle, D.C.L. 8vo. 10s. 6d.

Pollock and Wright. *An Essay on Possession in the Common Law.* By F. Pollock, M.A., and R. S. Wright, B.C.L. 8vo. 8s. 6d.

Poste. *Gaii Institutionum Juris Civilis Commentarii Quattuor;* or, Elements of Roman Law by Gaius. With a Translation and Commentary by Edward Poste, M.A. *Third Edition.* 8vo. 18s.

Raleigh. *An Outline of the Law of Property.* By Thos. Raleigh, M.A. 8vo. 7s. 6d.

Sohm. *Institutes of Roman Law.* By Rudolph Sohm, Professor in the University of Leipzig. Translated by J. C. Ledlie, B.C.L. With an Introductory Essay by Erwin Grueber, Dr. Jur., M.A. 8vo. 18s.

Stokes. *The Anglo-Indian Codes.* By Whitley Stokes, LL.D.
Vol. I. Substantive Law. 8vo. 30s.
Vol. II. Adjective Law. 8vo. 35s.
First and Second Supplements to the above, 1887-1891. 8vo. 6s. 6d.
Separately, No. 1, 2s. 6d.; No. 2, 4s. 6d.

Twiss. *The Law of Nations considered as Independent Political Communities.* By Sir Travers Twiss, D.C.L. Part I. *On the Rights and Duties of Nations in time of Peace.* New Edition. 8vo. 15s.

3. HISTORY, BIOGRAPHY, ETC.

Arbuthnot. *The Life and Works of John Arbuthnot, M.D.* By George A. Aitken. 8vo, cloth, with portrait, 16s.

Baker's Chronicle. *Chronicon Galfridi le Baker de Swynebroke.* Edited with Notes by Edward Maunde Thompson, Principal Librarian of the British Museum. 4to, stiff covers, 18s.; cloth, gilt top, 21s.

Bentham. *A Fragment on Government.* By Jeremy Bentham. Edited with an Introduction by F. C. Montague, M.A. 8vo. 7s. 6d.

Boswell's *Life of Samuel Johnson, LL.D.* Edited by G. Birkbeck Hill, D.C.L. In six volumes, medium 8vo. With Portraits and Facsimiles. Half-bound, 3l. 3s.

Calendar *of Charters and Rolls* preserved in the Bodleian Library. 8vo. 1l. 11s. 6d.

HISTORY, BIOGRAPHY, ETC.

Carte's *Life of James Duke of* Ormond. 6 vols. 8vo. 1l. 5s.

Casaubon (Isaac). 1559–1614. By Mark Pattison. 8vo. 16s.

Clarendon's *History of the Rebellion and Civil Wars in England.* Re-edited from a fresh collation of the original MS. in the Bodleian Library, with marginal dates and occasional notes, by W. Dunn Macray, M.A., F.S.A. 6 vols. Crown 8vo. 2l. 5s.

Earle. *Handbook to the Land-Charters, and other Saxonic Documents.* By John Earle, M.A., Professor of Anglo-Saxon in the University of Oxford. Crown 8vo. 16s.

Finlay. *A History of Greece from its Conquest by the Romans to the present time,* B.C. 146 to A.D. 1864. By George Finlay, LL.D. A new Edition, revised throughout, and in part re-written, with considerable additions, by the Author, and edited by H. F. Tozer, M.A. 7 vols. 8vo. 3l. 10s.

Fortescue. *The Governance of England:* otherwise called The Difference between an Absolute and a Limited Monarchy. By Sir John Fortescue, Kt. A Revised Text. Edited, with Introduction, Notes, &c., by Charles Plummer, M.A. 8vo, half-bound, 12s. 6d.

Freeman. *The History of Sicily from the Earliest Times.* Vols. I. and II. 8vo, cloth, 2l. 2s. Vol. III. The Athenian and Carthaginian Invasions. 8vo, cloth, 24s.

——— *History of the Norman Conquest of England; its Causes and Results.* By E. A. Freeman, D.C.L. In Six Volumes. 8vo. 5l. 9s. 6d.

Freeman. *The Reign of William Rufus and the Accession of Henry the First.* 2 vols. 8vo. 1l. 16s.

——— *A Short History of the Norman Conquest of England.* Second Edition. Extra fcap. 8vo. 2s. 6d.

French Revolutionary Speeches. (See Stephens, H. Morse.)

Gardiner. *The Constitutional Documents of the Puritan Revolution,* 1628–1660. Selected and Edited by Samuel Rawson Gardiner, M.A. Crown 8vo. 9s.

Gascoigne's *Theological Dictionary* ('*Liber Veritatum*'): Selected Passages, illustrating the Condition of Church and State, 1403–1458. With an Introduction by James E. Thorold Rogers, M.A. 4to. 10s. 6d.

Greswell. *History of the Dominion of Canada.* By W. Parr Greswell, M.A. Crown 8vo. With Eleven Maps. 7s. 6d.

——— *Geography of the Dominion of Canada and Newfoundland.* Crown 8vo. With Ten Maps. 6s.

——— *Geography of Africa South of the Zambesi.* With Maps. Crown 8vo. 7s. 6d.

Gross. *The Gild Merchant;* a Contribution to British Municipal History. By Charles Gross, Ph.D. 2 vols. 8vo. 24s.

Hastings. *Hastings and the Rohilla War.* By Sir John Strachey, G.C.S.I. 8vo, cloth, 10s. 6d.

Hodgkin. *Italy and her Invaders.* With Plates and Maps. By T. Hodgkin, D.C.L. Vols. I–IV. A.D. 376–553. 8vo.
Vols. I. and II. *Second Edition.* 2l. 2s.
Vols. III. and IV. 1l. 16s.

——— *The Dynasty of Theodosius;* or, Seventy Years' Struggle with the Barbarians. By the same Author. Crown 8vo. 6s.

Oxford: Clarendon Press.

HISTORY, BIOGRAPHY, ETC.

Hume. *Letters of David Hume to William Strahan.* Edited with Notes, Index, &c., by G. Birkbeck Hill, D.C.L. 8vo. 12s. 6d.

Johnson. *Letters of Samuel Johnson, LL.D.* Collected and edited by G. Birkbeck Hill, D.C.L., Editor of Boswell's 'Life of Johnson' (see Boswell). 2 vols. half-roan, 28s.

Kitchin. *A History of France.* With Numerous Maps, Plans, and Tables. By G. W. Kitchin, D.D. In three Volumes. *Second Edition.* Crown 8vo, each 10s. 6d.
   Vol. I. to 1453. Vol. II. 1453–1624. Vol. III. 1624–1793.

Luttrell's (*Narcissus*) *Diary.* A Brief Historical Relation of State Affairs, 1678–1714. 6 vols. 1l. 4s.

Lucas. *Introduction to a Historical Geography of the British Colonies.* By C. P. Lucas, B.A. With Eight Maps. Crown 8vo. 4s. 6d.

Lucas. *Historical Geography of the British Colonies:*
   Vol. I. The Mediterranean and Eastern Colonies (exclusive of India). With Eleven Maps. Crown 8vo. 5s.
   Vol. II. The West Indian Colonies. With Twelve Maps. Crown 8vo. 7s. 6d.

Machiavelli. *Il Principe.* Edited by L. Arthur Burd, M.A. With an Introduction by Lord Acton. 8vo. Cloth, 14s.

Ralegh. *Sir Walter Ralegh.* A Biography. By W. Stebbing, M.A. 8vo. 10s. 6d.

Ramsay (Sir J. H.). *Lancaster and York.* A Century of English History (A.D. 1399–1485). By Sir J. H. Ramsay of Bamff, Bart., M.A. With Maps, Pedigrees, and Illustrations. 2 vols. 8vo. 36s.

Ranke. *A History of England, principally in the Seventeenth Century.* By L. von Ranke. Translated under the superintendence of G. W. Kitchin, D.D., and C. W. Boase, M.A. 6 vols. 8vo. 3l. 3s.

Rawlinson. *A Manual of Ancient History.* By George Rawlinson, M.A. *Second Edition.* 8vo. 14s.

Rhŷs. *Studies in the Arthurian Legend.* By John Rhŷs, M.A. 8vo. 12s. 6d.

Ricardo. *Letters of David Ricardo to T. R. Malthus (1810–1823).* Edited by James Bonar, M.A. 8vo. 10s. 6d.

Rogers. *History of Agriculture and Prices in England,* A.D. 1259–1702. By James E. Thorold Rogers, M.A. 6 vols., 8vo. 7l. 2s.

—— *First Nine Years of the Bank of England.* 8vo. 8s. 6d.

—— *Protests of the Lords,* including those which have been expunged, from 1624 to 1874; with Historical Introductions. In three volumes. 8vo. 2l. 2s.

Smith's *Wealth of Nations.* With Notes, by J. E. Thorold Rogers, M.A. 2 vols. 8vo. 21s.

Stephens. *The Principal Speeches of the Statesmen and Orators of the French Revolution,* 1789–1795. With Historical Introductions, Notes, and Index. By H. Morse Stephens. 2 vols. Crown 8vo. 21s.

London: HENRY FROWDE, Amen Corner, E.C.

Stubbs. *Select Charters and other Illustrations of English Constitutional History, from the Earliest Times to the Reign of Edward I.* Arranged and edited by W. Stubbs, D.D., Lord Bishop of Oxford. *Seventh Edition.* Crown 8vo. 8s. 6d.

—— *The Constitutional History of England, in its Origin and Development. Library Edition.* 3 vols. Demy 8vo. 2l. 8s.

Also in 3 vols. crown 8vo. price 12s. each.

—— *Seventeen Lectures on the Study of Medieval and Modern History.* Crown 8vo. 8s. 6d.

—— *Registrum Sacrum Anglicanum.* An attempt to exhibit the course of Episcopal Succession in England. By W. Stubbs, D.D. Small 4to. 8s. 6d.

Vinogradoff. *Villainage in England.* Essays in English Mediaeval History. By Paul Vinogradoff, Professor in the University of Moscow. 8vo, half-bound. 16s.

Wellesley. *A Selection from the Despatches, Treaties, and other Papers of the Marquess Wellesley, K.G., during his Government of India.* Edited by S. J. Owen, M.A. 8vo. 1l. 4s.

Wellington. *A Selection from the Despatches, Treaties, and other Papers relating to India of Field-Marshal the Duke of Wellington, K.G.* Edited by S. J. Owen, M.A. 8vo. 1l. 4s.

Whitelock's *Memorials of English Affairs from 1625 to 1660.* 4 vols. 8vo. 1l. 10s.

---

4. PHILOSOPHY, LOGIC, ETC.

Bacon. *The Essays.* With Introduction and Illustrative Notes. By S. H. Reynolds, M.A. 8vo, half-bound. 12s. 6d.

—— *Novum Organum.* Edited, with Introduction, Notes, &c., by T. Fowler, D.D. *Second Edition.* 8vo. 15s.

—— *Novum Organum.* Edited, with English Notes, by G. W. Kitchin, D.D. 8vo. 9s. 6d.

—— *Novum Organum.* Translated by G. W. Kitchin, D.D. 8vo. 9s. 6d.

Berkeley. *The Works of George Berkeley, D.D., formerly Bishop of Cloyne; including many of his writings hitherto unpublished.* With Prefaces, Annotations, and an Account of his Life and Philosophy. By Alexander Campbell Fraser, LL.D. 4 vols. 8vo. 2l. 18s.

The Life, Letters, &c., separately, 16s.

Bosanquet. *Logic; or, the Morphology of Knowledge.* By B. Bosanquet, M.A. 8vo. 21s.

Butler's *Works, with Index to the Analogy.* 2 vols. 8vo. 11s.

Fowler. *The Elements of Deductive Logic, designed mainly for the use of Junior Students in the Universities.* By T. Fowler, D.D. *Ninth Edition,* with a Collection of Examples. Extra fcap. 8vo. 3s. 6d.

—— *The Elements of Inductive Logic, designed mainly for the use of Students in the Universities.* By the same Author. *Fifth Edition.* Extra fcap. 8vo. 6s.

Fowler. *The Principles of Morals.* (Introductory Chapters.) By T. Fowler, D.D., and J. M. Wilson, B.D. 8vo, boards, 3s. 6d.

Fowler. *The Principles of Morals.* Part II. By T. Fowler, D.D. 8vo. 10s. 6d.

Green. *Prolegomena to Ethics.* By T. H. Green, M.A. Edited by A. C. Bradley, M.A. 8vo. 12s. 6d.

Hegel. *The Logic of Hegel;* translated from the Encyclopaedia of the Philosophical Sciences. By W. Wallace, M.A. Second Edition, Revised and Augmented. Crown 8vo. 10s. 6d.

Hume's *Treatise of Human Nature.* Edited, with Analytical Index, by L. A. Selby-Bigge, M.A. Crown 8vo. 9s.

Locke's *Conduct of the Understanding.* Edited by T. Fowler, D.D. Third Edition. Extra fcap. 8vo. 2s. 6d.

Lotze's *Logic,* in Three Books; of Thought, of Investigation, and of Knowledge. English Translation; Edited by B. Bosanquet, M.A. Second Edition. 2 vols. Cr. 8vo. 12s.

—— *Metaphysic,* in Three Books; Ontology, Cosmology, and Psychology. English Translation; Edited by B. Bosanquet, M.A. Second Edition. 2 vols. Cr. 8vo. 12s.

Martineau. *Types of Ethical Theory.* By James Martineau, D.D. Third Edition. 2 vols. Cr. 8vo. 15s.

—— *A Study of Religion:* its Sources and Contents. Second Edition. 2 vols. Cr. 8vo. 15s.

5. PHYSICAL SCIENCE.

Chambers. *A Handbook of Descriptive and Practical Astronomy.* By G. F. Chambers, F.R.A.S. Fourth Edition, in 3 vols. Demy 8vo.
Vol. I. The Sun, Planets, and Comets. 21s.
Vol. II. Instruments and Practical Astronomy. 21s.
Vol. III. The Starry Heavens. 14s.

De Bary. *Comparative Anatomy of the Vegetative Organs of the Phanerogams and Ferns.* By Dr. A. de Bary. Translated by F. O. Bower, M.A., and D. H. Scott, M.A. Royal 8vo. 1l. 2s. 6d.

—— *Comparative Morphology and Biology of Fungi, Mycetozoa and Bacteria.* By Dr. A. de Bary. Translated by H. E. F. Garnsey, M.A. Revised by Isaac Bayley Balfour, M.A., M.D., F.R.S. Royal 8vo, half-morocco, 1l. 2s. 6d.

De Bary. *Lectures on Bacteria.* By Dr. A. de Bary. Second Improved Edition. Translated by H. E. F. Garnsey, M.A. Revised by Isaac Bayley Balfour, M.A., M.D., F.R.S. Crown 8vo. 6s.

Fisher. *A Class Book of Elementary Chemistry.* By W. W. Fisher, M.A., F.C.S. Second Edition. Crown 8vo. 4s. 6d.

Chemistry in Space. By Van't Hoff. Translated and edited by J. E. Marsh, B.A. Crown 8vo. 4s. 6d.

Goebel. *Outlines of Classification and Special Morphology of Plants.* By Dr. K. Goebel. Translated by H. E. F. Garnsey, M.A. Revised by Isaac Bayley Balfour, M.A., M.D., F.R.S. Royal 8vo, half-morocco, 1l. 1s.

Sachs. *Lectures on the Physiology of Plants.* By Julius von Sachs. Translated by H. Marshall Ward, M.A., F.L.S. Royal 8vo, half-morocco, 1*l.* 11*s.* 6*d.*

—— *A History of Botany.* Translated by H. E. F. Garnsey, M.A. Revised by I. Bayley Balfour, M.A., M.D., F.R.S. Crown 8vo. 10*s.*

Fossil Botany. *Being an Introduction to Palaeophytology from the Standpoint of the Botanist.* By H. Graf zu Solms-Laubach. Translated by H. E. F. Garnsey, M.A. Revised by I. Bayley Balfour, M.A., M.D., F.R.S. Royal 8vo, half-morocco, 18*s.*

Annals of Botany. Edited by Isaac Bayley Balfour, M.A., M.D., F.R.S., Sydney H. Vines, D.Sc., F.R.S., D. H. Scott, M.A., Ph.D., F.L.S., and W. G. Farlow, M.D.; assisted by other Botanists. Royal 8vo, half-morocco, gilt top.

   Vol. I. Parts I–IV. 1*l.* 16*s.*
   Vol. II. Parts V–VIII. 2*l.* 2*s.*
   Vol. III. Parts IX–XII. 2*l.* 12*s.* 6*d.*
   Vol. IV. Parts XIII–XVI. 2*l.* 5*s.*
   Vol. V. Parts XVII–XX. 2*l.* 10*s.*
   Vol. VI. Parts XXI–XXIV. 2*l.* 4*s.*
   Vol. VII. Part XXV. 12*s.*; Part XXVI. 12*s.*; Part XXVII. 12*s.*

Biological Series. (*Translations of Foreign Biological Memoirs.*)

I. *The Physiology of Nerve, of Muscle, and of the Electrical Organ.* Edited by J. Burdon-Sanderson, M.D., F.R.SS. L. & E. Medium 8vo. 1*l.* 1*s.*

II. *The Anatomy of the Frog.* By Dr. Alexander Ecker, Professor in the University of Freiburg. Translated, with numerous Annotations and Additions, by G. Haslam, M.D. Med. 8vo. 21*s.*

III. *Contributions to the History of the Physiology of the Nervous System.* By Professor Conrad Eckhard. Translated by Miss Edith Prance. *In Preparation.*

IV. *Essays upon Heredity and Kindred Biological Problems.* By Dr. A. Weismann. Translated and Edited by E. B. Poulton, M.A., S. Schönland, Ph.D., and A. E. Shipley, M.A. *Second Edition.* Crown 8vo. 7*s.* 6*d.*

Vol. II. Edited by E. B. Poulton, and A. E. Shipley. Crown 8vo. 5*s.*

Prestwich. *Geology, Chemical, Physical, and Stratigraphical.* By Joseph Prestwich, M.A., F.R.S. In two Volumes.
   Vol. I. Chemical and Physical. Royal 8vo. 1*l.* 5*s.*
   Vol. II. Stratigraphical and Physical. With a new Geological Map of Europe. Royal 8vo. 1*l.* 16*s.*
   New Geological Map of Europe. In case or on roller. 5*s.*

Rolleston and Jackson. *Forms of Animal Life.* A Manual of Comparative Anatomy, with descriptions of selected types. By George Rolleston, M.D., F.R.S. *Second Edition.* Revised and Enlarged by W. Hatchett Jackson, M.A. Medium 8vo. 1*l.* 16*s.*

⁎* COMPLETE CATALOGUES ON APPLICATION.

Oxford
AT THE CLARENDON PRESS
LONDON: HENRY FROWDE
OXFORD UNIVERSITY PRESS WAREHOUSE, AMEN CORNER, E.C.

www.ingramcontent.com/pod-product-compliance
Lightning Source LLC
Chambersburg PA
CBHW030014240426
43672CB00007B/940